VASANTOTSAVA

The Spring Festivals of India

Reconstructing Indian History & Culture
(ISSN 0971-3824)

1. Society in Ancient India by Sures Chandra Banerji (ISBN 81-246-0000-7)
2. Political Thought in Ancient India by G.P. Singh (ISBN 81-246-0001-5)
3. Early Indian Historical Tradition and Archaeology by G.P. Singh (ISBN 81-246-0005-8)
4. Vasantotsava: The Spring Festivals of India by Leona M. Anderson (ISBN 81-246-0011-2)
5. Ecological Readings in the Veda by M. Vannucci (ISBN 81-246-0009-0)
6. Vṛndāvana in Vaiṣṇava Literature by Maura Corcoran (ISBN 81-246-0024-4)
7. Social History of the Tamils (1707-1947) by P. Subramanian (ISBN 81-246-0045-7)
8. Ancient Indian Coinage by Rekha Jain (ISBN 81-246-0051-1)
9. Buddhism and Socio-Economic Life of Eastern India by Bimal Chandra Mohapatra (ISBN 81-246-0055-4)
10. Chandragupta Maurya by P.L. Bhargava (ISBN 81-246-0056-2)
11. Mṛtyu: Concept of Death in Indian Traditions by Gian Giuseppe Filippi (ISBN 81-246-0072-4)
12. Yama: The Glorious Lord of the Other World by Kusum P. Merh (ISBN 81-246-0066-X)
13. Sacred Complex of Ujjain by D.K. Samanta (ISBN 81-246-0078-3)
14. Vedic View of the Earth by S.R.N. Murthy (ISBN 81-246-0091-0)
15. Society in the Atharvaveda by B.S. Kharade (ISBN 81-246-0093-7)
16. Orissan History, Culture and Archaeology by S. Pradhan (ISBN 81-246-0117-8)
17. Education in Ancient India by Mitali Chatterjee (ISBN 81-246-0113-5)
18. Surā: The Liquor and the Vedic Sacrifice by M.B. Kolhatkar (ISBN 81-246-0114-3)
19. Human Ecology in the Vedas by Marta Vannucci (ISBN 81-246-0115-1)
20. Governance in Ancient India by Anupa Chandra Pandey (ISBN 81-246-0135-6)
21. The Cultural Glory of Ancient India: A Literary Overview by Sures Chandra Banerji (ISBN 81-246-0137-2)
22. Kauṭilya's Arthaśāstra in the light of Modern Science & Technology by Sunil Sen Sarma (ISBN 81-246-0187-9)
23. History of Jainism — With Special Reference to Mathura by V.K. Sharma (ISBN 81-246-0195-X)
24. Cultural Tourism in India: Museums, Monuments & Arts — Theory and Practice by S.P. Gupta; Krishna Lal; Mahua Bhattacharya (ISBN 81-246-0215-8)
25. Ancient Indian Historiography — Sources and Interpretations by G.P. Singh (ISBN 81-246-0228-X)
26. Republics, Kingdoms, Towns and Cities in Ancient India by G.P. Singh (ISBN 81-246-0237-9)
27. Facets of Ancient Indian History and Culture — New Perception by G.P. Singh (ISBN 81-246-0238-7)
28. Kamakhya — A Socio-cultural Study by Nihar Ranjan Mishra (ISBN 81-246-0251-4)
29. History and Culture of Tamil Nadu as Gleaned from the Sanskrit Inscriptions Vol. 1 (up to c. AD 1310) by Chithra Madhavan (ISBN 81-246-0308-1).

1. Festival of *Holī*, Bundelkhand
Upperpart of Central India, *circa* A.D.1750-60

Reconstructing Indian History & Culture, no. 4

VASANTOTSAVA

The Spring Festivals of India

~ Texts and Traditions ~

Leona M. Anderson

D.K.Printworld (P) Ltd.
New Delhi

Cataloging in Publication Data — DK
[Courtesy: D.K. Agencies (P) Ltd. <docinfo@dkagencies.com>]

Anderson, Leona M. (Leona May), 1951-
Vasantotsava: the spring festivals of India.
(Reconstructing Indian History & culture; no. 4).
Includes bibliographical references.
Includes Index.
ISBN 8124600112

1. Spring -- Religious aspects -- Hinduism.
2. Festivals -- India. I. Title. II. Series:
Reconstructing Indian history & culture; no. 4.

ISBN 81-246-0011-2
First Published in India in 1993
Second impression in 1994
Third impression in 2005

Published and printed by:
D.K. Printworld (P) Ltd.
Regd. office : *'Sri Kunj'*, F-52, Bali Nagar
New Delhi - 110 015
Phones : (011) 2545-3975; 2546-6019; *Fax* : (011) 2546-5926
E-mail: dkprintworld@vsnl.net
Web: www.dkprintworld.com

for

Mr. K. Venugopalan

Acknowledgements

The completion of this book would not have been possible without the assistance and support of numerous friends, colleagues and institutions in both India and Canada.

I thank the Social Sciences and Humanities Research Council of Canada and the Shastri Indo-Canadian Institute for funding which enabled me to travel to India in order to conduct research as well as affording me the time to write the initial and final drafts.

The *Annals of the Bhandarkar Oriental Research Institute* and *Purāṇa* undertook the publishing of earlier versions of chapters of this work for which I am grateful as I am to the National Museum, New Delhi for permission to reproduce paintings from its collection as the plates to this book.

I thank the faculty of the Religion Department at McMaster University who offered numerous insightful suggestions on the first drafts.

The staff of the Delhi office, Shastri Institute, especially Mr. P.N. Malik, ensured me consecutive hours of uninterrupted time during the final stages of the writing of this work. I thank Mr. S.D. Sayal, who seems to have a natural inclination in this regard, for his careful editing of the final draft and the DKs for undertaking its publication.

I wish as well to acknowledge my friends and colleagues in Pune for their assistance. Particularly, I must express my gratitude to Mr. Venugopalan for his patience and advice regarding the reading of a wide range of Sanskrit texts. He and his family have exhibited a generosity and hospitality over the past ten years which my family and I will never forget.

Finally, I thank my husband, Jack Anderson, for many hours of reading and discussion of what seems like practically every word of the text, and my daughters, Zoe and Lucy, who were born and almost grew up during this undertaking.

The translations from Sanskrit sources are my own unless otherwise noted. All errors and omisisons are also mine.

CONTENTS

List of Plates

1

Inroduction

The Indian Spring Festival, the *Vasantotsava*, is one of the multitude of celebrations which punctuates the ancient and medieval festival calendars. It is observed in the vernal season, in the interstices between winter and spring, sometimes signifying the departure of winter, at other times announcing the advent of spring. Most often, however, in anticipation of regeneration and rebirth, it plays upon the potential inherent in the hiatus between these two seasons. Although the *Vasantotsava* is not celebrated in contemporary India in its original form, literary evidence culled from Sanskrit texts belonging to the pre-modern period suggests that the *Vasantotsava*, in times past, was a signal event pivotally positioned within the Indian religious year.

A body of pertinent texts attests to the variability, complexity and multiplicity of the ritual and mythological framework of the Spring Festival as it was particularized in ancient and medieval India. Though our accounts by no means exhaust descriptions of the celebrations, they are distinct and plentiful, enriching our knowledge of the manner in which the spring season was perceived and practiced in medieval times. The two-fold purpose of this study of the *Vasantotsava* is first, on the basis of accounts in Sanskrit literature, to arrive at a description of the structures and forms through which the festival was celebrated and second, to shed some analytical light upon the panorama of ritual actions portrayed in these diverse sources.

My primary source material is drawn from a broad range of Sanskrit literature, including *purāṇas*, ritual texts, folk tales, drama, poetry and narratives in mixed prose and poetry (*campūs*). Five principle texts, the *Ratnāvalī*, the *Kathāsaritsāgara*, the *Vikramacarita*, the *Bhaviṣya Purāṇa* (ch. 132, 135) and the *Virūpākṣavasantotsavacampū*, have been selected here in pursuit of a fuller picture of the *Vasantotsava*.[1]

Composed in Sanskrit in the seventh century AD,[2] the *Ratnāvalī* of Śrī Harṣa is significant to our study on two counts: first, it was written specifically to be performed on the occasion of the *Vasantotsava* and second, it contains several detailed albeit sporadically positioned accounts of the constitutive format of the celebrations. The Spring Festival depicted herein spans a period of at least three days and is set in two separate locations. There are in the *Ratnāvalī*, two spatially distinct forums for spring ceremonies: one focussing on the festival as it was played in the city streets and a second focussing upon the celebrations in the garden. In each of these settings, the *Vasantotsava* takes on distinctive characteristics: in the urban environment the celebrations are characterized by the free and sometimes wild behavior of the citizens, while, in the garden, the attention is centered on the private worship of the deity Kāmadeva, the Hindu god of desire and love. Insofar as the *Ratnāvalī* was written to be performed on the occasion of the *Vasantotsava*, we may well assume that this play itself had some importance in the celebration of the festival. Plays of this type seem to have been commonly enacted on this occasion. The *Ratnāvalī*, then, is of special interest as it gives us a relatively complete picture of this festival as celebrated in the seventh century AD in the central Indian city of Kauśāmbī, thus affording us an understanding of the transitional development and regional variation of the festival with some degree of temporal and geographic precision.

Further descriptions are drawn from the *Kathāsaritsāgara* and the *Vikramacarita*. Both are collections of stories recorded in north India during the eleventh century AD.

Although the *Kathāsaritsāgara* is a relatively late compilation, the stories therein date to very early times.[3] The *Vikramacarita*[4] is a collection of thirty-two tales in praise of Vikramāditya which are alleged to have been discovered by Bhoja of Dhārā in the eleventh century AD. Most probably they were written for him or under his auspices.[5] These texts provide us with data concerning popular rites which were not necessarily codified in *purāṇic* or ritual literature. The descriptions of the *Vasantotsava* in both the *Kathāsaritsāgara* and the *Vikramacarita* are typical in that their brief vignettes of the Spring Festival function as *mise-en-scène*. They are significant for our discussion as well, for they both tend to highlight the role played by royalty in the celebration.

Two chapters from the *Bhaviṣya Purāṇa* amplify our picture of the *Vasantotsava* through the re-telling of myths germane to this festival celebrations. Here specific links between the *Vasantotsava* and the tradition of Hindu mythology are established and authenticated. My discussion centres on the role of mythological figures such as Kāma, Śiva and the *rākṣasī* Ḍhaunḍhā, the central role played by children in the celebrations, and an analysis of the activities which make up the festival, such as lighting and circumambulating a bonfire. Like all *purāṇas*, the *Bhaviṣya Purāṇa* is difficult to date[6] and like all *purāṇas* it clearly preserves popular, perhaps non-Sanskritic rituals, but in a form filtered through the Sanskrit language and culture. Although the *purāṇas* contain copious idiosyncratic material, they do give us information regarding orthodox ritual action which often comprises the basis of orthodox ritual manuals (*Nibandhas*).

Finally, the *Virūpākṣavasantotsavacampū*, a text in prose and verse dating from the fifteenth century AD has, as its principal subject, the documentation of the *Vasantotsava* as practiced during the Vijayanagara period of Indian history.[7] Location-specific, the *Campū* provides a different perspective on the festival: it is here described primarily as a Śaiva temple festival revolving around the deeds of Virūpākṣa (Śiva) and his consort Pampā (Pārvatī). Simultaneously, however, it validates the king of Vijayanagara, the capital of his kingdom, and his sovereignty over this realm.

Occasionally the information in these five primary texts is only briefly sketched and we must turn to other supplementary Sanskrit sources to flesh out our portrait of the *Vasantotsava*. The wealth of extant alternate representations of this festival, for the most part containing brief descriptions of it, have not been included in full primarily due to the brevity of their descriptions. They are, however, large in number and their significance lies in that they either confirm or contradict the information contained in our more complete textual sources. Ritual texts including, for example, the *Gṛhya Sūtras*, *Śrauta Sūtras*, and *Nibandhas* enumerate the figures to be worshipped, the rituals to be performed, and, specifically, how they are to be performed. These sources are repositories of pertinent information regarding rituals and procedures which are, or ought to be, undertaken by individuals and groups of individuals either to gain merit or to fulfill a particular social obligation. These materials also contain significant data with respect to the mythological context in which the festival is set. So, for example, we learn of the exploits of various deities of the Hindu pantheon and their particular roles in the context of these celebrations. In short, our five primary texts coupled with these explanatory ritual texts reveal the panoply of vernal celebrations described and prescribed by the Sanskrit literati of the Hindu tradition. In formalizing our understanding of the festivities, we shall rely on these five primary texts as guides.

We can glean from these Sanskrit portrayals of the Spring Festival information which delineates the festivities within the parameters of a particularized and ritually circumscribed environment exclusive to a select elite and also information regarding the celebration of spring that is more generalized, more *popular*, in which a majority of individuals from all sectors of society is engaged. Each text formulates the festival in accordance with its own frame of reference. Each portrayal of the celebrations is, indeed, a portrayal, a stylized vision filtered through the media of the text. Just as each festival is celebrated in a particular way at a particular time, so too, each of our descriptions is unique to a specific author, time, and place. Just as the rites and myths of which this festival is composed are negotiated or renegotiated in every celebration, so too, are they recast in every textual description.[8] The sketch generated from these specific and general source materials becomes more sharply delineated by analyzing the various elements of which this festival is composed, the manner in which they combine and re-combine, as well as by examining some of the major themes which the festival embodies. When examined *in toto,* this body of Sanskrit texts gives us a broader description of the celebration of the *Vasantotsava* than any single text. The vigourous and colourful modern Spring Festival is one of the few spring festivals described in both ancient and medieval texts to survive into modern times. Since this is the case, our analysis may provide some background through which the modern Spring Festival may be more readily understood.

The Date of the *Vasantotsava*

Although it is clear from our textual descriptions that the *Vasantotsava* was a major festival in classical India, establishing its position in the Hindu calendar is a somewhat baffling operation as texts describing it are not unanimous as to precisely when in the spring season it was to be celebrated. Confusion is due, in part, to the number of apparently similar festivals which cluster around the vernal equinox. The texts themselves occasionally refer to *a Vasantotsava* without sufficient mention of the specifics of its celebration, thus further compounding the confusion. In the literature, where a festival is incidentally mentioned in the context of some other event in a story, rarely do we find a date specified even though we may find the festival itself both named and described.

Traditionally, the advent of spring is celebrated at the time of the vernal equinox which occurs in the Hindu calendar at the end of the lunar month of Phālguna (February-March) and the beginning of the month of Caitra (March-April). The *Vasantotsavanirṇaya,*[9] a medieval text devoted almost entirely to the question of when the *Vasantotsava* is to be celebrated, is of great importance to our study. It tells us:

> *caitrakṛṣṇapratipadi vasantotsavah sā caudayikī grāhyā pravṛtte madhumāse tu pratipadyutite ravau* /
>
> (The *Vasantotsava* is to be celebrated on the first day of the dark half of Caitra: specifically, when the sun rises. As it is said, on the first day in the month of Madhu [Caitra, spring] when the sun first comes up at the new fortnight.)

This is corroborated by the *Varṣakṛtyādīpikā*[10] which reads verbatim, thus identifying the date of the *Vasantotsava* as the first day of the dark half of Caitra or the day after the full moon in Phālguna.

The *Nityotsava*[11] which belongs to the *tantric* tradition and dates to medieval times, is in variance with the *Vasantotsavanirṇaya* and the *Varṣakṛtyādīpikā* when it states that the *Vasantotsava* is to be celebrated on the full moon day of Caitra.. Thus:[12]

> *Caitrapūrṇimākṛtyam asyāmeva pūrṇimāyāṁ vasantotsavo'pi vihitah*
>
> (The *Vasantotsava* is also to be performed on the full moon day of Caitra [It is a festival of the full moon of Caitra].) (108.7)

A wide variety of texts, both ancient and medieval, tells us simply that the *Vasantotsava* is a festival celebrating the advent of spring (*vasantasamayotsava* or *vasantārambha* [*varṣa*]).[13] Several texts mention a festival specifically called the *Vasantotsava* but do not actually tell us when it is to occur. The eleventh century AD Jain *Triṣaṣṭiśalākāpuruṣacaritamahākāvya*[14] falls into this latter category, giving us no precise date for the festival but rather indicating simply that the *Vasantotsava* is anticipated with eagerness.

ko 'pyavācaihi bhagavan! gṛhānyanugrhāna nah /
vasantotsavavad deva! cirādasi nirīkṣitah //

> *vasantotsavavad deva! cirādasi nirīkṣitaḥ* //
> (O honoured one! Come to my house. It has been so long since I've seen you - as long as the *Vasantotsava* itself. You are welcome after such a long time, i.e., the eagerness in looking forward to the visit of a seer is like the eagerness one experiences in looking forward to the *Vasantotsava*).
> (1.3.253)

Various modern scholars give correspondingly different views. Chattopadhyaya, basing his analysis on the *Kathāsaritsāgara* which originated in north India, asserts that the *Vasantotsava* is to be celebrated on the full moon day of Caitra.[15] L. Babb on the other hand notes that it is to be celebrated in Chhattisgarh in north India on the first day of the light half of Caitra (the day of the new moon).[16]

The dates for the celebration of the *Vasantotsava* thus range from the first day of the dark half of Caitra, the day of the full moon in Caitra and the first day of the light half of Caitra. The perplexity in determining the exact date of the *Vasantotsava* is partially dispelled when we consider that spring season extends from as early as the month of Māgha (January-February) to Vaiśākha (April-May). During this breadth of time a number of celebrations occur; some clearly belong to the Spring Festival, the *Vasantotsava* variety, while others do not. Our texts describing the *Vasantotsava* incorporate a wide range of seasonal motifs together with all the connotative and denotative associations appropriate to the spring.[17]

NOTES

1 Śrī Harṣa, *Ratnāvalī* , preface and trans., by C.R. Devadhar and N.G. Suru (Poona: 1954); Somadeva, *Kathāsaritsāgara*, ed. by Pandit Durgaprasad and K.P. Parab (Bombay: 1899) and Somadeva, *Kathāsaritsāgara or The Ocean of the Streams of Story*, trans. by C.H. Tawney (Calcutta: 1880); *Vikrama's Adventures (Thirty-Two Tales of the Throne)*, ed. and trans. by F. Edgerton (Cambridge: 1926); and Ahobala, *Virūpākṣavasantotsavacampū* , intro. by V. R.S. Panchamukhi (Dharwar: 1953).

[3] M. Krishnamachariar, *History of Classical Sanskrit Literature* (3rd ed., Delhi: 1974), pp. 419-20.

[4] This text is also known as the *Siṁhāsanadvātriṁsikā.* There are various versions the *Vikramacarita* attributed, for example, to Kālidāsa, Rāmacandra, Śiva, and the Jain author Śiva Siddhasena Divākara Kṣemaṅkara. The Jain recension is the latest and dates to the fourteenth century AD (Krishnamachariar, pp. 428-9). Vikrama's adventures are also the subject of a variety of other works, including the *Vīracarita* of Ananta and the *Vikramodaya.*

[5] A. Berriedale Keith, *A History of Sanskrit Literature* (Indian ed., Delhi: 1973), pp. 191-3.

[6] Certain sections of the *Bhaviṣya Purāṇa* may be as late as the sixteenth or seventeenth century AD while others are probably earlier, dating to the eighth or eleventh century AD.

[7] The Vijayanagara period dates approximately from the fourteenth to the sixteenth century AD.

[8] S. Hanchett's usage of the term 'negotiable' in her discussion of the various elements in south Indian festivals seems appropriate also to our discussion of the components of which the Spring Festival is composed. S. Hanchett "The Festival Interlude" in G.R. Welbon and G.E. Yocum, *Religious Festivals in South India and Sri Lanka* (Delhi: 1982), pp. 219-242, pp. 225f.

[9] *Vasantotsavanirṇaya,* np., nd., pp. 1ff.

[10] Nityānanda, *Varṣakṛtyādīpikā (A Treatise on the Hindu Rites during the Year),* Kasi Sanskrit Series 96 (Varanasi: 1967), p. 117.

[11] Umānandanātha, *Nityotsava,* ed. by A. Mahadeva Śastri (Baroda: 1948), 108.7.

[12] In addition to these methods, another manner of calculating the festival date with reference to fixed stars (the sidereal year) is employed in such texts as the Pāñcarātra *Paremeśvara Saṁhitā:*

> *caitre māsi punarvasvoh/ vasantotsavam ācaret //*
>
> (The *Vasantotsava* should be performed in the month of Caitra on the occasion of the *punarvasu* star).

When the *punarvasu* star occurs in the month of Caitra, the celebration of the *Vasantotsava* is prescribed. We may take this to mean that celebrating the *Vasantotsava* on the full moon of Caitra is not required, but it is fortuitous when the full moon happens to coincide with the day of the *punarvasu* star. The *punarvasu* star belongs to the fifth and seventh lunar mansions and is associated with either Viṣṇu or Śiva.

[13] E.g., *Varṣakṛtyādīpikā,* p. 287.

[14] Hemachandra, *Triṣaṣṭiśalākāpuruṣacaritamahākāvya,* 2 vols. (Bhāvnagar: 1936), VII. 1.3.253 [*parvan, sarga, śloka*].

[15] A. Chattopadhyaya, "The Spring Festival and Festival of Indra in the *Kathāsaritsāgara*," in *Journal of the Oriental Institute, Baroda*, XVII (Dec. 1967), part 2, pp. 137-141.

[16] See, for example, L. Babb, *The Divine Hierarchy* (New York: 1975), p. 124.

[17] H. D. Smith in his survey of festivals in Pāñcarātra literature refers to a number of festivals which incorporate seasonal motifs. "Festivals in Pāñcarātra Literature" in G.R. Welbon and G. E. Yocum, *Religious Festivals in South India and Sri Lanka*, pp. 27-50, p. 35.

2

The *Vasantotsava* and its Variants

Even a cursory examination of the abundance of descriptions of Indian spring festivals (*Vasantotsavas*) in the Sanskrit literary tradition reveals that it is difficult to isolate a single *Spring Festival*, a single *Vasantotsava*. Strict circumscription of *the Vasantotsava* is problematic due primarily to the variety of festivals which cluster around this season. Our textual evidence suggests that certain identifiable spring observances are intimately related and should therefore legitimately be examined under the title '*Vasantotsava*.' Historically, the festivals which are to be celebrated at the advent of the vernal season include the *Vasantotsava, Holākā,* (*Holī*), *Phālgunotsava, Caitrotsava, Phaggu, Madhūtsava, Madanamahotsava, Madanatrayodaśī, Anaṅgotsava, Madanadvādaśī,* and *Kāmotsava*. So, for example, the Spring Festival is called the *Yātramahotsava* of Madana in the *Śṛṅgāramañjarīkathā* and the *Kāmamahotsava* in the *Kāvyaviveka*.[1] It is referred to as both the festival of Madana (*Madanamahotsava*) and the *Caitrotsava* in both the *Ratnāvalī* and the *Bhaviṣya Purāṇa* (135). In the *Bhāvaprakāśa* it is called the *Madanotsava* of Vasanta.[2] The *Deśīnamāmālā* refers to it simply as *Phaggu* (Spring Festival) whereas the *Dāyabhāga, Bhaviṣya Purāṇa* (132) and the *Kāṭhaka Gṛhya Sūtra* identify it as *Holī* or *Holākā*.[3] The *Kathākośa* names it *Madanotsava* and the *Gāthāsaptaśatī* and the *Bhaviṣya Purāṇa*

(132) both refer to the *Vasantotsava* as *Phālgunotsava* and *Madanamahotsava*.[4]

The problem of whether or not this cornucopia of names refers to interchangeable festivals can be resolved in a number of ways. First and most directly, we could assume that all these terms are synonymous with the *Vasantotsava* and that there is only one Spring Festival. This seems to be true for many of the names enumerated above. The *Kamotsava, Anaṅgotsava, Madanamahotsava, Madanatrayodaśī* and *Madanadvādaśī* are likely the same festival, festivals in which the god of love/desire is worshipped. Anaṅga, Madana, and Kāma all are names of the god of love. Similarly, the *Madhūtsava* and the *Caitrotsava* would seem to be synonyms for the term *Vasantotsava*. *Vasanta* and *Madhu* are both words meaning spring; the month of Caitra is also called Madhu.

From these variously named festivals then, three potentially distinct clusters emerge. These are: festivals designated simply as spring festivals, festivals of Kāma and festivals called *Holī*. As to the relationship between these clusters, the most manageable hypothesis is to assume that the *Vasantotsava* is a generic festival which accommodates the widest variety of observances bearing structural similarities but exhibiting many regional variants. According to this hypothesis, there would appear to be no one normative *Vasantotsava* but a number of *Vasantotsava*s which are offtimes identified by the general term 'Spring Festival' or '*Vasantotsava*' but which every so often are given a more specific designation such as '*Kāmotsava*' or '*Holī*.'[5]

Scholars generally agree that there are separate components to the spring festivities and that there are separate festivals that cluster around the spring season, although in numerous instances there is confusion as to the general nature and nomination of these celebrations. Opinion differs as well regarding their formulation and number. V. Raghavan who has published prolifically in this field identifies the *Vasantotsava* (*Madanotsava* or *Madanatrayodaśī* or *Anaṅgotsava*) and *Holī* as separate festivals and describes the *Madanotsava* as only a component aspect of the *Vasantotsava*.[6] Hence when discussing the *Vasantotsava*, Raghavan says:

> This is the Spring Festival proper, for celebrating the advent of Spring, the most pleasant of the seasons....People drink and rejoice in the company of women, throw water through Syringes, and coloured powder, on each other. (p. 86)

With reference to the *Madanotsava* or the *Madanatrayodaśī*, he says:

> This is the worship of the God of Love and comes off on the 13th of the bright half of the *Caitra-Śukla-Trayodaśī* and is hence called *Madana-trayodaśī*. Manmatha and his spouse Rati, as also their friend and aid, the Spring, Vasanta, are worshipped on this day by ladies. (p. 86)

An excellent picture of this festival is in the same play *Ratnāvalī* (Act 1) where the Queen performs this worship. It is part of the Spring Festival [*Vasantotsava*?] and the series of happy celebrations. (p. 87)

And under the heading of *Holī*, Raghavan remarks:

> We may notice lastly a festival which completes the cycle of the year and brings us back to the Spring festival of the God of Love with which we began. In the month of Phālguna, the signs of the coming Spring are already seen. The chief festival which occurs at this time on the full moon day is the *Holī* or Holikā or Holākā.... (p. 193)

Raghavan goes on to describe the destruction of the demoness Holākā as outlined in the *Bhaviṣya Purāṇa* (132), and the wide-spread tossing about of coloured powder which is also characteristic of *Holī*. Then he remarks:

> In much later times, the earlier phase of the anti-child demoness and her killing recedes completely. The worship of the God of Love, which follows on the next day becomes prominent, and *Holī* and its

bonfire coalesces with the story of the God of Love being burnt in Śiva's third eye. (p. 201)

These statements are somewhat baffling. The worship of Kāma (*Madanotsava*) by Raghavan's own admission is on the thirteenth day of Caitra, not on the day after *Holī*, i.e., not on the day following the full moon in the month of Phālguna. If we take the worship of Kāma to mark the beginning of spring, then what is the distinction between the *Madanotsava* and the *Vasantotsava*? Moreover, Raghavan describes both *Holī* and *Vasantotsava* as festivals of over-all merriment and powder throwing popular amongst women. If it is not possible to distinguish these festivals in terms of time or content, how, then, are they to be differentiated?

Similarly, B.N. Sharma also makes a distinction between the *Vasantotsava* and *Holī*. Concomitantly, he identifies the *Vasantotsava* as *Ṛtūtsava* as is described in the *Raghuvaṁśa* of Kālidāsa (fifth century AD), the *Yātramahotsava* of Madana as portrayed by King Bhoja in the *Śṛṅgāramañjarīkathā* (eleventh century AD) and the *Kāmamahotsava* as defined by Jīmūtavāhana.[7] P. Thomas in *Festivals and Holidays of India* describes the Spring Festival succinctly as *Holī* and omits any reference whatsoever to the *Vasantotsava* or to the *Kāmotsava*.[8] A. Chattopadhyaya in "The Spring Festival and Festival of Indra in the *Kathāsaritsāgara*" argues that *Holī* and the *Vasantotsava* are different and separate festivals.[9]

Contradistinctively, there appears to be a tendency amongst scholars to differentiate between various spring festivals as much as there is also a tendency to establish equations between them. Raghavan as noted above, seems to equate the *Vasantotsava* and the *Madanatrayodaśī* or *Madanotsava* or *Anaṅgotsava*. Sharma clearly likens the *Vasantotsava* to the *Ṛtūtsava*, the *Yātramahotsava*, and the *Kāmamahotsava*. Basham, in *The Wonder That Was India* matches *Holī* with the *Vasantotsava* of ancient times.[10] Clearly, an assessment of these conclusions in the light of more extensive textual evidence than has been used by previous scholars is in order.

The *Vasantotsava* and the Worship of Kāma

One of the more profitable equations we could examine would be that between the *Vasantotsava* and the festival of Kāma. Under the rubric of a 'festival of Kāma' we can include the following: *Madanamahotsava, Madanatrayodaśī, Madanadvādaśī, Anaṅgotsava* and *Kāmotsava*. Both Raghavan and Chattopadhyaya describe the festival of Kāma as one associated with the *Vasantotsava*. Raghavan assumes the Madana festival to have been part of a larger festival for which he retains the title *Vasantotsava* (p.87), while Chattopadhyaya sees the two as essentially identical. Chattopadhyaya further describes the *Vasantotsava* as a festival of love with the worship of Kāma as its primary distinguishing feature (*Kāmotsava*). However, we know that the *Madanadvādaśī* is to be celebrated on the twelfth day of Caitra, the *Madanatrayodaśī* on the thirteenth. Neither of these dates agree with those given for the *Vasantotsava* by either Raghavan (the first day of Caitra [1 Caitra]) or Chattopadhyaya (30 Caitra). Some reconciliation is necessary.

One possible solution to this conundrum is that the *Vasantotsava* is not specific to one day but is celebrated over a span of time. The spring season after all is not just one day in the year. The well-known *Ratnāvalī* of Harṣa, which dates to the seventh century AD contains an important description of this festival in which the celebrations appear to last for a minimum of three consecutive days. In this play, which is often cited as an exhaustive description of the *Vasantotsava*,[11] the festival is specifically called the *Vasantotsava, Madanamahiyāṅs* (Madana's festival), *Madanamahotsava* and simply *Madhu* lending support to the interpretation that equates the festival of Kāma with the *Vasantotsava*.[12] This text is not explicit regarding the date of the Spring Festival but seems to give us yet another day in Caitra for its commencement. C.R. Devadhar and N.G. Suru in their introduction to the text, tell us that the festival probably commences on the thirteenth day of the bright half of Caitra and lasts through to the full moon day. The dramatic scenario comprises five or six days.[13] There is no transition in the *Ratnāvalī* from one festival to another and no procedural distinction is made between the celebrations described. Under the designation *Vasantotsava*, the festivities in the *Ratnāvalī* include those noticed elsewhere as separate festivals.[14] Thus, the day set aside for the worship of Madana (Kāma), known as the *Madanatrayodaśī*, is in the *Ratnāvalī*, described as part of the *Vasantotsava*[15] while the overall festival occurs under the umbrella or blanket term of *'Vasantotsava'* or *'Madanamahotsava.'*

The linkages among these festivals, be they implicit or explicit, are indicated further by the *Kāmasūtra* which declares that the *Madanamahotsava* is the *Vasantotsava*.[16] The *Kathāsaritsāgara* describes a festival very similar to that in the *Ratnāvalī* which it identifies as either *Madhūtsava* or simply *'Madhu'*.[17] The *Kathākośa*, a compilation of Jain folklore, contains a story of Sanatkumāra which reports a festival called the *Vasantotsava* identifying the details of this festival (earlier referred to as the *Vasantotsava*) with those of the *Madanotsava* of spring:[18]

> *āpānakelīh śakrārcā vasantamadanotsavāh* /
>
> (The festivities of the *Vasantotsava* and the *Madanotsava* involve drinking and the worship of Indra.) (23.11)

The *Bhaviṣya Purāṇa* calls a similar celebration *Madanamahotsava*[19]

Texts making specific reference to the spring celebration as an aspect of the worship of Kāma include the *Pārijāta-Mañjarī*, a play transcribed from an inscription dating from the twelfth century AD.[20] The festival herein is alternately mentioned as the *Vasantotsava* or the *Caitrotsava*. The celebration consists simply of the worship of Madana.[21] In Rajasthan during Cauhan rule, one of the most important festivals was the *Vasantotsava* or Spring Festival, celebrated in honour of Madana or Kāma.[22] Thus ancient and more modern authors in dealing with a Spring Festival (*Vasantotsava, Caitrotsava*) stress the worship of Kāma, often explicitly naming the Spring Festival as the festival of Kāma.

Complicating further the present discussion is the existence of yet another festival, the *Śrīpañcamī*, which although usually associated with the worship of Lakṣmī is, in the *Varṣakṛtyādīpikā*, described as the day set aside for worshipping Kāmadeva and his consort Rati. Clearly, this is the *Vasantotsava*.[23] It is to take place on the bright half, fifth day of Māgha. The text reads as follows:

> *māghe śukla pañcamī śrīpañcamī /*
> *asyām ratikāmayoh pūjanādinā vasantamahotsavah kāryah //*
>
> (On the fifth day of the bright half of Māgha is the *Śrīpañcamī*. On this day the great festival of spring [*Vasantotsava*] is to be performed by worshipping Rati and Kāma and other activities.)

The *Śrīpañcamī* is as well described in the *Haribhaktivilāsa*.[24]

> 167. *māghasya śuklapañcamyāṁ mahāpūjām samācaret /*
> *navaih pravalaih kusumairanulepair viseṣatah //*
>
> 170. *kṛtva vasantapañcamyāṁ śrīkṣṛṣṇārcanotsavaṁ /*
> *syād vasantiva preyavanavihāriṇah //*
>
> (On the bright fifth of Māgha one should perform an elaborate ceremony with new shoots, flowers and unguents.
>
> Having performed this worship of the image of Kṛṣṇa on the spring fifth one becomes beloved of that one sporting in Vṛndāvana, just as the spring is beloved of him.)

This Vaiṣṇava text, written before the middle of the sixteenth century AD, characterizes the *Śrīpañcamī* as a festival of spring[25] to be celebrated on the fifth day in that season. Kṛṣṇa is the object of devotion in this text while Kāma fails to make an appearance.

In summary, what we have is a festival dedicated to Kāma which sometimes is *included* as part of the *Vasantotsava* and sometimes is *equated* with the *Vasantotsava*. In at least one instance, the *Madanadvādaśī* is transformed into a sectarian festival where Kṛṣṇa, worshipped as lover (*Madanagopāla*), assumes the function of Kāma. A celebration identified as the *Śrīpañcamī* and associated closely with the *Vasantotsava*[26] finds a form in the *Haribhaktivilāsa* in which the focus is neither on Kāma nor Lakṣmī. This festival is still, however, celebrated on the fifth of spring (*Vasantapañcamī*). It is thus clear that the identification of the *Vasantotsava* with the *Madanotsava* has support from ancient and medieval texts alike. Even in those cases where one cannot assert the absolute identity of these two festivals, it is clear from the texts that the worship of Kāmadeva, the god of love, was very intimately linked to the celebration of spring.

Vasantotsava and *Holī*

While many modern scholars equate the *Vasantotsava* with the *Madanadvādaśī*, others, including Chattopadhyaya and Raghavan, refuse to accept the correspondence of *Holī* and *Vasantotsava*. Chattopadhyaya's primary argument against this is that the two festivals are celebrated a month apart (*Holī* is celebrated on 30 Phālguna, *Vasantotsava* on 30 Caitra). Yet this temporal question does not deter him from equating the *Kāmotsava* with the *Vasantotsava* which are situated anywhere from thirteen to seventeen days apart. Raghavan's position that *Holī* and *Vasantotsava* are different festivals is based on the argument that *Holī* marks the end of the old year and *Vasantotsava* celebrates the beginning of the new year: hence *Holī* is celebrated on 30 Phālguna; *Vasantotsava* on 1 Caitra. Again, Raghavan's position, based on a difference in dating, is not entirely consistent: a time difference did not deter him from identifying the *Madanamahotsava* and the *Vasantotsava* as the same festival.

As previously noted, texts as early as the *Kāmasūtra*[27] equate the following: *Holākā*, *Vasantotsava* (or *suvasantaka*),

2. Kṛṣṇa and Rādhā playing *Holī*
Kangra, *circa* A.D. 1780

Madanamahotsava, Caitrotsava and *Phālgunotsava*. According to Mayuravamāli's commentary on the *Mīmāṁsaka* text, the *Śāstradīpikā*, the *Vasantotsava* is *Holākā*.[28] Hence:

> *holāketi / vasantotsava holāko*
>
> (*Holākā* is a Spring Festival [*Vasantotsava*].)

Yet another *Mīmāṁsaka* text, the *Nyāyamālāvistara*, specifically describes *Holākā* (the modern *Holī*) as the *Vasantotsava*.[29] Hence:

> *holākādattah prācyair eva kriyante /*
> *vasantotsava holākā*
>
> ([Festivals] like *Holākā* are performed only by easterners. *Holākā* is a Spring Festival [*Vasantotsava*].)

The section in the *Bhaviṣya Purāṇa* entitled *Phālgunotsava*[30] tells us that the *Phālgunotsava*, or *Holākā*, takes place on the fourteenth and fifteenth day of the bright fortnight in Phālguna (i.e., the full moon of Phālguna) and the day following the full moon (1 Caitra). It refers to the *Phālgunotsava* as *Phālgu*.[31] In addition, the *Deśīnamāmālā*, a lexicon compiled in the eleventh century AD, also speaks of a festival called *Phaggu*.[32] K. Deshpande has commented that the description given of the festival in the *Deśīnamāmālā* indicates that it is a counterpart of the Spring Festival described in the *Ratnāvalī*.[33] *Holī* is to be celebrated according to the *Nāradīya Purāṇa*[34] on the last day of Phālguna, suggesting that *Holī*, *Phālguna* and *Vasantotsava* are thus cognate festivals. Finally, when the *Varṣakṛtyādīpikā* ;and the *Vasantotsavanirṇaya* describe the *Vasantotsava* which occurs on the first day of the dark half of Caitra, they both cite the *Bhaviṣya Purāṇa* as the evidence for its performance. The section of the *Bhaviṣya Purāṇa* to which they refer is the portion describing the destruction of the demoness Holākā.[35] Hence, Holākā and Phālguna are cognates and the Spring Festival of ancient and medieval times survives thematically as the modern *Holī*. Curiously, among the myriad of Spring Festivals described in ancient Sanskrit texts, it is only *Holī* to have survived.

Unfortunately, however, to regard *Holākā* simply as a synonym for the *Vasantotsava* is not sufficient. In some textual instances there is an indication that *Holākā* is not *the Vasantotsava* but rather simply *a vasantotsava* (a spring festival). Texts like the *Nyāyamālāvistara*, for example, imply that the festival was local and confined to the east where it was called *Holākā*.[36] Whether the festival is called *Holākā* or *Vasantotsava*, it is given general authority and is said to be enjoined for all Hindus. It is thus difficult to maintain strict distinctions between *Holākā* and the *Vasantotsava* as in their Sanskrit descriptions they coincide, cross boundaries and disengage from each other. The *Vasantotsava* would seem to be a festival which, depending on circumstance and region, takes a variety of forms. One such form would be *Holākā* which was largely confined to the east. This seems to hold true today in that *Holī* is celebrated primarily in north and northeast India. Safely, we can say that *Holī* is the *Vasantotsava* of north-east India.

A further question to be considered, in addition to the nature and number of the *Vasantotsavas*, is their antiquity. The name *Holākā* is found, in fact, in the *Atharvaveda Pariśiṣṭas*.[37] The *Pariśiṣṭas (addenda)* are early, ritual texts which follow the *Śrauta* and *Gṛhya Sūtras*.[38] This seems to indicate that *Holākā* is an old and independent celebration rather than simply a modern manifestation of the ancient *Vasantotsava*.

In sum, the '*Vasantotsava*,' literally 'Spring Festival,' is probably an inclusive term used in the sources as a generic name for festivals occurring in the spring season. Its parameters are broadly sketched and often include the worship of Kāma as at certain times in history and in certain places, the *Vasantotsava* is a *Kāmotsava* or contains a *Kāmotsava*. Given the contextual origins of the particular text, be they historical, geographical or sociological, the signification of language and rituals described require variant interpretations. Thus, given the prominence of the worship of Kāma in the Spring Festival as described in the *Ratnāvalī*, we might suggest here that the *Kāmotsava* represents a central Indian version of the festival.[39] In other times and places the *Vasantotsava* is *Holī*, a festival in the *Bhaviṣya Purāṇa* (132) associated with the burning of a demoness. In all cases, the term *Vasantotsava* is applicable to such local festivals. In no case, is it strictly definable as one limited term.

Vasantotsava and Regional Celebrations

One possibility which we might entertain and which might dispel some of the confusion surrounding the celebration of this festival is to suggest that the *Vasantotsava* was largely a regional celebration, strongly coloured by local customs. This would, at least in part, account for the bewildering variety of descriptions and nomenclature. As some texts seem to tell us that the festival was local and confined to certain regions of the subcontinent (as, for example, the *Nyāyamālavistara*, above) while others suggest that it is to be considered a pan-Indian celebration imbued with generalized authority (as, for example, the *Varṣakṛtyādīpikā* and the *Vasantotsavanirṇaya*, above), there is no simple way to approach this eventuality.

The *Śāstradīpikā* suggests that the *Vasantotsava* was in practice *both* a local event and that it was supported by scriptural authority valid for people living in all parts of the country. *Holākā* in this instance is not performed by everyone but only by those in the east (*prācya*).[40] Hence:

> *Holākādayo hi kaiścideva prācyādyabhimānibhir anusthīyante na sarvaih* /
>
> (Festivals like *Holākā* are performed by those who consider themselves as coming from the east and not by everyone.) (1.3.8)

The *Śāstradīpikā* also discusses the question of the scriptural basis for festivals like the *Holākā* or *Vasantotsava*.[41] It begins with a *purvapakṣa*, an objection, stating that because the *Vasantotsava* is not recorded in Manu or in the *vedic* texts, there is no basis for observing it. However, the reply is given that although it is not recorded in the *Veda*, it is observed by people who are accepted as *śiṣṭhas*, i.e., those who, in the matter of their conduct, strictly adhere to *vedic* injunctions. Hence because it is observed by *śiṣṭhas*, it is implicitly graced with *vedic* sanction. That the *Vasantotsava* is not mentioned specifically in Manu is here considered to be irrelevant: Manu did not write the rules of conduct for all observances, for then his text would have been overwhelmingly long! After some debate, the *Śāstradīpikā* finally declares that the Spring Festival is, indeed, sanctioned by *vedic* authority.

In a section of his *Bhāsya* on the *Pūrvamīmāṁsa Sūtra*, Śabara argues that this *vedic* authority is a general one, applicable to all people even though the actual performance of *Holākā* is limited to certain regions in the country.[42] This author argues that, in fact, we observe only easterners performing *Holākā*. It is at this point that the question arises as to what is the scriptural basis for the Spring Festival. Śabara answers that it must be some *vedic* text and further on in his *Bhāsya* he treats the problem of the kinds of scriptural injunction we may infer. Since only easterners practice *Holākā*, he asks, are we to assume an injunction that is specific to easterners? The *purvapakṣa* declares this to be the case but Śabara replies that this is impracticable since we see that it is impossible to define the term 'easterners.' Does it mean people living in the east? Well, not all people living in the east do *Holākā*. Some are immigrants from the south, for example, and they do not observe *Holākā*. Does it mean people born in the east? Well, in that case think of easterners who moved away generations back and are now living in the north. Their grandchildren, though born in the north, still do *Holākā*. Ultimately, there is no satisfactory way to define a limited injunction and we must therefore assume a general injunction that enjoins all people to perform *Holākā*. If they do not, other causes must attribute. Śabara considers *Holākā* then as a *Vasantotsava* and a local one, specific to the east. This would imply the possibility of other spring festivals occurring elsewhere under other names such as, for example, *Kāmotsava*.

It is necessary to evaluate the information provided by Śabara in the light of all of our many other texts. Śabara regards the Spring Festival as both synonymous with *Holākā* and as a regional celebration which, though backed by a generalized *vedic* injunction valid for everyone in the country, was in fact observed only by easterners. It is interesting to note that Śabara is correct about *Holākā* itself, for modern ethnographic information corroborates his statement that it is a festival of the east.[43] But the corpus of texts available and referred to for this study broadens the base of the *Vasantotsava* beyond the regional and confirms the accuracy of Śabara's second presupposition: the *Vasantotsava* could indeed be celebrated by people all over the country. For example the *Nāradīya Purāṇa* and the *Kathāsaritsāgara,* both of which describe the Spring Festival, originated in Kashmir confirming the existence of a spring celebration there. The *Ratnāvalī* hails from central India while the *Dolayatraviveka* was written by a Bengali and the *Virūpakṣavasantotsavacampū* was composed in Vijayanagara.[44] Thus, texts record the practice of this festival all over India. Śabara's recognition of *Holākā* as the *Vasantotsava,* as coupled with the fact that *Holākā* is specific to the east, led him to conclude wrongly that the Spring Festival was a purely regional phenomenon. The modern scholar would be more accurate to surmise instead that the festival differed greatly from place to place, a fact that led ancient scholars like Śabara to identify the observance as a purely local manifestation failing to recognize the existence of related celebrations.

Moreover, the texts indicate that the festival for which Śabara was at such great pains to establish *vedic* authority, was celebrated equally by the non-*vedic* religions of Jainism and Buddhism as well as by those normally taken to fall outside the purview of *vedic* injunctions, i.e., the lowest castes or *śūdras.* Hence in Burlingame's *Buddhist Legends,* Buddhists also play *Holī.*[45] The festival is called *Bālanakkhatta* (*Bālanakṣatra*) and it is observed for seven days. The *Bālanakkhatta* was popularly engaged with such vigour that, at Śrāvastī, the Buddha was unable to enter the city for seven days during which the festival was being observed. During this time the lower castes smear their bodies with cow dung and ash, engage in coarse talking and insults, while extracting money from each other.

The Jain *Kathākośa* contains a story wherein Sanatkumāra, the son of the king, goes into the forest to celebrate the Spring Festival.[46] And again, in the same text, King Sāgarachandra is described attending the festival of spring adorned with royal splendour. Even today Jains observe special fasts on the full moon of Caitra and, if possible, enter onto pilgrimages. They fast on *Phālgun Punema* (the full moon in Phālguna) and decorate their temples. *Oli* or *Āmbella* which occurs eight days before the full moon in Caitra is observed annually by Jain adherents. Great fairs are held at the chief places of pilgrimage and these are attended by Jains from all over India. At this time men and women take special vows as to what they will eat, promising, for instance, to consume only one kind of grain throughout the day and to drink only boiled water. *Oli* is the fast *par excellence* of women, for it is recorded that on this occasion a royal princess, Mayanā Sundarī, by worshipping the saint-wheel, won health and restoration of the kingdom for her husband, Śrīpāla, who had been a leper. Thus, women who want a happy married life have been specially diligent in observing this fast, giving up (for the time) any food they particularly like, such as melted butter or molasses, and eating only one sort of dish.[47] Tradition has it moreover that on *Caitra Punema* (the full moon of Caitra) the chief disciple of Ṛṣabhadeva, Puṇḍarīka Ganadhara, obtained *kaivalya* along with fifty million monks.

The Śaiva *Lokāyatikas* and the *Kāpālikas*, according to D.R. Shastri, observed a year which was replete with festivals. They made it a rule to meet twice a year, on the *Vasantotsava* and the *Kaumudīmahotsava*, specifically for enjoying pleasures with full freedom.[48]

According to Raghavan, among the multiple elements of this day's sanctity are the Brāhmaṇic tradition which states that this is the birthday of one of the fourteen Manus as well as the Buddhist tradition which states that the Sun, the Moon, Sumeru and the Himālayas were created on this day.[49] He also suggests that the unbridled behavior typical of the *Vasantotsava* underlies the fact that the festival has a special vogue among lower castes. In some parts of the country there was *even* a practice of the higher castes ceremoniously touching the lower castes prior to their daily bath.[50] The *Vasantotsava*, it seems, was a festival kept by all castes. According to Khare in *The Hindu Hearth and Home* some popular Hindi books classify major festivals in terms of the *varṇa* classification. Here *Holī* is for *śūdras, Dīvāli* for *vaiśyas*.[51]

From the array of titles examined above, a definitive picture of the *Vasantotsava* fails to emerge. Yet we are able to cull some broad generalizations concerning it: the *Vasantotsava* was a festival composed of a wide variety of elements as described in the texts (sometimes equating it with the *Madanamahotsava* and at other times identifying it with *Holī*) which make clear that the *Vasantotsava* was celebrated in diverse ways throughout the different regions of India. Depending upon the text consulted, it occurred at various times. It was a festival which, according to certain other sources, overlapped chronologically with other festivals and occasionally was an admixture of these many diverse celebrations. Modern scholars admit to puzzlement as to what exactly comprises the *Vasantotsava* and much of this is due, in fact, to the textual confusion. Most modern scholars refer to the description in the *Ratnāvalī* as typical. This account includes the *Madanamahotsava* and if we distill the *Madanamahotsava* from within the *Ratnāvalī* we are left with a description of general merriment and powder throwing (i.e, the usual description of *Holī*). In fact there is a dearth of descriptions of the *Vasantotsava* that fail to refer either to Kāma-worship or to *Holī*.

Given all of these discrepancies, it may be suggested that the *Vasantotsava* was not, in fact, a specific Spring Festival composed of *specific* ritual practices to be celebrated at a *specific* time but rather that the term *Vasantotsava* was an umbrella term which meant simply and literally 'Spring Festival.' *Vasantotsava*, as a blanket term, may include a large number of festivals celebrated in the spring and it may or may not itself be treated as a festival separate from these other festivals. This would account for the tendency of the authors of Sanskrit texts to commingle numerous festivals of different names under the term *Vasantotsava*. Once it is accepted that the *Vasantotsava* is a term to be understood in a generic sense then it is easy to reconcile the discrepancies in the descriptions of it. Some of these differences must clearly be regional differences; spring is celebrated differently in different regions. Others may be due to historical changes in patterns of worship and sectarian differences. Often, if not always, there occurs a direct connection between Hindu mythology proper and the Spring Festival, e.g., sometimes Kāma and his destruction by Śiva are associated with the *Vasantotsava* while at other times it is Holākā and her destruction by Kṛṣṇa that occasions the Festival.

NOTES

[1] B.N. Sharma, *Festivals of India* (New Delhi: 1978), p. 17.

[2] Śāradātanaya, *Bhāvaprakāśa*, ed. by B. Bhattacharyya (Baroda: 1930), 111.99.18.

[3] Hemachandra, *Deśīnamāmālā*, ed. by R. Pischel (Bombay: 1938), VI. 82; Jīmūtavāhana, *Dāyabhāga*, trans. by H.T. Colebrooke (Calcutta: 1868) and also the *Kāṭhaka Gṛhya Sūtra*, ed. by Dr. W. Caland (Lahore: 1925), 73.l.

[4] *Ratnāvalī* (Poona: 1954), Act 1ff.; Hāla, *Gāthāsaptaśatī*, ed., intro., trans. by R. Basac (Calcutta: 1971), 4.69; *Bhaviṣya Purāṇa* (Bombay: 1959), chapters 132, 135.

[5] The *Kāmotsava* would refer specifically to the worship of Kāma while *Holī* would refer to the throwing of coloured powder.

[6] V. Raghavan, *Festivals* (Ahmedabad: 1979), pp. 86-88, 193-203.

[7] B.N. Sharma, *Festivals of India*, pp. 12, 14.

[8] P. Thomas, *Festivals and Holidays*, p. 7.

[9] A. Chattopadhyaya, "The Spring Festival and the Festival of Indra in the *Kathāsaritsāgara*," p. 139.

[10] A.L. Basham, *The Wonder That Was India* (New York: 1959), p. 207.

[11] For example, Raghavan, Chattopadhyaya, Sharma and Thomas cite this text in reference to the Spring Festival.

[12] *Ratnāvalī*, pp. 4, 8, 10 and 12 respectively.

[13] *Ibid.*, p. 15, 21.

[14] That is to say that festivals like the *Madanadvādaśī* as described in texts like the *Matsya Purāṇa* (154) are not specifically described as part of the *Vasantotsava*. Rather, they are mentioned without reference

to it. See also the *Nīlamata Purāṇa* which describes *Madanatrayodaśī* without reference to the *Vasantotsava*. (*Nīlamata Purāṇa*, trans. by Dr. Ved Kumari, 2 vols. [Srinagar: 1973], II. 679)

15 *Ratnāvalī*, Act l, p. 4.

16 Vātsyāyana, *Kāmasūtra*, Chowkhambha Sanskrit Series LIV (Benares: 1929), p. 42.

17 *Kathāsaritsāgara*, lV.35; X.87, 88, 98; XXXV.6; LXXlX.6.

18 *Kathākośa*, 23.11 (page, line). This story may also be found in *Kathākośa*, trans. by C.H. Tawney (Delhi: 1975), pp. 31-32.

19 *Bhaviṣya Purāṇa* (Bombay: 1959), ch. 135.

20 Raja-Guru Madana *alias* Bala-Sarasvati, *Pārijāta-Mañjarī alias Vijayaśrī*, ed., trans. by S.K. Dikshit (Bhopal: 1963).

21 The description of the festival begins 1.3,13. For a discussion of the dating of the play see the introduction to the *Pārijāta-Mañjarī alias Vijayaśrī*,. p. vii.

22 D. Sharma, *Early Cauhan Dynastiess* , p. 266 as cited by Chattopadhayaya, "The Spring Festival and Festival of Indra," pp. 138-9.

23 *Varṣakṛtyādīpikā*, p. 288.

24 Gopala Bhatta, *Haribhaktivilāsa* (Bengali script [Transliteration provided for me by Dr. P. Granoff]), p. 733.

25 S.K. De, *Early History of the Vaiṣṇava Faith and Movement in Bengal* (Calcutta: 1961), p. 139.

26 As for example the *Varṣakṛtyādīpikā* cited above.

27 *Kāmasūtra*, 1. lV. 42.

28 *Śāstradīpikā*, Commentary of Mayuravamālī (np., nd.), 1.3.8.

29 Jaiminīyanyāyamāla, *Nyāyamālāvistara*, ed. by A. Saṁskṛta (np., 1946), 35. 10-18.

30 *Bhaviṣya Purāṇa*, 132.

31 *Ibid*., 132.32.

32 Hemachandra, *Deśīnamāmālā*, vi.82.

33 K. Deshpande, "Some Observances (*Vratas*) and Festivals (*Utsavas*) mentioned in the *Deśīnamāmālā*," *AIOC* XVII, 1955 (Annamalai University, *Proceedings and Transactions*, 1958), pp. 483ff. The translation of the relevant passage is:

> Oh shameless one! Why are you wielding like a shield that twig of a cotton bush that you have held in your hand? For in the vernal festival when creepers abound, the arrows, which are discharged by love, do not miss their aim.

34 *Nāradīya Purāṇa*, 1.124.81 and Raghavan, *Festivals*, p. 199.

35 *Varṣakṛtyādīpikā*, p.117; *Bhaviṣya Purāṇa*, 132, vs. 36,37.

36 *Nyāyamālāvistara*, 35.10-18.

[37] *Atharvaveda Pariśiṣṭa (The Pariśiṣṭas of the Atharvaveda)* (Varanasi: 1976) and Raghavan, *Festivals,* p. 194.

[38] M. Winternitz, *A History of Indian Literature,* 2 vols. (Reissue; 1972), I. p. 281.

[39] The *Ratnāvalī* hails from central India. We might suggest further that a southern version of the Spring Festival is the *Paṅkuni* festival. This festival is described by P. Younger in "Ten Days of Wandering and Romance" in *Modern Asian Studies* and F. Clothey in "Chronometry, Cosmology, and the Festival Calendar in the Murukan Cult" in Welbon and Yocum, *Religious Festivals,* pp. 157-188.

[40] *Śāstradīpikā,* 1.3.8

[41] *Ibid.*

[42] Jaiminī, *Pūrvamīmāṁsa Sūtra,* (chapters 1-3), trans. by Mahamahopadhyaya Ganganatha Jha (New York: 1974), III. VII. 1.3.15-23.

[43] See for example, *Festivals of India* (Delhi: 1977), pp. 12, 20.

[44] Śulapani, *Dolayatraviveka,* cited by Kane, *History of Dharma Śāstra,* V. 238.

[45] E.W. Burlingame, *Buddhist Legends* (London: 1969), p. 310.

[46] *Kathākośa* (Lahore: nd.), p. 30.

[47] Margaret Stevenson, *Jaina Festivals and Fasts,* cited by Sharma, *Festivals of India,* p. 142.

[48] Dakṣiṇa Ranjan Shastri "The *Lokāyatikas and the Kāpālikas*" in *Indian Historical Quarterly,* VII (1931).

[49] Raghavan, *Festivals,* p. 200.

[50] *Ibid.,* p. 198.

[51] R.S. Khare, *The Hindu Hearth and Home* (Delhi: 1976), p.147

3

The *Ratnāvalī*: The City

The *Ratnāvalī* is the most famous of several Sanskrit sources to narrate the exploits of the popular King Udayana of Vatsa. He is a monarch whose *raison d'etre* is the pursuit of pleasure: the security of his kingdom lies in the hands of his skillful and effective minister Yaugandharāyana. In the *Ratnāvalī* it is Yaugandharāyana's mission to arrange the political alliance through marriage of King Udayana and Ratnāvalī, a princess of Siṁhala. This marital *cum* political compact which, in turn is achieved through a series of complex intrigues, at least one purpose of which is to ensure that the match is authenticated by mutual adoration. As a political entente, the betrothal and wedding of King Udayana and the Princess Ratnāvalī is simply a technicality, easily solemnized by ceremony. Yet in the *Ratnāvalī*, the action revolves around the arousal of amour of future husband for future wife and *vice versa*. The *Vasantotsava*, the Spring Festival, with its exuberance, its amorous overtones and all the attendant implications thereof is the ideal occasion for the couple to 'fall in love.'

Manners and Ways

The temper of the season is signified by paroxysms of merriment and gaiety: music, song, dance, the imbibing of wine, the general sporting of the citizens with water-filled syringes and the throwing of red powder are specific to the celebration of the *Vasantotsava* as ceremonialized in urban space. The streets of the city of Kauśāmbī are here saturated with colour, music and song. The senses are assaulted; the mood is infectious. Day-to-day conventional, hum-drum modes of behavior are turned topsy-turvy resulting in much that is simultaneously enticing and alarming, alluring and dangerous. Hence:[1]

> Since in front rises the hum of people's merriment, sweet with music played to the accompaniment of a mellow drum, I believe that His Majesty is proceeding to the mansion to witness the rejoicing of the citizens, intense because of Madana's festival (*madanamahamahīyāṁsaṁ*)
>
> -spoken by Yaugandharāyana, *Ratnāvalī*, p. 9

> Observe the charm of this Love's festival which interests one with the citizens who are dancing at the touch of water from syringes. Citizens are voluntarily seized by lovely women now under the exhilaration of wine. The openings of the roads all round are seething with the swelling music of wild songs, and all the quarters are rendered yellowish-red with a mass of fragrant powder scattered all about.
>
> -spoken by Yaugandharāyana, *Ratnāvalī*, pp. 11, 13

> Dear friend! Behold the sporting of courtesans who are charming on account of their hissing uttered when struck by water from syringes discharged by naughty gallants.
>
> -spoken by the *vidūṣaka*, *Ratnāvalī*, p. 13

> Look! Look! Friend! Here comes Madanikā with Cūtalatikā. She is dancing the spring dance in an

3. Ladies Enjoying Wine
Deccan-Golkonda, *circa* A.D. 1700-1725

unsteady manner as she is under the influence of love.

-spoken by the *vidūṣaka, Ratnāvalī,* p. 15

The dance is referred to here in the *Ratnāvalī* as the *vasantābhinayam,* literally, the dance of spring.[2] The *Nāṭyaśāstra,* a text the primary concern of which is dance, elaborates on this description and identifies this spring dance specifically as *lāsya*[3] which, according to Basham, in his *Cultural History of India,* is one which represents a story or part of a story.[4] The *lāsya* is regarded as the prototype of the profusion of independent popular ballets which have always accompanied and counterpointed the more serious and classical theatre of India.[5] The *Nāṭyaśāstra* tells us that, indeed, the *lāsya* is imitative of the activities of ordinary people (*laukikavṛtta*).[6] Thus, the popularity of this dance amongst common folk suggests that the spring festival celebrations do not revolve around any one specific social group but, apart from royalty, cross all caste and economic boundaries. They are *laukikavṛtta.* Another medieval text, the *Daśakumāracarita,* particularizes the nature of the spring dance by suggesting that the *lāsya* is a dance of love, i.e., it is a dance in which the emotions of love are represented by means of various gesticulations, attitudes and postures.[7] The rhythm of the music and motions of the dance of love suggest enticement and beckoning which, on the occasion of the *Vasantotsava,* is a more than welcome 'seduction.'

The foregoing textual reference mentions the singing of special festival songs which are termed *caccarī* (or *carcari*) in the *Ratnāvalī* and *Holī* or *Hori* in other sources. Various texts treating music specify and define the exact qualities of these songs. The twelfth century AD *Saṅgītaratnākara* points to the songs of the Spring Festival as *prākṛt* songs[8] and, according to the *Vāsavadattā* , the mass dancing and mass singing of vulgar songs, typical of this occasion, were performed most often by women. Raghavan reports that in north India musical compositions called *Holī* or *Hori* are derived from songs sung by common folk during the *Holī* festival[9] and Apte tells us that in southern India on the day after *Holī* (*Kāmandī*), the new year is celebrated with songs sung in the common Marathi mode.[10]

Further, indulging in alcoholic beverages is commonly identified in festival literature as an aspect of the celebration of Vasanta. The *Ratnāvalī* describes quaffing of wine in mixed gatherings of men and women in the streets. Other texts confirm that this activity is given sanction only on festival days and particularly on Spring Festival days. Liquor is mentioned in Bhoja's eleventh century AD text, the *Sarasvatīkaṇṭhābharaṇa*, as being consumed on the *Vasantotsava* as a reasonable means of heightening the exhilaration and achieving intoxication. Hence:[11]

> *kṣanapiṣṭadhūsarastani madhumadatāmrākṣī* /
> *kasya kṛte cūtamañjarī putri tvayā maṇḍito grāmah* //
>
> (O Cūtamañjarī!, whose breasts are smeared dusty with coloured powder and whose eyes are red from intoxication with liquor, for whose sake have you graced our village?)

And in Śāradātanaya's *Bhāvaprakāśa* which dates from the thirteenth century AD, drinking bouts occur as a part of the regular festivities at the *Madanamahotsava*.[12]

> *udāyana-salila-drīḍāsumāpacaya-krīyā* /
> *āpānalekelih śakrārcā vasantamadanotsavah* //
>
> (The *Madanotsava* and spring festivities are attended with plucking of flowers , sports in the pool of the garden, drinking bouts and the worship of Indra.)

Traditional forms of engagement during festival periods which lend to the general merriment involve then singing, dancing, the entertaining of courtesans and the ritual consumption of liquor. Evidence suggests that celebrants comported themselves similarly in *vedic* times during the performance of ritual sacrifice (*yajña*). On the occasion of the autumn *Sautrāmaṇī* sacrifice, for example, drinking and the entertainment of courtesans are prescribed[13] and, according to descriptions of the *Mahavrāta* sacrifice such as those found in the *Aitreya Āraṇyaka*, *Śāṅkhāyana Āraṇyaka* and the *Taittirīya Saṁhitā*,[14] licentious behavior of a type similar to that found in the *Vasantotsava* was common.

The jocundity engendered by drinking, dancing and singing could easily be delineated as licentiousness. The abandonment of normal codes of conduct giving way to sexual license is frequently noted in the literature of spring festivals. This connection between the ritual consumption of wine and fertility rituals has been noted by Crooke in *Religion and Folklore of North India*.[15] Briffault, in a rather standard if not voyeuristic reading of the Spring Festival in India, comments as follows:[16]

> The *Holī* festival, which is celebrated in every part of Hindustan in honour of the goddess Vasantī is an occasion on which the most licentious debauchery and disorder reign throughout every class of society. It is the regular Saturnalia of India. Persons of the greatest respectability, without regard to rank or age, are not ashamed to take part in the orgies which mark this season of the year.' Phallic emblems operated mechanically are carried, and the loves of the gods are represented in 'tableaux vivants' on stages and chariots. In ancient times the festival was called Basantotsava, and the noblest princesses danced in public in honour of the god of love. The original intention of the carnival, says Mr. Crooke, is to promote the fertility of man, animals, and crops. In Chota Nagpur, among the Hos, the harvest is the signal for general license, and such license is looked upon as a matter of absolute necessity. Men set aside all conventions and women all modesty, and complete liberty is given to the girls. In Orissa, among the Bhuiyas, during the spring festival called Magh Porai, "as well respect for blood relations and husbands is at nought." The Parganait, a caste of husbandmen in the Rājmahāl Hills, have a great yearly agricultural festival, called Sohrai, at which the unmarried of

> both sexes indulge in promiscuous sexual intercourse. In Jeypore promiscuity and changes of partners last for a month at the new year festival of the Punjas. The Kotas of the Nilgiri Hills have a similar festival of continuous licentiousness. In Assam spring festivals are observed by all the tribes, and women are allowed complete freedom without "any stain, blemish, or loss of reputation." Similar festivals are observed in Khondistan, among the wild tribes of Manipur and of northern Burma.

Though Briffault's description verges on stereotypical hyperbole, it draws our attention to the general high spirits of the celebrants apparently concomitant to the blurring of social categories as well as to the spontaneous creation of new relationships and hence the possibility for the formation of new social orders. Evidence of the relaxation of restrictions prohibiting physical contact between castes and sexes is in abundance at the point in the *Ratnāvalī* when the crush of individuals celebrating the festivities is uncontrolled and, in consequence, unpredictable. With respect to social hierarchy, general descriptions of the *Vasantotsava* including those in the *Ratnāvalī* as well tend to accentuate a society functioning *en masse.* Harṣa makes profuse reference to the lively engagement of all members of the social body regardless of caste without making specific reference to their role in the festival.[17] Citations to dances which are *laukikavṛttam* (activities of common people) and the songs of common folk sung in common dialects (i.e., non-sanskritic dialects) clearly indicate that all strata of society participated in the festival.

Within this generalized field, amorphous as it is, we find that women (often courtesans) can be identified as distinct players. In the above description from the *Ratnāvalī* as well as in a variety of other texts, it will be recalled that it was women who were the primary targets in the matter of powder throwing and it was women who appeared as singers and dancers. In the *Ratnāvalī* the *vasantābhinayam*, the spring dance, is performed by the women, Madanikā and Cūtalatikā.[18] Someśvara in the

Mānasollāsa tells us the songs are sung by women (*yoṣit*)[19] and the *Kāvyamīmāṁsā* tells us that at this time:[20]

> *mano adhikam cātra vilāsalāsye prenkhāsu dolāsu ca sundarīnāṁ |*
> *gīte ca gauricaritāvataṁse pūjāprapañce ca mano-bhavasya ||*
>
> (The minds of women on this occasion [i.e., on the *Vasantotsava*] should be on graceful dance, on swinging in a swing, on singing and on the hearing the stories of Gaurī and on the worship of Kāma.)

The *Kāvyamīmāṁsā* clearly points to the prominent role women are to take and, in this case, makes specific reference to the worship of Gaurī and Kāma. Gaurī (Pārvatī) is often said to be worshipped at the advent of spring[21] and the worship of Kāmadeva by women, according to many medieval descriptions, is a prominent ingredient in the festival mix. The above quote from the *Kāvyamīmāṁsā* specifically connects women with particular activities: it is primarily the female participants whose dances, songs and worship create the gay ambiance suffusing the festival of spring.

The body of diverse textual references to the worship of Pārvatī as it is performed by women during the Spring Festival links this performance with specific goals much in the manner of a *kānya* rite or *vrata* designated for specific ends. The Jain author Nemichandra in his *Ākhyakamanikośa*, for example, specifically describes a fertility ritual wherein ladies worship Gaurī on the occasion of the *Vasantotsava* for conjugal happiness.[22] The *Holākāmāhātmya*, which is a late text appended to the *Matsya Purāṇa* enumerates the ways of worshipping the goddess on this day.[23] Rājaśekhara in the *Karpūramañjarīsara* speaks of a festival exclusively for women which consists solely of the pleasurable act of swinging to and fro in honour of Gaurī on the night of the full moon of Phālguna.[24] In modern times women fashion an image of Pārvatī out of the ashes of the *Holī* fire. Mrs. Sinclair Stevenson in *Rites of the Twice Born* reports that celebrants place an ashen image of Pārvatī in the centre of a circle and circumambulate it for fifteen days, the sole purpose of which is to gain a good husband.[25] Clearly, the collective evidence of classical text and modern observance suggests that one of the primary foci of this celebration was the auspicious opportunity for women to worship specific gods or goddesses in order to secure marital bliss, a state synonymous in the Indian tradition with fecundity.

Yet the *Vasantotsava* was not the exclusive domain of women even in medieval times. In the *Ratnāvalī* the king is described as proceeding to the mansion of Madana to observe the citizens of the city celebrating Kāma's festival. The sovereign is one of the few individuals who, at this place and time, retains his distinct social status; he is situated physically at some distance from the locus of the celebrations. Harṣa has noted in his instructions for the play that the king does not participate directly in the crush of the crowds in the streets but, rather, observes the festival from the confines of his mansion, a safe distance high above the mobs. He is an observer, an overseer. Śulapani tells us in the *Dolayatraviveka* that while *Holākā* was instituted first by King Indrayumna in Vṛndāvana,[26] he does not engage directly in the jubilations except in a supervisory capacity. This is confirmed also in the *Kathāsaritsāgara* wherein Prince Naravāhanadatta amuses himself by watching the festivities of the citizens who dance without restraint at the Spring Festival.[27] However, there are a few textual descriptions such as the *Pārijāta-Mañjarī* in which the king and queen engage directly in the ritual of throwing powder and musk, although they do this in one of the uppermost rooms of the palace, isolated and towering far above the crowds. (Act 1) The *Vasantotsava*, it would appear, receives sanction by the mere appearance of the king at the celebrations. In a culture which often delimits itself by its traditions and customs, the king is historically the functional and theoretical primary representative of order in the social system. He is responsible not only for maintaining the social order within the kingdom, but for the prosperity of his citizens as well. As symbolic overseer of the festival, he articulates that order; as convener, he establishes the legitimacy of the celebration.

Colours, Powders, and Syringes

Perhaps one of the most widespread and unusual characteristics of the relaxing of social restrictions specifically associated with the Spring Festival is that of the slinging/tossing/drenching of one another with such substances as mud, coloured powders, coloured waters, flower dusts and musk. In the *Ratnāvalī* it is vividly described thus:

> O! How excessive has been the merriment of the people. Thus the scattered heaps of fragrant powder, tinted yellow with saffron dust create (an illusion of) daybreak. This Kauśāmbī, whose wealth is manifest from her attire, seeming to outvie the treasures of the lord of wealth, appears one yellow mass, as though her sons were dressed in molten gold. Moreover the pavement in front is reddened by the people with the tread of their feet. It is pink with vermillion tints that drop from the cheeks of boisterous women in the yard which is flooded all over with ceaseless flow of water spouted by fountain-jets and where they are sporting in mud that is created by the heavy crush (of hurrying feet).
>
> -spoken by the king, *Ratnāvalī*, p.13

This activity is not confined to the *Ratnāvalī* but is found in many other accounts of this festival and is so widespread and so ripe metaphorically that it deserves special attention.

The *Taittarīya Āraṇyaka* which forms part of the *Taittirīya Brāhmaṇa*, one of the oldest of the *Brāhmaṇas*[28] and plausibly the earliest reference to this behavior, gives evidence of the ritual activity of throwing coloured water in Vasanta (spring). Although the *Vasantotsava* as it is described in the *Ratnāvalī* is not found in *vedic* texts, there is a spring sacrifice akin to it which admits of the throwing of coloured water. In the *Kāmasūtra*, which probably dates to the fourth century BC, the spring festivities are said to be accompanied by powder slinging.[29] A precedent then, for such activities, more deliberately described in medieval texts (such as the *Ratnāvalī*) under the name of *Vasantotsava*, indeed does exist in texts describing *vedic* rituals.

Outside of the context of festival but within the textual tradition and also in the context of spring, one can observe an historical growth in the popularity of this same practice as a favoured pastime.[30] Beginning with the *Kāmasūtra* the squirting of coloured water occurs as a separate spring entertainment called *'udakakṣvedikā'* or, in Jayamaṅgalā's commentary, *'sṛṅga krīḍa.'*[31] The penchant for more and more elaborate descriptions of this observance continues with Someśvara, for example, in the tenth century AD, where it is described as *'secana krīḍa'* or squirting each other with tinted and fragrant water through the medium of syringes (*sṛṅgas*).[32] Here it is a vernal amusement but dissociated from any particular ritual context. Further evidence of this playful yet erotic 'wetting' sport appears both in prose and poetry in such works as the *Śiśupālavadha*, the *Kādambarī*, and the *Āvantisundarī*[33] but is in these works situated outside of the festival proceedings. These texts contain yet more detailed descriptions of increasingly elaborate mechanical gadgets for launching or discharging waters or powders. In Someśvara's *Mānasollāsa* the horns of wild bulls or silver and gold replicas thereof are identified as containers for water and the like behavior described is not confined to any specific festival occasion.

In other instances the tossing of flower-balls, or balls made of silken threads form part of the overall merriment of spring-time.[34] Occasional manuscripts of the *Kāma Sūtra* mention a festival called *Yavacaturthī* which the commentator, Jayamaṅgalā, elucidates as a spring rite of flinging fragrant *yava*-flower-dust at one another. In his eleventh century AD *Śṛṅgāra Prakāśa*, Bhoja of Dhārā mentions this same *Yavacaturthī* as a ritual of spring revolving around *yava* twigs.[35] Here women roll in *yava* flowers but elsewhere mango blossoms are ingested, trees are touched by women to make them flower, and the like. Perhaps the tossing of flower-dust, i.e., pollen, is directed at effecting a transference of the fertile powers of flowers which blossom in spring to the performers on whom the flower-dust is thrown. In any case, as a visual image it surely affirms human affinity, if not union, with nature and the forces of nature. But this by no means exhausts its symbolic potential.

The Ratnāvalī specifically describes the materials to be flung as coloured powder, coloured water or mud. This corresponds with the *Nīlamata Purāṇa* which prescribes mud on this occasion and for this purpose; the *Sarasvatīkaṇṭhābharaṇa* which names the substance as powder (*kṣanapiṣṭhadhūsarastāni*); and the *Śāstradīpikā* which identifies water (*kriyamānah parasparajalaseko vasantotsavah*).[36] Texts, including the *Varṣakṛtyādīpikā,* vividly portray the exuberance of the occasion when men and women smear their bodies with ashes and red powder, sing, dance, and roam the streets behaving like ghosts (*krīḍitavyam piśācavat*).[37] The *Gāthāsaptaśatī* tells us that on this day (*Phālgunotsava*) decorative mud is to be flung, especially at women:[38]

> Why do you wash off the decorative mud flung by someone innocently during the vernal festival (*phālgukṣana*) even when it (mud) has been wiped away by sweat rolling down from the tips of your jar-like breasts? (4.69)

Finally, a vivid and sexually charged description of this behavior is to be found in the *Pārijāta-Mañjarī alias Vijayaśrī* of Rāja-Guru Madana *alias* Bāla Saraswati.[39] This is a text known only by an inscription found in Dhar which dates to the twelfth century AD. The following excerpts describe the festival in terms of the pure and playful mood of *eros*:

> Look at it! At some places the vermillion flies sky high with the peals of reverberating laughter; at others (it is) quantities of musk-powder, and at (still) others (it is) the whiff of the powder of the sandal-wood. With the showers of the waters of the *desara* (or *kumkuma)* thrown up high from the outlets of the syringes, the Spring Festival, that has

> been started by the town-folk at will in numerous ways, has now become tumultuous. Again, the ladies of the town, with their bodies made charming by flowery ornaments, now wearing at pleasure on their foreheads streaks of vermillion, that have turned their hair reddish, and dancing in an intoxicating and faltering manner, so as to cause a confusion in the lilt (of the music), look smilingly at the faces of their lovers, the drummers in sports. (p. 9)

The king and queen referred to in this text watch the festivities of the citizens from the uppermost rooms of the palace whereupon the queen's handmaiden surreptitiously slips her a handful of vermillion. The queen playfully casts the powder into the king's face. The handmaiden and the *vidūṣaka* (the court wit) toss vermillion at each other and subsequently this wit advises the king to discharge musk powder onto the queen. The king then says:

> The southern wind (lit., the wind of the hill of the sandal-wood, i.e., the Nilgiri Hills) blows, bringing (with it droplets of) tears of joy, that have come out of the shutting eyes of the musk deer, that got wet at the soft touch of the horns of the female deer, meeting him with an ardent pining for copulation; and dexterously removing the perspiration due to exertion in the sports of love, in which were engaged the wives of the Kinnaras (the heavenly musiians), that were seated, singing, in solitude.
> (p.11)

The musk, derived from the Sanskrit word *muskā* (testicles), with which the king smears the queen is clearly the stuff of sexual ardour. In the context of this particular narrative, the act of flinging, tossing or drenching a member of the opposite sex with colours, powders waters (or any combination thereof), takes on more than a hint of sexual playfulness becoming clearly a form of seduction and a prelude to sexual union.

Motifs

Dissolution motifs typical of end of the year rituals and described by scholars such as Eliade and Turner[40] are clearly operative in the literature thus far. Here conventional boundaries and social distinctions dissolve into ambiguity: men and women smear each others' bodies with mud, powder, flower-dust, coloured water and musk, concealing the individuating distinctions between them. A. Béteille remarks that '...religious festivals provide occasions for the coming together of different castes in the village...'[41] By the shedding of their established 'skins' and by the assumption of unconventional behaviors the participants in these rituals position themselves outside 'normative' values and constrictions. Unexpected and illegal activities occur, new patterns emerge. Sexual distinctions remain operative and the sexual overtones which are clearly evidenced in the *Gāthāsaptaśatī* and the *Ratnāvalī* are even more explicit in a further investigation of the literature. Sexual licentiousness points to dissolution in its contravention of social mores at the same time as it signals and asserts the renewed vitality of the oncoming spring. The division between the old year and the new year, between winter and spring, is ambiguous: neither of the two competing cycles is given ascendence over the other.

The blossoming of spring is relentless in its onslaught, in its victory over winter. Its arrival is in a sense, inevitable, just as the arrival of the following summer and the following winter and the following spring. This changing of the seasons is a phenomenon over which humankind has little control. These rituals of imbruement are mimetic of the shifting of the seasons, signifying both the waning of winter and the burgeoning of spring. As such they are essential components of the *Vasantotsava*.

Unlike the inevitability of the seasons, social structures are mutable: in human affairs there is some potential for change, for new relationships and new social orders to take form. The implications of these ritual actions are multivalent and point directly to sexuality and fertility. In this context there is both re-newal (in the sense of continuation of the old, making new again, reactivating old and forgotten patterns) as well as the opportunity to fashion something altogether new (in the sense of destroying what is old and worn out, starting over, creating new social patterns).

Given its prevalence in the festival, particular note must be taken to emphasize the colour red.[42] The most straightforward and in many ways the most appropriate symbolic interpretation is to associate red with blood and hence life, fertility, sexuality and vigour. The abundant promiscuity licensed during the festival, the numerous references to female sexuality and the colour red must form a configuration which somehow link together under the umbrella of a Spring Festival.

The most obvious starting point for an interpretation of red powders and waters is the direct link between the colour red and blood. In India, as well as in cultures across the globe, the sign of blood imparts vital energy; it also delineates or creates boundaries.[43] Thomson writes:

> It is a worldwide custom for menstruating or pregnant women to daub their bodies with red ochre, which serves at once to warn the men away and to enhance their fertility. In many marriage ceremonies the bride's forehead is painted red...a sign that she is forbidden to all men save her husband and a guarantee that she will bear him children...[44]

Thus, blood and red (its symbolic or metonymic counterpart) may be linked with the fertility-invoking behavior which accompanies the discharge of powder in our descriptions of this festival. The Bhils, for example, prior to sowing their crops, smear stones with vermillion, probably symbolic of menstrual blood.[45] In a parallel act akin to the smearing of vermillion on the bride, the act of smearing vermillion on the stone implies the infusion of productive energy into the stones, into the earth and perhaps as well, it marks a territorial claim, isolating and separating one from the rest. O'Flaherty is adamant that the smearing of an erotic substance (blood, red powder, ashes, sandalwood paste) on cult objects sanctifies them (i.e., separates them?) especially when the object of worship was the female and her sexual essence.[46] An alternative to tossing red powder is the drenching of one another with liquids squirted from syringes. This is an activity associated with fertility and sexuality and one practiced with almost as much frequency as the flinging of powders. Clearly, it is the blood of nurturing that is here implied. When, in a crowd, men saturate women with blood-red water, they are not only sanctifying her femaleness but also, perhaps, staking a claim. That men also hurl powder at each other and women drench men may be likened to territorial battles. There is also clearly an element of fun, a childlike game of splash and run.

The visual change brought about by plastering one or another's body with colour must have some bearing on our understanding of this activity and in an imaging of the festival of spring, three categories of signification have emerged. First, in a uniform field of one colour individual differences become glossed: all participants become alike. Second, if one defines social structure as the organization of individuals into distinct, functional groups operating together then that structure, which itself assures the continuance of the society, becomes inoperative when the distinctive and determining roles of the individual participants are obfuscated. The powder conveys a sense of social, but not sexual, dissolution. Third, as symbolic of blood, particularly menstrual blood, red powder is simultaneously one of the most ritually potent of substances and one of the greatest of pollutants.[47] Blood, or shall we say its symbolic substitute, vivifies the participants by positively affecting fertility at a time of the year when this is precisely the effect for which one would wish. The primary aims of the Spring Festival have been achieved.

Finally, the *Vasantotsava* celebrates the termination or destruction of winter. The hurling of substances at one another is essentially an aggressive act. These colour wars are clearly combative. The throwing of symbolic blood, here of death, reflects the theme of the bloody victory of life over death. Life is the waxing of blood; death its waning. In the sphere of human relations, these same wars reflect a struggle between the sexes but also a struggle to establish new social patterns. In this struggle there is an element of chance. Playing *'Holī'* is both a contest and a game, the outcome of which is unpredictable. As the participants in the *Ratnāvalī* are one indistinguishable mass covered with vermillion and performing rites of the *Vasantotsava*, so too is this one indistinguishable mass covered with vermillion and performing rites celebrating the inevitable death of winter. In nature as well as in human society, fertility and eroticism, destruction and death co-exist.

NOTES

[1] These excerpts are paraphrased from the translation of N.G. Suru and C.R. Devadhar, *Ratnāvalī*, pp. 9-15.

[2] *Ratnāvalī*, p. 14, line, 2, 5.

[3] *Nāṭyaśāstra*, III.67.15 (vol., page, line).

[4] *A Cultural History of India*, ed., Basham (Oxford: 1975), p.172.

[5] This also is the dance which Kālī performs in her contest with Śiva. O'Flaherty, *Women, Androgynes and Other Mythical Beasts* (Chicago: 1982), p. 141.

[6] *Nāṭyaśāstra,, loc. cit.*

[7] *Daśakumāracarita*, 2.5 cited by V.S. Apte, *Sanskrit-English Dictionary*, III.1365.

[8] Śārṅgadeva, *Saṅgītaratnākara*, 5 vols. (Madras: 1959), V. 291. For the date of this text see Krishnamachariar, p. 120.

[9] Raghavan, *Festivals*, p. 194.

[10] Apte, *The Sacrament of Marriage*, p. 71.

[11] *Sarasvatīkaṇṭhābharaṇa*, 314.12.

[12] Śāradātanaya, *Bhāvaprakāśa*, ed. by B. Bhattacharyya (Baroda: 1930), III.99.18. For the date of this text, see Krishnamachariar, p. 837.

[13] Raghavan, *Festivals*,. p. 15.

[14] A.B. Keith, *Religion and Philosophy of the Veda and Upaniṣads*, 2 vols. *HOS* 31, 32 (Second Indian Ed.; Delhi: 1976), 31, pp. 349ff.

[15] Crooke, p. 100.

[16] R. Briffault, *The Mothers*, III, pp. 198-9.

[17] There is scant reference in our texts to the participation of Brahmins in the celebrations. An exception is found in the *Varsa-*

kṛtyādīpikā which tells us that one should listen to the *vasantarāga* after the worship of Kāma and Ratī is completed. Thus:

> *tatra dine brāhmaṇamukhena vasantarāga śravanaṁ*
> (On that day the *Vasantarāga*, sung by Brahmins, should be heard.)

References like this, however, are comparatively rare and, one suspects, somewhat artificial. Most accounts describe the participants as an homogeneous mass. Hence, although Brahmins most probably did participate in the festivities the lack of direct textual reference suggests that their identity as authorities in religious matters was probably in this context unimportant. Minimizing the role of Brahmins even further, it must be restated that according to some sources, the Spring Festival is a celebration particularly appropriate for *śūdras*. See, for example, Khare, *Hindu Hearth and Home* (p. 147) and Chapter Two, above.

18 *Ratnāvalī*, p. 14, line, 2, 5.

19 Someśvara, *Mānasollāsa*, 297.16.

20 *Kāvyamīmāṁsā*, ed. by C.D. Dalal and R.A. Śastri (3rd. ed.; Baroda: 1934), 104.

21 See the following chapters on the *Bhaviṣya Purāṇa* (135) and the *Virūpakṣavasantotsavacampū* below.

22 Sharma, *Festivals of India*, p. 17 cites this text.

23 Chatterjee, *Padma Purāṇa: A Study* (Calcutta: 1967), p. 181.

24 Rājaśekhara, *Karpūramañjarīsara*, ed. S. Konow, trans. by C.R. Lanman (2nd. ed.; New Delhi: 1971), pp. 281-7.

25 pp. 281-7.

26 Śulapani, *Dolayatraviveka*, ed. by S. Banerji in the volume of papers presented to Kane, pp. 56-62. See also Kane, *History of Dharmaśāstra*, p. 238.

27 *Kathāsaritsāgara*, XIV, 58.

28 *Taittirīya Āraṇyaka*, 1.3.4. and M. Winternitz, *A History of Indian Literature* (New York: 1972), I. pp. 235-6.

29 *Kāmasūtra*, I. iv. 46.

30 i .e., outside of the context of a specific spring celebration.

31 *Kāmasūtra*, I. iv. 46.

32 Someśvara, *Mānasollāsa* or *Abhilasitārthacintāmaṇi*, ed. by B.J. Sansesara (Baroda:1925, 35, 61), no. 138, p. 102. See also V. Raghavan, *Festivals*, pp. 74-5.

33 Raghavan, *Festivals*, p. 200.

34 See, for example, V. Raghavan, *Bhoja's Shṛṅgāra Prakāśa* (Madras: 1978), pp. 628-33.

35 Raghavan, *Śṛṅgāra Prakāśa*, pp. 631-2. During this ritual (also referred to as *kundacaturthī*), women spread *yava* twigs in the garden and frolic amongst them.

[36] *Nīlamata Purāṇa* trans., intro. by Dr. Ved Kumari, 2 vols. (Srinagar-Jammu: 1968, 1973); Dhareśvara Bhojadeva, *Sarasvatīkaṇṭhābharaṇa*, commentary of Ramsiṁha and Jagaddhara, ed. by P.K. Sarma and W.L.S. Pandurang Jawaji (Bombay: 1934), 314.12 (page, line); *Śāstradīpikā*, 1.3.8..

[37] *Varṣakṛtyādīpikā*, p. 301.

[38] Hala, *Gāthāsaptaśatī*, ed., intro., trans. by R. Basak (Calcutta: 1971), 4.69.

[39] Rāja-Guru Madana *alias* Bāla Saraswati, *Pārijāta-Mañjarī alias Vijayaśrī*, re-edited by S.K. Dikshit (Bhopal: 1963), p. 9.

[40] M. Eliade, *Cosmos and History* (New York:1959); V. Turner, *The Ritual Process* (Reprint; Ithaca: 1977), pp. 94ff.

[41] A. Béteille, *Caste, Class, and Power* (Berkeley and Los Angeles: 1965), p. 101; also quoted in S. Hanchett "The Festival Interlude" in G. Welbon and G. Yocum, *Religious Festivals in South India and Sri Lanka*, pp. 219-243, p. 225.

[42] Secondary sources like Kane's *History of Dharmaśāstra* confirm the importance of propelling water and coloured powder in the course of modern *Holī*. (V. 237f.) Field studies such as those conducted by Lawrence Babb in the *Divine Hierarchy* touch upon similar behaviors in Chhattisgarh as does the work of McKim Marriot on the *Holī* festival wherein he recounts his experience in Kishan Garhi in northern India during the Spring Festival as follows: 'The state of the clothes in which I ultimately fell asleep told me the next morning that I had been sprayed and soaked repeatedly with libations of liquid dye, red and yellow. My face in the morning was still a brilliant vermilion, and my hair was orange from repeated embraces and scourings with coloured powders by the bereaved and probably by many others.'(p.204) Bhattacharyya comments: 'The most important rite of the festival of *Holī* is the use of a red powder (*abir* or *phag* as it is generally called) which is to be smeared on the bodies of friends and relatives and even on the bodies of strangers. Sometimes water is coloured red with this powder and is sprinkled on human bodies. Now-a-days young men and women also use other colours, but the approved colour is red.' (N.N. Bhattacharyya, *Ancient Indian Rituals* (Delhi: 1975), p.121)

[43] Red substances are featured in certain cases of the worship of goddesses, particularly during her menstrual cycle. Often the temples of the *devī* are closed for this period as, for example, the temple of Kāmākhyā in Assam which is dedicated to Pārvatī and where a red liquid is sold to devotees as her blood. See, for example, N.N. Bhattacharyya, *Indian Puberty Rites*, p. 16. In *tantric* literature menstrual blood is a prescribed offering to the great goddess. See, for example, the *Mundamala Tantra*, *patala* II, cited by Bhattacharyya, *Indian Puberty Rites*, p. 17.

[44] G. Thomson, *Studies in Ancient Greek Society*, pp. 209-10 cited by Bhattacharyya, *Indian Puberty Rites*, pp. 17-18.

[45] W. Crooke, *Religion and Folklore of North India* (3rd ed.; New Delhi: 1926), p. 250 and Saraswati, pp. 46ff.

[46] W. O'Flaherty, *Śiva, The Erotic Ascetic* (London and New York: 1981), p. 246. The basis for this identification is the use of sandalwood paste on the bodies of females (especially Pārvatī) to enhance their sexuality. This is seen particularly in opposition to Śiva who smears his body with ash.

[47] See, for example, Mary Douglas who argues that the most polluting substances are also the most ritually potent. *Purity and Danger* (London: 1979), pp. 7ff.

4

The *Ratnāvalī:* The Pleasure Grove

From the urban setting, where citizens regale themselves in the streets and lanes of the city, our focus now shifts to the sanctuary of the pleasure grove. The festivities described in the second half of the *Ratnāvalī* exhibit a marked dissimilarity to those found in the previous section. Here in the garden, a pleasure grove inherently rife with burgeoning fecundity, the action revolves not on the generalized revelry of the citizens but rather on the relationship of the queen and the king. Here in the garden of enchantment the Princess Ratnāvalī and the King Udayana fall in love. Amidst its refined and serene beauty, Kāma, the god of love and desire is ritually invoked and worshipped.

Flowers and Trees

Both king and queen and their respective retinues proceed to the garden separately. The king and his attendant (*vidūṣaka*) arrive first and remark as follows:

> This Makaranda garden seems now to hail your approach with a silk canopy formed by a mass of pollen from the opening blossoms of mango trees which are waving in the Malaya breezes. The garden is charming with the choirs of Koil's sweet

song which blends with the humming of the giddybees (spoken by *vidūṣaka, Ratnāvalī,* p. 23

The trees yonder appear to be drunk with the wine offered at the Spring Festival. They are glowing red with the new leaves which have the lustre of sprouting coral; and they seem to talk in an indistinct manner because of the sweet murmur of the bees; and they seem to swagger and reel as their branches, struck by the Malaya breezes, are ever and anon waving. The mouthful of wine sprinkled at the root of the Bakula trees seems now to be flavored with thick dripping blossoms by the Bakula trees; and the Campaka flowers bloom even while the moon-faces of young damsels are flushed with wine; while the bees give back in harmony and thus seem to imitate the music of the anklets ringing loud as the delicate feet are raised against the Aśoka trees.

-spoken by Udayana, *Ratnāvalī,* p. 23

There is a close association between the worship of certain plants and the occasion of the *Vasantotsava* as evidenced in texts like the *Ratnāvalī* as well as in the previously mentioned *Śāstradīpikā* and *Nityotsava.* According to the commentary on the *Śāstradīpikā,* family groups perform worship to specific trees during this festival.[1] In the *Nityotsava* one is enjoined to offer Damana flowers simultaneous with the performance of the *Vasantotsava.*[2] In describing each of the seasons Sanskrit authors follow certain poetic conventions regarding vegetation. Rituals related to specific flowers and trees are understandably typical of spring celebrations and are said to initiate erotic desire and love which frequently leads to reproduction. Specifically, both the Aśoka (*Saroca Indica*) and the mango (*Magnifera Indica*), are harbingers of spring and as such figure largely in accounts of the our festival. Though the Aśoka and the mango are by no means exclusive to ritual worship in spring, they are central and it is to an examination of the rituals associated with these that we now turn.

The Aśoka Tree

The Aśoka is a small evergreen tree considered to be one of the most sacred trees of the Hindus by virtue of its beauty and the perfume of its flowers.[3] This tree is associated with eroticism (it is dedicated to the god Kāma), fertility (Siddhārtha Gautama's mother, Māyā, gave birth under the Aśoka tree) and chastity (Sītā, the wife of Rāma, when abducted by Rāvaṇa, the king of Laṅkā, escaped from the caresses of the demon and found refuge in a grove of Aśoka trees).[4]

As depicted in the *Ratnāvalī*, devotees are garlanded with Aśoka wreaths and worship the tree with yet more flowers and sandal unguents. The trunk of the tree, in another play called the *Priyadarśikā*, is decorated with saffron fingerprints. Further, a queen plants an Aśoka tree near her door thereby on this occasion inviting prosperity into her home in Rājaśekhara's *Karpūramañjarī* (composed in the tenth century AD in the western Deccan).[5] The *Ratnāvalī, the Priyadarśikā* and the *Daśakumāracarita* further link this tree with the adulation of Kāmadeva: an image of Pradyumna (Kāma) is placed at its foot and then worshipped.[6] The specific ritual with which Kāma is associated is known as the *dohada*, a ritual which is intimately linked to trees and often described in the context of the *Vasantotsava*.

Dohada means 'pregnancy longing,'[7] In this context, trees are represented as feeling, like women, such longing, such desire, that they cannot blossom until their craving is satisfied. The term *dohadikā* is given in the *Sāhityamīmāṁsā* as different ways of fulfilling the yearnings of trees and thus prompting them into blossom.[8] The *Ratnāvalī* describes the Bakula tree (*Mimusops Elengi*) which, according to the conventions of poets, desires a mouthful of wine to be discharged upon it. When this longing is fulfilled it puts for its flowers.[9] The Campaka craves to hear the loud laughter of a beautiful damsel. (1.18)

The Aśoka longs for a kick from the foot of a beautiful woman. Vāsavadattā in the *Ratnāvalī* performs the ritual of *aśokadohada*, or the kicking of an Aśoka tree, during her worship of Kāma. The king describes her as follows:

> While thus employed in worshipping Kāma, you resemble a creeper twining round a tree with fresh foliage, the border of your robe shining bright with the dye of the Kusumbha flowers and your complexion remarkably bright from the fresh bath. Moreover:
> The Aśoka tree appears to have put forth a new and lovelier shoot, while your hand, engaged in the the worship of Kāma, rests upon it. (p. 31)

Aśokadohada (or *aśokottamsikā* as it is sometimes referred to) is integral to the spring festivities in a number of texts such as the *Raghuvaṁśa*.[10] The *Karpūramañjarī* links this ceremony with Kāma when it tells us the ritual is efficacious only if 'Kāma abides in you.' The qualifications for this presence are springtime, youth and beauty.[11] In Kālidāsa's *Meghadūtam*, the exiled Yakṣa longs for his wife no less than the Aśoka tree desires her foot.[12] In the *Mālavikāgnimitram* of Kālidāsa,[13] the moment of arousal (spring), the substance to be aroused (the tree), the environment of desire (the pleasure grove) and the colour of life (red) coalesces, creating a powerful symbolic motif of enchantment. Thus Mālavikā, the princess, first has her foot decorated with red powder, then adorns her ear with a shoot of the tree and finally kicks the tree. The foot, having intimate knowledge of the earth, is first smeared with red powder, symbolic of life's blood. The power associated with and attributable to the colour red is subsequently transferred from the foot of Mālavikā to the tree. It blossoms. Mālavikā thus fulfills the longing of the Aśoka: the kick effectively wakes up the tree from its slumber and nature's spring cycle is set in motion. The ritual has a corresponding effect on her king. He says:

> This person also has not been putting forth similar flowers in the form of peace of mind since a long time. With the nectar of touch, fulfill the longing of this one also who has no taste for anything else (that is, is devoted to you alone). (*Mālavikāgnimitram*, p. 60)

The *aśokadohada* clearly affects fertility through the union of woman with nature: by striking the tree with her foot a beautiful female leads a tree into blossom. The *dohada* motif suggests a connection, if not a transference between natural fecundity and human life, a continuity between human fertility and the fertility rising out of the earth. Here women play a central and mediating role between the human world and the world of nature: women are both forces of the erotic, as their relationship to the tree is provocative and sensual, as well as forces of fertility, as the tree awakens and bursts into blossom.

Spring rites of the Aśoka tree are performed not only as positive rituals in order to prompt new growth but also as parallel ceremonies enacted to remove negative obstacles. The *aśokāṣṭamī*, another spring performance in which the festivities focus upon the Aśoka tree,[14] is celebrated on the eighth day of the bright fortnight of Caitra and consists, in part, of the drinking of eight buds of the Aśoka tree in order to alleviate sorrow. In Anantadeva's fourteenth century AD *Nibandha*, the *Smṛtikaustubha*, this very ritual is referred to as *aśokakalikābhakṣana* (drinking Aśoka buds). On this occasion participants recite the following *mantra*:[15]

> *tvām aśoka harābhiṣṭa madhumāsā-samudbhava* /
> *pibāmi śokasaṁtapto mam aśokaṁ sadā kuru* //
>
> (O Aśoka! You are the favourite of Hara (the provider) and you are born of Caitra [spring]. I drink thee, make thou me, who am oppressed with grief, ever griefless.)

Moreover, in Orissa the *aśokāṣṭamī* is associated with Pārvatī who performs penance to attain Śiva at the foot of the Aśoka tree.[16] Here drinking eight Aśoka buds is prescribed for women to alleviate suffering.[17] The *aśokakalikābhakṣana* in this light becomes a ritual of purification aimed at cleansing the participants of grief through the ingestion of new blossoms. The relationship between the Aśoka flowers and the conquest of sorrow is expressed through Sanskrit homonyms: '*aśoka*' means both 'freedom from grief' and the tree of this name. Such word-plays commonly motivate magic rituals in the *Atharva Veda*.

The Mango Tree

Although not mentioned specifically in the *Ratnāvalī*, mango trees like Aśoka trees, are symbolic of the advent of spring. Parallel to the ingestion of Aśoka buds during spring festivities is the prescription of *āmrakusumāśana* (eating mango blossoms). Described as occurring on the day after *Holī*, the ritual enjoins women to drink mango water on the morning of the new year day after worshipping Kāma in a *pūrṇakalaśa* (full pitcher): palm, sandal water and fresh mango blossoms are to be consumed on :his day. The auspiciousness engendered by eating new nango buds on the first day of the new year is still prescribed in the *Pañcāṅgas* (*Almanacs*) of today.[18] It is recorded in *Ancient Indian Festivals* that on the day of *Vasanta Pañcamī* wandering bards congratulate each other with the presentation of mango blossoms.[19]

The *Bhaviṣya Purāṇa* enjoins participants to consume mangos at daybreak in the courtyard before making the offering during the *Madanamahotsava*.[20] This same injunction is found, juxtaposed with rituals to be observed on the New Year's Day (*Caitra Śukla Pratipad*), in texts which seem to draw from information in the *Bhaviṣya Purāṇa*. Among these sources we include the *Smṛtikaustubha* of Anantadeva which prescribes the recitation of certain verses when imbibing the mixture of mango blossoms and sandal paste.[21] The *Puruṣārthacintāmaṇi* of Viṣṇubhaṭṭa, another *Nibandha*, says the performer, in honour of Kāma, must be daubed with sandal paste before he swallows the mango blossoms.[22] The eating of mango blossoms is further prescribed as part of the *Vasantotsava* in the *Vasantotsavanirṇaya*.[23]

Mango blossoms are not the only portion of this tree to exhibit efficacious properties. According to the *Pārijāta-Mañjarī*, the queen queens:and mango twigsoffers the king a mango-twig in blossom at the commencement of the *Vasantotsava.* The king responds as follows:

> This off-shoot of the mango-tree, which is being offered by you and which is the arrow of the god of love (literally flower-armed one), is being accepted by me as a mark of submission to your commands. (p. 7)

This quote exemplifies descriptions of the spring rite of *cūtalatikā* or *navalatikā* in which men and women actively select their lovers.[24] It is in accordance with descriptions of the same rituals found in the *Deśinamāmālā* and Bhoja of Dhārā's *Śṛṇgāra Prakāśa* that ladies take mango twigs or new Palāśa twigs in their hand and go about asking each other about the identities of their lovers. A lady so accosted points out her paramour by striking him with the twig. Gaster in his *Thespis*, remarks that in Europe these 'May-boughs,' as they were used in the spring festivals, origianlly symbolized the entire wealth of fertility which nature had brought to birth and, further, that they were believed to be endowed with specially beneficent properties by virtue of the power dwelling in them.[25] The mango-twig ritual is an apparent reversal of the above-mentioned *dohada* in which the tree is struck. Here, the lover is struck by the tree (twig). Yet in both cases there is a recognition of power: the woman wakes up the tree; the tree wakes up the woman's sweetheart.

The prominence of Kāma in these rituals is unmistakable. Kāma, the god of love, is traditionally armed with five arrows: the lotus, Aśoka twig, mango, jasmine and lily.[26] Each year at the onset of spring his arsenal is replenished by young women who pluck the mango blossoms, offering them as arrow-tips to Manmatha (Kāma). Kālidāsa, in his *Śākuntala*, describes this feature of spring festivities as follows:[27]

> *tvamasi mayā cūtāṅkura dattah kāmaya gṛhītadhanuṣe /*
> *pathikajanayuvatilakṣyah pañcamyadhikah saro bhava //*
> (act VI. 130)

(Oh, mango bud, I offer you. Be you his choicest dart, your mark. Some maid whose lover wanders far.. To Kāma, grasping now his bow.)

The ramifications of the mango-as-arrow are clear. In the *Ṛtu Saṁhāra*, Kālidāsa describes the mango tree in spring as bent with bunches of coppery red leaves, its branches covered with yellow fragrant blossoms, shaken by the March breezes and which kindle the flame of love in the hearts of women. Intimate desire, love, new growth, ingestion of raw blossoms and the rearmament of Kāma form an assemblage of attributes ripely connotative in the context of the spring and the festivals which celebrate it.

Further illustrative of the interplay between the natural and the human domain is the *Pārijāta-Mañjarī* which tells us that after the king and the queen have witnessed the citizens' tossing of powder, the queen as participant in the celebrations, retires to the garden to 'marry the creeper of Mādhavī to the mango tree.' The king, on seeing the newly wedded couple (i.e., the Mādhavī creeper and the mango tree) muses:

(45) Blessed, indeed, is the handsome youth (of) the mango tree, who, (as) a lover, imperiled by the to-and-fro movement of the breezes of the month of Caitra, longs to climb to his beloved (the creeper), resting on his left. (*Vāmāṅga-viśrambhinī* virtually means a *vāmāṅgī* or wife). (Blessed is) also this young creeper, the betrothed one getting often low and turning away in the face of (the lover's) pressing request, does not countenance (even) the idea of boldness (of lover to lover) (i.e., she is too coy to submit to the bold demands of her lover). (p. 19)

Parallel to this is the practice of marrying trees, in more recent times found amongst certain tribal groups in Bengal. K.N. Sahay in "Tree Symbol Worship In India" reports that among the Oraon and Kharia it is considered essential to marry trees before they bear their first fruits (i.e., in their virgin state)[28] as un-wedded tress are believed to be likely to breed worms. Very often this ceremony is enacted concurrently with the nuptial rites of a member of the family to which the tree belongs, as, for example, amongst the Mundari tribes of Bengal. In this latter case the bride and groom are anointed with turmeric and subsequently escorted to two trees (very often two mango trees). Once there, they are made to daub the trees with vermillion and then embrace them.[29]

Notable here is that again the cleavage between things human and things of nature (i.e., marriage) is rendered indistinct and ambiguous: people marry people, people marry trees and trees marry trees. The fruit engendered by wedded trees is believed to be an efficacious food, for example, amongst the Oroans and Kharia who will only eat fruit of trees sanctified in this way. The marital bond between trees lends itself easily to sexual symbology creating what might be called a sustained triple entendre: ever-present is the oscillation of life-invoking power between the humans and trees, both imparting fecundity to each other and sanctifying their respective unions. Marriage rituals, both human and arboreal, are thus central acts in spring festivals.

With the participation of Kāma in flower or vegetation rituals, the bifurcation of the mortal and the immortal becomes similarly blurred. In the context of the flower rituals, Kāma becomes a mythological counterpoint to the tree. The conjunction of Kāma and spring rituals, particularly those rites involving the mango tree, is notable above and is illustrated further in the *Matsya Purāṇa*. Here Śiva sets Kāma afire and, for the sake of the universe, divides this fire among the mango, spring and the moon, flowers, bees and cuckoos.[30] The mango tree is hence reborn of Kāma; it is one of his incarnations. Indeed, Kāma is occasionally pictured as a tree whose sprouts are women. The hand of Śākuntala, in Kālidāsa's famous play of that name, is said to be a new sprout begotten of the tree of Kāma while Pārvatī, in the act of making love to Śiva, is said to be a new sprout from the charred, consumed tree of Kāma.[31] Clearly, the placement of an image of Kāma at the foot of the Aśoka tree in the *Ratnāvalī* emphasizes these arboreal associations and calls our attention to the divine, natural and human arenas intermingling in the continuance of life.

The pleasure grove as *mise-en-scene* for the private celebration of the Spring Festival is integral to the relationship of king and queen as it is performed in the *Ratnāvalī*, but the garden is the context also in a number of other non-dramatic texts. Several stories in the *Kathāsaritsāgara* mention that the *Vasantotsava* is enacted in pleasure groves, particularly the pleasure groves of kings. The garden in the city of Pratiṣṭhāna, created under the auspices of the goddess Durgā, is one such venue mentioned in the *Kathāsaritsāgara*[32] as is the garden in the city of Śivapura in Nepal where Princess Śaśīprabhā watches the Spring Festival procession.[33] There the princess is spotted by a Brahmin who instantly falls prey to desire for her and she for him. The affection thus engendered eventually leads to their marital union. In the "King who did not know his Sanskrit Grammar," King Sātavāhana sports with his wives in the lake of the pleasure grove at this time.[34] The *Daśakumāracarita*, describing the festival of Kāma, tells us that the king in spring sits in the garden surrounded by hundreds of damsels who entertain him.[35]

The pleasure grove provides the surroundings for a specific type of Spring Festival scenario where kings cavort privately with their queens: here love between individuals is engendered. The enchantment is purely personal, purely emotional. In the *Ratnāvalī* (and in the *Kathāsaritsāgara*) the initial meeting in the garden between a king and future queen takes place in the pleasure grove. King Udayana falls hopelessly and madly for the princess Ratnāvalī and she for him. Their fascination with each other results in the legitimized public sanction of marriage. A like situation occurs in the *Kathāsaritsāgara* in the turn of affairs for Princess Śaśīprabhā and her Brahmin suitor. The privacy and security of the garden lead to few distractions and on warm and fragrant spring evenings quite naturally thoughts of love are in the air.

Figuratively and functionally the garden is a setting which stands in opposition to the urban core. This 'contrast of place' is a common dramatic device used to impart meaning. If we follow the notion of opposition by characterizing the settings as they appear in the *Ratnāvalī*, we find two parallel lines diametrically opposed descriptively yet equally rich connotatively. The urban space is as we would expect, set in a humanly constructed environment; the pleasure grove, a natural though controlled environment.[36] The city is bustling and crowded with an indistinct mass of all manner of humanity: the garden scene is peopled by only three specific individuals who directly or indirectly are part of the privileged classes. And most importantly the city stage is active while the garden stage is passive. Despite these contrasting elements or rather as a result of them, we form two different images created on the same theme: in both, it is the element of fecundity and love which unifies and clarifies the settings.

Kāmadeva

The *Ratnāvalī* situates the character of Queen Vāsavadattā when she performs a ceremony in honour of Kāmadeva. She enjoins King Udayana as follows:

> I am going today to the Makaranda garden to offer worship to the image of the flower-armed deity who stands at the foot of the red Aśoka tree; so my lord will be pleased to be present there. (p. 20)

The queen queries her attendant, Kāñcanamālā, as to the whereabouts of the Rāktaśoka tree where she is to pay homage to Madana (p. 25). Finding it, she commands Kāñcanamālā to 'place the divine Pradyumna at the foot of the Aśoka tree.'[37] The king arrives and Kāñcanamālā directs Queen Vāsavadattā to adorn the Aśoka tree with flowers, saffron, sandal and unguents offered by the queen's own hands. She is also enjoined to worship the deity Pradyumna.[38]

As the ceremony draws to a close, Queen Vāsavadattā's attendant directs her to worship her husband which she proceeds to do using flowers and unguents.

Finally, as the sun is setting on the festivities, Kāñcanamālā, the queen's attendant, herself offers to Vasantaka, the king's attendant, the same flowers, unguents and ornaments which he, like the king, accepts.

The worship of Kāma, 'the flower-armed deity,' amid the budding natural beauty of the pleasure grove is of sufficient importance to warrant the presence of both queen and king. Kāma seems to play a pivotal role in the *Vasantotsava*, yet he is not worshipped today to any great extent. Evidence however, suggests that he was at one time a mythological figure of some importance. Kāma is mentioned often in Sanskrit texts, characteristically as the god of love necessary to the arousal of desire, but rarely as a featured player. Kāma appears in the texts typically in reference to his exploits on the occasion of spring-time celebrations and it is in this context in the *Ratnāvalī* that ritual worship of him by the king and the queen, among others, occurs. Even texts not specifically associated with the *Vasantotsava* inform us that Kāma's worship is associated with the spring season,[39] while numerous others directly link co-laterally the festival of spring with his worship.[40]

A variety of sources, *purāṇic*, poetic and iconographic, detail Kāma's intimate relationship with spring. Kālidāsa, in the *Kumārasaṁbhava*, tells us this season is an aid to Kāma's effectiveness[41] as he replenishes his arsenal in spring, while, by contrast the winter season inhibits his effectiveness. In the *Gaṅgāvatarama* of Nīlakaṇṭha Dikṣita,[42] Kāma's characteristic weapons, his arrows, are destroyed at the onset of the winter season. Notable is the representation of Kāma accompanied by his companion Vasanta (spring). According to the *Kālikā Purāṇa*,[43] the birth of Manmatha (Kāma) together with the birth of Vasanta (spring) is reported. In this text Vasanta is born out of a sigh of Brahmā for the specific purpose of augmenting Kāma's power. According to the *Vāmana Purāṇa*, Vasanta is introduced in the account of the penance of Nara and Nārāyaṇa.[44]

kandarpaśca sudurdharṣascūtaṅkuramahāyudhah |
samam sahacareṇsadive vasantenāśramaṁ gatah ||

> (And the extraordinary unassailable Cupid (Kandarpa, Kāma), armed the mighty weapon the tender mango shoots and accompanied by his companion Spring entered the hermitage.) (6:7)

Vasanta and Kāma together disturb the penance of Śiva in texts like the *Kumārasaṁbhava*[45] and the *Matsya Purāṇa*.[46] In this latter text, Indra directs Kāma as follows:

> Array yourself with Madhu, the vernal season, the king of all the seasons. (154.111)

Kāma Rituals: the *Matsya Purāṇa* and the *Sanatkumāra Saṁhitā*

While it is not possible to examine all the rituals dedicated to Kāma in full detail, two primary rites have been selected to provide a basis for an understanding of this deity and to have a clear point of departure for an examination of his role in the *Vasantotsava*. I hope it will become clear from the following discussion that there is a definite link between these Kāma festivals and the *Vasantotsava*; a link which has led me to suggest earlier the essential identification of Madana festivals with the *Vasantotsava*.

Two primary rituals centering around Kāma are the *Madanadvādaśī* from the *Matsya Purāṇa* and the *Kāmayāga* from the *Sanatkumāra Saṁhitā*. Inclusion of descriptions of these two rituals here is a result of a consideration of a number of factors. First, descriptions of rituals akin to those of the *Matsya Purāṇa* occur in the *Viṣṇudharmottara Purāṇa*, *Nārada Purāṇa* and the *Kāvyamīmāṁsā*,[47] confirming a commonality in the manner in which Kāma was worshipped. Second, these recapitulations of Kāma rituals illustrate that he was historically a figure of greater importance than he is today. Third, these two rituals, the *Madanadvādaśī* and the *Kāmayāga*, are similar to and hence validate each other. Fourth and most importantly, these rites clearly parallel those of the *Vasantotsava*.

The following set of liturgical parameters defining the *Madanadvādaśī* ritual is located in the *Matsya Purāṇa*.[48] The worship of Kāma here commences in spring on the twelfth day of the bright fortnight of Caitra. We are told that the *Madanadvādaśī* ceremony was performed by Diti, the mother of the demons who, subsequent to her correct execution of this rite, gave birth to the Maruts. The entire rite spans the period of one year.[49]

> One who observes this fast should place a jar of gold, silver, copper, brass or earth, according to his means, on an earthen platform, after filling it with different fruits, pieces of sugar cane and white rice. Before placing the jar on the platform, it should also be painted with white sandal and covered with two pieces of white cloth. After this, a small plate of copper containing some fruits, gold and raw sugar should be placed on the top of the jar. Above it should be placed a plantain leaf, being an image of Kāma and to the left of it should be placed the image of Rati made of sugar. After this, the worship of Kāma and Rati should be performed in the following manner. The images should first be bathed with incense and water, then white flowers, rice and sesame should be offered. Afterwards, one should perform the *aṅgapūjā* (body worship) as follow: after pronouncing *'Om Kāmāya,'* worship the feet; after pronouncing *'Om Saubhagyadāya,'* worship the legs; after pronouncing *'Om Smarāya,'* worship the thighs; after pronouncing *'Om Manmathāya,'* worship the waist; after pronouncing *'Om Svaśchodarāya,'* worship the stomach; after pronouncing *'Om Anaṅgāya,'* worship the breast; after pronouncing *'Om Padmamukhāya,'* worship the mouth; after pronouncing *'Om Pañcasarāya,'* worship the hands; after pronouncing *'Om Sarvātmane,'* worship the head. On the completion of this worship, sandal and incense should be offered and then prayers should be sung accompanied by music. In case there is no one to sing prayers and play the music, then the glories of Kāma and Keśava

(Viṣṇu) should be narrated and listened to. On the following morning, the jar should be given to a Brāhmaṇa. After making over the jar to a deserving Brāhmaṇa, the worshipper should feast a number of Brāhmaṇas with devotion and afterwards he should have his own meal devoid of salt. Then, the invited Brāhmaṇas should be dismissed with presents and the following prayer should be uttered before giving them presents:

'O Lord Janārdana (Viṣṇu), in the form of Kāma! Who brings bliss to every soul, be pleased with thy devotion.'

The same routine of worship should be observed each month, on the twelfth day of the bright fortnight and continued on for a whole year. The worshipper should observe a fast on the thirteenth day of the bright fortnight and worship Viṣṇu. On the twelfth day of every bright fortnight, he should live only on fruits and sleep on the floor. At the beginning of the thirteenth month, he is to finally complete his cycle of fasts by performing worship as mentioned before and on its completion he should worship the golden image of Kāma. Afterwards, white sesame mixed with clarified butter, should be poured into fire and at the time of each sacrificial offering the various names of Kāma, already mentioned, prefixed with *'Om'* and suffixed with *'Svāhā'* should be pronounced. At the close of the sacrifice, the worshipper should also worship the officiating priest and his consort and then dismiss all his Brāhmaṇa guests after feasting, garlanding and giving them presents of clarified butter, cows, decently-arranged beds, clothes, ornaments and sugar-cane, The golden image of Kāma should be given to the officiating priest along with other presents mentioned above, according to the means of the worshipper.

One who observes the *Madanadvādaśī* fast in this way becomes liberated from evils, begets worthy children and finally passes away in peace, for Viṣṇu and Smara are the same.

The second of the two rituals honouring Kāma, as mentioned above, is the *Kāmayāga* and the following account of it is drawn from a text belonging to the *Pañcarātra* sect of Vaiṣṇavism, the *Sanatkumāra Saṁhitā*.[50] The ritual is prescribed for the thirteenth day of the lunar month[51] as follows:

> In the middle of the village or in a corner one should make a place for Kandarpa (Kāma). Having constructed this sacred area[52] with the door facing west, one should mark the area with those items which are special to Kāma, namely, the trident,[53] the Aśoka and the Makara (fish-banner). One should then make an image nine *talas* high and adorn it as follows: it should be yellow, the corner of its eyes white and it should be adorned with red clothes. It should also be smeared with red sandal and adorned with red flowers, a garland of red Aśokas and the palms of its hands and the soles of its feet should be red (vs. 296-297). The image should appear wearing a crown made of various gems and a cloth over both shoulders. The image should have a thin belly, a slender waist and a broad chest (vs. 298). It should look like a sixteen-year-old, carry a bow and arrow of flowers and resemble molten gold in its colour (vs. 299). The image should be seated on a throne or in a chariot with right foot folded under the left leg and the left foot resting on a pedestal (vs. 300). The image should be attended by the images of two female attendants who stand behind him holding whisks. They are Halī (the plough-share) and Varuṇī (wine). Images of Vasanta and Soma should be placed at his sides (vs. 302). Images of Rāga (with red garlands) and Mada (with white garlands) should appear standing at the back wall. The five arrows of Kāma should be painted on this wall..

They are called Tapanī (burning), Mohinī (delusion), Mardanī (destruction), Pramāthinī (harassment, tormenting) and Harinī (stealing). The arrows should be drawn in the form of women who have their heads adorned with flowers. Tapanī (fire) should be red in colour and wear in her hair the red Aśoka flower (vs. 304). Mohinī (delusion) should be yellow and wear the red lotus flower (*rāktaśoka*). Mardinī (destruction) should be green and wear the red lotus (*rāktotpala*) (vs. 305). Pramāthinī should be pale yellow and wear a blue lotus (kumunda) and Harinī should be smokey colour and wear blue lotuses (*utpala*) (vs. 306). The images should be placed beginning in the south and ending in the north. In front of the temple one should prepare a place for the Makara (fish banner) (vs. 307). The image of Kāma should be installed with *Sāntihoma* and the *Gāyatri Mantra* which is:

'Let us know Kāma, think of Kāma, let Kāma impel us!' (*manobhavāya vidmaha pañcabāṇāya dhīmahi tannah Kāmah pracodyāt)* (vs. 309)

One should worship Kāma with a diagram of a lotus while concentrating on the *Gāyatrī Mantra*. In the center of the diagram one should place a branch of the Aśoka tree uttering, '*Om.*' The branch of the Cūta or Mādhavī tree also may serve the same purpose (vs. 311). Then, invoking Kāma with *Gāyatri mantra*, one should place the image on the platform and then perform *nyāsa* (laying on of hands) accompanied by the utterance of seven syllables which are contained in the phrase 'praise to the flower arrowed one' (vs. 312). With this same *mantra* places of asylum should be created. Vasanta should be on the east, Mada on the south, Raga on the west, Soma on the north, Rati on the southeast, Vārunī on the southwest, Makara on the northeast and Usas on the northwest. Then one should offer water for the feet with the same seven syllables. Following this, one should worship Kāma with unguents, red flowers, rice covered with sugar and bowls of *dal*. One should fast day and night on the thirteenth lunar day in order to gain control of all women (vs. 317).

These two descriptions epitomize Kāma worship and establish four primary thematic affinities with accounts considered previously in this study: by worshipping Kāma in the prescribed manner, Diti is able to give birth to the Maruts; secondly, as Diti is, in the *Matsya Purāṇa* (above), the primary figure to worship Kāma, it is implicitly acknowledged that Kāma is worshipped primarily by women, particularly when conception is the aim; thirdly, the moment for commencement of the Kāma-ritual is the spring, the God of Love's most auspicious season; and, finally, given the final line in the *Kāmayāga*, worshipping Kāma may be a rite connected with sexual prowess when performed by men as its execution results in the winning of women.

Kāma and Women

Pragmatically, for women seeking favours or boons from the God of Love/Desire, the ambient richness and productiveness inherent in this season of beginnings must seem not only conducive to the propitiation of Kāma, but absolutely opportune. In the *Ratnāvalī* it is the queen who performs the liturgy of Kāma at the advent of spring;[54] in the *Bhaviṣya Purāṇa* his worship in the context of the *Vasantotsava* is specific to women. The concatenation of these Kāma rituals with rites of fertility directed toward getting, keeping and satisfying husbands is much in evidence.

The *Ākhyakamanikośa* prescribes the worship of Kāma for ladies wishing to secure a husband[55] who, according to Bhoja of Dhārā, if they are from villages, go to this ceremony bedecked with flowers, their eyes red with drink.[56] In the ritual of *āmrakusumāśana* (the eating of mango blossoms), the worship of Kāma on New Year's Day is enacted specifically by women (see flower festivals above). He is worshipped in a pitcher of plenty (*pūrṇakalaśa*).[57] Occasionally Kāma is worshipped as one aspect of the binary male/female couple as, for instance, in the *Kāvyamīmāṁsā* wherein he is called Kandarpa and is venerated by women only alongside Gaurī.[58] In Siddharsi Suri's *Upamitibhāvaprapañcakathā*, women worship an image of Kāmadeva and his consort Rati sleeping side-by-side on a bed cushioned with pillows.[59] This rite is prescribed for the express purpose of fulfilling one's desires (we can assume these dreams consist solely of finding a mate).

Unmarried women worship Kāma in order to find a husband; married women worship him to secure long life for their husbands. The purpose of the *Ratikāmavrata*, as detailed in the *Nārada Purāṇa*, is to achieve a long married life and prolific progeny.[60] A woman or girl undertaking this fast is to worship gold, silver, copper or mud images of Rati and Kāma and then to offer these images to a Brahmin couple along with food and other gifts. The ritual is to be performed annually for fourteen years. In the *Bhaviṣya Purāṇa* we find thus:

> A woman should honour her husband with ornaments, garlands and clothes, thinking of him as Kāma with her mind full of happiness (135. vs. 27).

And in the *Matsya Purāṇa* we find that courtesans were to worship Kāma in order to avoid the sin inherent in their occupation.[61]

An exception to this active role taken by women is the description of *kāmayāga* in the *Sanatkumāra Saṁhitā* where the participants engaged in the ritual play reverse their normal roles: men rather than women perform the ritual to gain favour relative to their relationship *vis-à-vis* women. The aims and results of the performance of this ritual, however, are identical for men as for women In the majority of our sources, women worship Kāma to gain control over men, i.e., a good husband and children; here, men worship Kāma to gain control over women. It would seem that the worship of Kāma can thus be turned to advantage regardless of one's sex.

The ritual described in the *Sanatkumāra Saṁhitā* (above) as men enact it, has decidedly *tantric* overtones. The worship of a diagram of a lotus with a branch of an Aśoka tree placed in the centre corresponds roughly to the *tantric* practice of *yantra*, a diagram or figure engraved, drawn or painted on metal, stone, pater, etc. Kane in *History of Dharmaśāstra* tells us that *yantra* is similar to the *mandala* but that the former is employed for the worship of a particular deity or for a particular purpose.[62] The use of such a diagram, the practice of *nyāsa* or equating parts of ones own body with the body of god and the utterance of *mantras* all have counterparts in *tantric* ritual practice. A. Bharati in *The Tantric Tradition* tells us that the *tantras* do not teach one to subdue the senses, but to increase their power and then to harness them in the service of achievement of lasting ecstasy, the target of these methods thus being the same as that of orthodox methods.[63] Kāma's association with eroticism and the creative powers of the universe renders him a particularly appropriate focus of meditation in this tradition. Further, that Kāma is worshiped in a specifically *tantric* context is confirmed by the sixteenth century AD work, the *Śrītattvacintāmaṇi*, the author of which was a *rāḍaya* Brahmin and a great tantric *sādhaka*.[64] This text describes the worship of Kāma along with Rati and Prīti and Spring (Vasanta).

The description of Kāma worship in the *Sanatkumāra Saṁhitā*, despite the fact that it is performed by men, is overwhelmingly feminine. Kāma is surrounded by damsels; his arrows are even to be fashioned in the form of women. He is flanked by the maiden wine (Varuṇī) and the plough-share (Halī): the first, indicative of intoxication (and eroticism), the second of the fertility of the soil (planting and tilling the soil). Both of these figures are appropriate companions to the god of love, especially at this season, when fertility and eroticism are central.

Images of Kāma and Image Worship

A final detail to be considered is the worship of an image of Kāma as recorded in the *Ratnāvalī*. We are told here that one is to adorn an Aśoka tree with flowers, saffron, sandal and worship an image of Pradyumna (Kāma) placed at its foot. Further, evidence found in descriptions of the *Vasantotsava* and in descriptions of Kāma worship in general tells us that images of Kāma of some form, be they pictorial or sculptural, were a common feature of both these rituals. Moreover, an image of Kāma of some type is specific to the worship of Kāma during the *Vasantotsava*. Given that images of Kāma are not worshipped to any extent today, it is only this textual evidence which suggests that in previous times these images did indeed exist.

The *Priyadarśikā* gives the following evidence for the worship of an image of Madana on this occasion:

> On the full moon day of spring an image or picture of Madana was placed in the garden under an Aśoka tree. The trunk of the tree is to be decorated with saffron finger prints. The deity (Kāma) is worshipped with offerings of flowers, turmeric, perfumes, rice, silk, clothes, etc. (Act I)

To this we add the commentary of Jayamaṅgalā on the *Kāmasūtra*[65] which states that an image of Madana was to be fashioned and subsequently worshipped with Damana flowers.[66]

> *madanotsavo madanapratikṛtipūjanam, damanabhañjikā paraśparam damanaka puṣpāvataṁsanaṁ*
>
> (The festival of Madana is worshipping an image of Madana. This adorning with Damana flowers on each other is the sport of Damana.)

In the *Mālatīmādhava* and the Tamil *Śilappatikāram*, separate temples dedicated to Kāmadeva in a garden referred to as *madanodyāna* (the grove of Kāma) are described.[67] And in the Jain *Kathākośa*, the maiden Kesarā performs the worship of Kāma on the day prior to her marriage. It is the custom, the text tells us, that such worship be performed in solitary in the temple of Kāma.[68] The above passage from the *Matsya Purāṇa* describing the *Madanadvādaśī* tells us that a golden image of Kāma was worshipped confirming a similar description in the *Nārada Purāṇa*.[69] The *Bhaviṣya Purāṇa* cites an image of Kāma, worshipped during the *Vasantotsava*., which is painted under an Aśoka tree together with similar images of his consorts, Rati and Prīti. Other figures to be drawn include his assistant, Spring (Vasanta) and Śiva.[70]

In the *Sanatkumāra Saṁhitā* an image of Kāma is constructed to celebrate the *Kāmayāga*. The description of this image is fairly elaborate and reflects the vitality of Kāma's overall persona: it is to have the features and aura of a sixteen-year-old, i.e., eternal youth and virility and should be attended by women, specifically Halī (the plough-share) and Varuṇī (wine). He is here accompanied by Vasanta (spring) as well as Soma and he possesses five arrows called fire (*tapanī)*, delusion (*mohinī)*, destruction (*mardini)*, torment (*pramāthinī)* and loss (*harinī)*.

Thus, it is clear that images of Kāma and, in some cases, temples housing his image were constructed. These images very often are brought forth in the specific context of the *Vasantotsava*. The fashioning of images of Kāma, frequently accompanied by an image of his consort, Rati, and their subsequent worship, proceeds in a manner typical of image worship as it is practised throughout Hinduism: they are bathed with incense and other rich substances, offerings are presented to them and celebratory *mantras* are uttered. Thus, for example, in the *Matsya Purāṇa* one is enjoined to worship the feet of Kāma and utter '*Om Kāmāya*,' to worship the legs of the Kāma image and utter '*Om Saubhagyadāya*,' and so on.

Despite these abundant and detailed textual references to images of Kāma, archaeological evidence supplies us with surprisingly few extant representations of him. An image of Kāma is found in Assam at Sibsagar. Made of sandstone, the deity is standing in a *dvibhaṅga* pose on a lotus pedestal. He is wearing a conical cap and jewelry (bracelets [*hara, keyūra, kaṅkana*] and earrings [*kuṇḍala*]). This particular image conforms to the *dhyāna* of both the *Matsya Purāṇa* (ch. 261 vs. 54) and the *Kālikā Purāṇa* (ch. 80 vs. 131). As this sculptural representation of Kāma belongs to the eleventh or the twelfth century AD,[71] a connection can be suggested between the medieval *purāṇic* textual descriptions of rituals and ritual paraphernalia and their actual iconographic representations.

Coomaraswamy, however, traces Kāma's iconographic origin much further back when he likens him to a *yakṣa* representation. The *yakṣa* figure is characterized by the mark of the Makara (fish); there are images of Kāmadeva and Rati at Bādāmī, Kailasanatha and Ellora where Kāma is identified by his *makaradhvaja*. Coomaraswamy maintains that this Makara which generally is linked to water and virility is a symbol sympathetic with any fertility deity. *Yakṣas* were in essence fertility figures and it was in this capacity that they appear, usually in scenes of abundant vegetation, as objects of worship. Coomaraswamy's descriptions of *yakṣa* shrines and of their worship is parallel in many respects to the shrines and worship of Kāma as described in our texts.[72] In a large number of instances *yakṣa* worship was performed in a *caitya* which may perhaps have been a building of some sort but was more likely scarcely more than a sacred tree. The essential element of a *yakṣa* shrine is a stone table or altar placed beneath the tree sacred to the *yakṣa*; in the above accounts of images of Kāma, they are all placed beneath trees. Coomaraswamy's statement that Kāma is indeed a *yakṣa*[73] strongly reinforces an interpretation of both the rituals performed in his honour and the attributes and actions of his person as intimately and straightforwardly linked with fertility, fecundity and simple *amour*.

In the final page of the *Ratnāvalī*, but while still in the pleasure grove, the princess who has become captivated by the king, sketches a portrait of her anamorato in the guise of Kāma. Her handmaiden Susamaṅgatā catches Ratnāvalī brush in hand and remarks that the image is incomplete. Susamaṅgatā finishes the picture by drawing the likeness of the princess in the guise of Rati, the consort of Kāma (pp. 41-45). The king, laying his eyes on the portrait, falls immediatelyin love with the princess.

NOTES

[1] *Śāstradīpikā,* 1.3.8.

[2] *Nityotsava,* 108.7.

[3] The Aśoka tree is found in decorations not only on Hindu temples but also in abundance at Buddhist sites such as Sanchi. See S. Sen Gupta, ed., *Tree Symbol Worship in India* (Calcutta: 1965), p. 95.

[4] B.C. Sinha, *Tree worship in Ancient India* (Delhi: 1979), p. 19.

[5] Rājaśekhara, *Karpūramañjarī,* ed., trans. by C.R. Lanman (Delhi: 1963), 1.47.

[6] The *Priyadarśikā,* ed. intro., trans. by N.G. Suru (Poona: 1928), Act I and the *Daśakumāracarita,* trans., notes by M.R. Kale (Delhi: 1979) which accord with the description in the *Ratnāvalī.*

[7] Coomaraswamy cites as evidence for the antiquity of the *dohada* motif, a railing pillar in the Mathura Museum (J-55) which represents a woman (or *yakṣī)* performing this ceremony. The motif survives in sculpture to the eighteenth century AD. These *dohada* rituals may, further, be related to the prolific appearance of the *Sālabhañjikā* or 'woman touching a tree' motifs on Indian temples.

[8] *Sāhityamīmāṁsā,* p. 151 cited by Raghavan, *Festivals,* p. 89. This is a twelfth century AD text according to Krishnamachariar, *History of Classical Sanskrit Literature,* p. 765.

[9] See also *Priyadarśikā* , Act II p. 23 of Nariman's translation.

[10] *Raghuvaṁśa,* VIII.62.

[11] Rājaśekhara, *Karpūramañjarī,* 1.47.

[12] Coomaraswamy, *Yakṣas* p. 35. G. Southerland in *Yakṣa* remarks that Kālidāsa uses the stock figure of the yakṣa to symbolize and embody the extremity of the sensual, poetic temperament that is inextricably bound to Sanskrit poetry (p. 150).

[13] *Mālavikāgnimitram,* Act III.

[14] According to Raghavan there are two of these festivals. One features the worship of the goddesses and is performed in autumn while the other celebrates spring. Raghavan, *Festivals,* p. 83. See also the *Bhaviṣya Purāṇa* (135) below for the overlapping of spring and autumn rituals.

[15] Anantadeva, *Smṛtikaustubha* (Bombay: 1909) p. 422. Trans. by K.C. Ray in "Aśokāṣṭamī," in the Royal Asiatic Society of Great Britain and Ireland (1901), pp. 127-40, p. 127. The date of this text is difficult to ascertain though it seems to be later than the *Bhaviṣya Purāṇaa* Raghavan in *Festivals* identifies it as a *Nibandha.* (p. 203)

[16] See also *Nīlamata Purāṇa* (787-90) which tells us that *aśokāṣṭamī* involves the worship of Umā for conjugal happiness. (Raghavan, *Festivals,* p. 83.)

[17] Kunjabehari Das, *Study of Orissan Folklore* (Santiniketan: Visva Bharati Series, no. 16, 1953), cited by Raghavan, *Festivals,* p. 83.

[18] Raghavan, *Festivals,* p. 201.

[19] A.C. Mukerji, *Ancient Indian Fasts and Festivals* (London: 1932), p. 30.

[20] *Bhaviṣya Purāṇa,* 132.

[21] Raghavan, for example, cites the following verse:

cūtamagryaṁ vasantasya mākanda kusumaṁ tava /
sacandanaṁ pibāmyadya sarvakāmārthasiddhaye //

He comments as follows: 'As mango-blossoms usher in the spring season and form also the arrows of Kāmadeva, they are now taken. As the days warm up now and as it is the season of enjoyment, sandal paste comes into use.' (*Festivals,* p. 204)

[22] *Puruṣārthacintāmaṇi* (Bombay: 1927), pp. 81-82 cited by Raghavan, *Festivals,* p. 203.

[23] pp. 1ff.

[24] Raghavan, *Festivals,* p. 93.

[25] Gaster, *Thespis,* p. 382.

[26] Raghavan, *Festivals,* p. 89.

[27] Kālidāsa, *Śākuntala,* Vi. 130. Translation by A Hjalmar Hedgren in "Śākuntala" in *Six Sanskrit Plays,* p. 256.

[28] K. N. Sahay, "Tree Symbol Worship in India", in S. Sen Gupta, ed., *Tree Worship in India* (Calcutta: 1965), p. 73.

[29] *Ibid.* One might note here that Brenda Beck records the spring marriage of Mariyammam in Kannapuram, Tamil Nadu, to a demon represented by a tree. The marriage of the tree and the Goddess is dissolved at the end of eight days and the tree uprooted. During these eight days, however, the Goddess is extremely dangerous and unpredictable. (B. Beck, "The Goddess and the Demon" in *Puruṣārtha* [Paris: Centre d'Etudes de l'Inde et de l'Asie du Sud, 1980])

[30] *Matsya Purāṇa,* 154, 250-2, also O'Flaherty, *Śiva,* p. 158.

[31] O'Flaherty, *Śiva,* p. 159.

[32] This particular garden is special in a number of respects. The story tells us that the goddess Durgā, gave a Brahmin devotee, who sacrifices himself to her, divine seed and directed him to create a garden. In this way he was told he would remain eternally near her. (*Kathāsaritsāgara,* VI. 108-9 ([rans. pp. 36-7])

[33] *Kathāsaritsāgara,* pp. 301-2.

[34] *Kathāsaritsāgara,* VI. 108-9 (trans. pp.36-40). This defect in the character of the unfortunate king is pointed out by one of his wives and thereupon the king becomes extremely despondent. The situation if remedied by one of his ministers who, with the aid of Kārttikeya, is able to teach the king his grammar.

[35] Daṇḍin, *Daśakumāracarita*, ed. with critical notes by R. Pischel (Bombay: 1938), p. 51.

[36] The garden is, of course, cultivated and not a natural environment in the sense of a wilderness or wild, uncontrolled nature. My point is merely to point out that the pleasure-grove appears here in sharp contrast to the urban environment.

[37] This is a reference to an image of Kāma (Pradyumna) which is placed at the foot of the tree.

[38] *Ratnāvalī*, p. 31,. See also above p. 50.

[39] We may include the *Sanatkumāra Saṁhitā*, *Matsya Purāṇa* and Kālidāsa's *Śākuntala* in this group of texts which mention of the worship of Kāma in the spring but do not make reference to a specifically named festival. *Sanatkumāra Saṁhitā*; ed., by P.V. Krishnamacharya (Madras: 1969), pp. 128-131; *Matsya Purāṇa*, ed. by B.D. Basu, trans. by a Taluqdar of Oudh, SBH 17 (2 Parts) (New York: 1974), 7. 154, etc. and Kālidāsa, *Śākuntala*, trans. by H. Edgren in H.W.Wells, *Six Sanskrit Plays*, pp. 221-329, Act IV.

[40] See, for example, the tenth century AD text, the *Tilakamañjarīsāra* of Pallīpāla Dhanapāla, ed. by N.M. Kansara (Ahmedabad), p. 52. See also *Śṛṅgāra Mañjarī* of Bhoja, pp. 20-1 and Haricandra's Jīvadharacampū as cited by Raghavan, *Ṛtu in Sanskrit Literature* (Delhi: 1972), p. 92.

[41] Kālidāsa, *Kumārasaṁbhava*, trans. by S.R. Sehgal (Delhi: 1959) p. 16, śloka 50, 66.

[42] Nilikantha Dikṣita, *Gangāvatarama*, Canto four, cited by Raghavan, *Ṛtu*, p. 93.

[43] *Kālikā Purāṇa*, ch.4 cited by Raghavan, *Ṛtu*, p. 23.

[44] *Vāmana Purāṇa*, ed. by A. Gupta, trans. by Mukhopadhyaya, A. Bhattacharya, N. C. Nath and V.K. Verma (Varanasi: 1968), 6.7.

[45] *Kumārasaṁbhava*, III. 25-7.

[46] *Matsya Purāṇa*, 154.111.

[47] See *Sanatkumāra Saṁhitā* and *Matsya Purāṇa* above and *Viṣṇudharmottara Purāṇa* (Bombay: 1834), III.183; *Nārada Purāṇa*, 122.16-18 cited by D. Nambiar, *Nārada Purāṇa: A Study* (Poona: 1968), p. 327; *Kāvyamīmāṁsā*, ed by C. D. Dalal, R.A. Śastri (3rd ed.; Baroda: 1934), pp. 104-6.

[48] *Matsya Purāṇa*, ch. 7.

[49] It should be noted at the outset that this is not the only myth which records the birth of the Maruts, but rather one version of their birth. Kāma is not central in all of the versions recording this myth.

[50] *Sanatkumāra Saṁhitā*, vs. 293-317, pp. 128-131.

[51] The thirteenth lunar day is often cited as auspicious for Kāma. See, for example, the "Rājadharmakhaṇḍa" of Lakṣmīdhara in *Kṛtyakalpataru* (Baroda: 1944) wherein this day is set aside for the worship of Kāma by kings.

[52] The sacred area is described here as *hastipṛṣṭha,* the meaning of which is obscure.

[53] My thanks to Mr. Venugopalan for his suggestion regarding the reading of *'pratimāśūla'* as trident. This reading would associate Kāma with the Śaiva tradition.

[54] *Ratnāvalī*, Act I.

[55] Sharma, *Festivals of India,* p. 17 cites this text but gives us no further information as to its date. Krishnamachariar in *History of Classical Sanskrit Literature*, p. 235 lists Nemichandra as a Jain author. The text dates to 1073-1083 AD (ed. Prākṛt Text Society, Varanasi: vol. 5 of the Prākṛt Text Series, 1962).

[56] *Śṛṅgāra Prakāśa,* p. 575 cited by Raghavan, *Festivals,* p. 88.

[57] Raghavan, *Festivals,* p. 201.

[58] Rājaśekhara, *Kāvyamīmāṁsā,* 104-6.

[59] B.N. Sharma, *Festivals of India,* p. 16. This text dates to the tenth century AD and is a lengthy allegory containing a great deal of folk material. M. Krishnamachariar, *A History of Classical Sanskrit Literature,* 233.

[60] *Nārada Purāṇa,* 122.28-32.

[61] *Matsya Purāṇa,* ch. 70. Pertaining to the relationship between courtesans and Kāma, S.C. Banerji, *Society in Ancient India* (Delhi: 1993) quotes an interesting verse from the *Saduktikarṇāmṛta,* a twelfth century AD anthology compled by Śrīdharadāsa: 'I think, Cupid, formerly reduced to ashes by the flames of the fire of the wrathful Śiva, is brought back to life by the glances of a prostitute.' (p. 195)

[62] Kane, *History of Dharmaśāstra,* V. 1021.

[63] A. Bharati, *The Tantric Tradition* (New York: 1970), p. 290.

[64] Paramahaṁsa Pūrnānanda. *Śrītattvacintāmaṇi,* intro., P. Bagchi, notes, C. Bhattacharya, Calcutta Sanskrit Series XIX (Calcutta: 1936), pp. 806-7.

[65] *Kāmasūtra* , I.iv.42.

[66] The Damana flower is usually associated with Viṣṇu. This relationship will be examined further in the chapter on the *Vikramacarita.*

[67] Bhavabhūti, *Mālatīmādhava,* ed., notes, intro. by R.D. Karmakar (Poona: 1935), Act I; Raghavan, *Festivals,* p. 88 cites the *Śilappatikāram.*

[68] *Kathākośa,* trans. by C.H. Tawney, p. 75.

[69] *Nārada Purāṇa,* 121. 2-16.

[70] *Bhaviṣya Purāṇa* , 135, 19-20.

[71] Arun Bhattacharjee, *Icons and Sculpture of Early and Medieval Assam* (Delhi: 1978), p. 50.

[72] A. Coomaraswamy, *Yakṣas* (New Delhi: 1971), pp. 22-27.

[73] R.D. Banerji, *Bas Reliefs of Badami,* p. 34 and Burgess, A.S.W.I., V. p. xxvi, 2 cited by Coomaraswamy, *Yakṣas,* p. 54.

5

The Spring Stage

The staging of dramas is a familiar conjunctive to festive celebrations in India and it is not surprising to encounter this type of performance in the course of the ancient, medieval and modern *Vasantotsava*. As a form of ritual behavior, the enactment of theatrical production during festivals touches upon the religious tradition: just as people celebrated momentous and auspicious junctures such as the advent of spring with gaiety, powder flinging, dancing and the worship of Kāma, they marked these occasions too with the enactment of plays.[1]

Although it is impossible to locate precisely the roots of the Indian tradition of dramaturgy, embedded in the texts are clues as to its date as well as the context of its origins. The earliest detailed text treating the subject of dramatic theory is Bharata's *Nāṭyaśāstra*.[2] Here is an elaborate description of the fully developed, sophisticated court drama complete with a body of specialized rules governing its creation and production. The *Nāṭyaśāstra*, self-styled as the fifth *Veda*, indicates that at least one explanation for the origin of the dramatic art is to be located in the context of religious festivals and that the first dramatic performance revolved around the story of the defeat of the demons by the gods.[3]

Other authorities on Indian drama including G.H. Tarlekar, suggest that plays were always staged in the courts of kings or in connection with religious festivals. Thus:

> From the Prologues of the plays we know that the plays were performed by the troops during the religious festivals in temples before the public. At the courts of the kings also the dramas were produced before the appreciative audience. Festive occasions like the Spring Festival were the most common for the performance.[4]

Such an intimate connection between drama and festive celebrations has prompted cultural historians like Rawlinson to cite the importance of festivals in the genesis and performance of Indian drama. Hence:

> ....dramatic representations at religious festivals are referred to in Aśoka's inscriptions. No doubt the first plays resembled the *yātra* still popular in Bengal and on occasions such as the spring festival, episodes such as the death of Rāvaṇa, the abduction of Sītā, the binding of Bali, the slaying of Kaṁsa, or Krishna's adventures with the Gopīs were ... enacted. (p. 134)

The prologue (*prastāvanā*) to the *Ratnāvalī* informs us that the play itself was composed specifically for production during the Spring Festival. The events described around which the play revolves are set not coincidentally in the context of the festival. An examination of the corpus of Indian dramatic literature reveals that there are other Sanskrit plays which are akin to the *Ratnāvalī* in respect to their being scripted specifically for the *Vasantotsava* stage as well as set during the course of the actual celebrations. The sequence of events and the content of Kālidāsa's *Mālavikāgnimitram* as well as Madana's *Pārijāta-Mañjarī* fall into this category, both exhibiting marked similarity to the information we find in the *Ratnāvalī*. Further, Śrī Harṣa's *Priyadarśikā* was written for performance on the occasion of the Spring Festival and, although it is set during the

Kaumudīmahotsava, the scenarios are remarkably similar to those above mentioned dramas revolving as they do around seasonal transition. Themes parallel to those of the Spring Festival are echoed throughout these particular dramas underscoring the concordance and symmetry of festival sentiment with ritual action. Our analysis focuses on the thematic affinity of the *Vasantotsava* with the *Ratnāvalī*, *Priyadarśikā*, *Pārijāta-Mañjarī* and the *Mālavikāgnimitram*.

Śrī Harṣa's *Ratnāvalī* and his *Priyadarśikā*, both written in the seventh century AD, Kālidāsa's *Mālavikāgnimitram* and Madana's *Pārijāta-Mañjarī* are plays written to be enacted on the *Vasantotsava* and all, with the exception of the *Priyadarśikā*, are set in the context of this occasion.[5] They thus, both literally and extra-literally, come into being at the onset of spring. All turn on a similar plot-line concerning the arrangement and accomplishment of the politically advantageous marriage between a king and a princess from another state. In each play the marriage is either arranged or foretold resulting in the potential bride's sojourn to the king's territory. Before the marriage has been solemnized some calamity befalls the princess and she is subject to a curious loss of identity. Silent with regards to her true identity, she steps into the king's palace as a servant who is, in some capacity, responsible to the king's chief queen. When the princess Ratnāvalī and Priyadarśikā appear at the palace, they assume different names. Ratnāvalī becomes Sāgarikā (one who has emerged from the ocean), Priyadarśikā becomes Āraṇyakā (one who has emerged from the forest).[6] No attention is drawn to the princess' sudden inability or unwillingness to reveal their true identity and few, save the audience, is privy to this information. The princess acts until the final scenes as if she were a drudge, subject to the commands of the queen. When the true identity of the princess is revealed there is no attempt to construe this silence, no astonishment as to it, nor is this issue raised by any other character in the play. This unclarified 'amnesia' of the princess seems essential to the development of the story. The knowledge of the true identity of the princess is concealed even, or especially, from the king and the chief queen who are both portrayed as oblivious to it. If the princess, the king or the queen knew that this chattel was in fact destined to marry the king, there would be no question employing her in this capacity.

The 'amnesic' condition of the princess and the chief queen affords an opportunity for these two women to become acquainted and perhaps even friends. Should the princess, a stranger, have been brought into the palace and identified as a new bride or bride-to-be of the king, her relationship with the chief queen might indeed have been different. During the interval in which the princess is in the employ of the queen as her personal servant, an intimate relationship develops between these two of apparently unequal status.[7] Most importantly, amity develops between the queen and the princess. Any potential rivalry between the two is mediated by this interval of anonymity.

As each drama unfolds, the young serving-girl cum princess and the king fortuitously encounter each other in the verdant garden during the spring celebrations. Both fall instantly in love. The queen, though fond of this handmaid, assumes she is unbefitting of the king's attentions and, distressed by his displays of affection towards this menial, she attempts to isolate her. Eventually the true identity of the princess is discovered, the queen, already fond of the princess is appeased and the match between the two lovers is secured by marriage.

The *Ratnāvalī*

Ratnāvalī, the Princess of Siṁhala, was destined by prophecy to become the wife of a universal monarch and on that account Yaugandharāyana, the minister of King Udayana, solicits her hand for his sovereign, the master of the kingdom of Vatsa. The marriage proposal is accepted but the ship in which the princess had embarked on her sojourn to her new home is wrecked in a storm. Ratnāvalī, catching hold of a plank, safely reaches the shore and is transported to King Vatsa's capital by a merchant of Kauśāmbī. Once there, Yaugandharāyana places her in the custody of the queen, Vasāvadattā, without disclosing her identity. Without comment Ratnāvalī assumes the name Sāgarikā, 'the one who emerged from the ocean.' During the time in which Ratnāvalī is under the protection of Queen Vasāvadattā, King Udayana casts his eyes upon her and becomes instantly enamoured. The princess, already bewitched by the king's beauty and suave demeanor, begins, from this point onwards, to pine for him. A rendezvous of the lovers is soon arranged in which Sāgarikā is to come disguised as the queen but the intrigue is discovered by the queen who, in a jealous fit of anger, has Sāgarikā bound and pitched into prison. The astute Yaugandharāyana, in the meantime, is watching the progress of his designs. A magician is sent to the palace and he casts a spell, creating the illusion of fire. The queen, now aghast, requests the king to rescue Sāgarikā from imminent peril. At this instant, Vasubhūti, the minister of Siṁhala who had accompanied the princess on the ship and escaped from the wreck in which the Princess Ratnāvalī was thought to have been lost, is ushered into the royal presence and he recognizes Sāgarikā as the Ratnāvalī who is pledged in marriage to King Udayana. The queen, learning that Sāgarikā is her own cousin, accepts her as a co-wife and, just at this moment, the joy of the occasion is doubled by the happy news that Rumaṇvat, the victorious general of King Udayana, has subdued the rival monarch of Kosala.

Priyadarśikā

The *Priyadarśikā* proper begins with praise of Gaurī and Śiva, that paradigm of marital bliss in Indian myth. The marriage of Priyadarśikā (the daughter of Dṛḍhavarman) and King Vatsa Udayana of Kauśāmbī has been arranged by Priyadarśikā's father. The rival king of Kaliṅga had wanted to marry the princess but had been rebuffed and consequently had waged war upon Dṛḍhavarman, taking him captive. During the confusion of the battle, Priyadarśikā is rescued and sheltered in the forest by King Vindhyaketu, an ally of her father. King Udayana then, unaware of the whereabouts of Priyadarśikā, marries Vāsavadattā and mounts a military campaign against

Vindhyaketu who is slain in the battle. Among the spoils of war is the maiden Priyadarśikā who is given to the queen to educate. The true identity of the princess is unknown: she is believed to be the daughter of King Vindhyaketu but is called Āraṇyakā because she was found in the forest. A year or so later the queen dispatches her to the palace garden to gather lotuses. There, in the pleasure grove, the king casts his eyes upon her and is instantly enchanted. At that moment, the princess is suddenly and fortuitously attacked by bees and falls crazed into the king's arms. In the third act we learn that a play on the subject of the marriage between King Udayana and Queen Vāsavadattā has been arranged and that Priyadarśikā is to play the role of the queen. The *vidūṣaka* ensures that the king will play himself. The queen, unaware of the identity of the actors, watches the performance but the intensity of the passion between the king and Priyadarśikā on-stage arouses her suspicions. Vāsavadattā rushes out of the hall and discovers that her husband (King Udayana) and Priyadarśikā are the chief actors. She incarcerates the princess who, stricken with grief, attempts to poison herself. The king administers a magical potion which saves her and, at last, the queen is appeased. Priyadarśikā's true identity becomes known; Vāsavadattā rejoices, having found that her servant and the lover of her husband is, in reality, her long lost cousin. The marriage between king Vatsa and *Priyadarśikā* is approved.

Mālavikāgnimitram

As the title suggests, the Princess Mālavikā and the King Agnimitra are the two destined for love and marriage in this drama of Kālidāsa.[8] The Princess Mālavikā arrives at the palace incognito and takes up a position as a maid-servant of the chief queen of Agnimitra, Dhāriṇi.[9] In this capacity Mālavikā appears in a group portrait of the queen and her entourage. The king, seeing her in this portrait, instantly falls in love with her. He asks his court wit (*vidūṣaka*) to discover some means of seeing her again. Mālavikā is enrolled in dance lessons and the *vidūṣaka* conveniently arranges for a quarrel between two dancing masters, one of whom is Mālavikā's teacher. A dance contest is arranged to determine who is the superior instructor. The queen, Dhāriṇi, becomes suspicious after she sees Mālavikā dance and, fearing that the king will fall in love with the beautiful drudge, refuses to allow him to witness the performance.

The scene shifts to the garden where Dhāriṇī has had a minor accident swinging and has asked Mālavikā to perform the *dohada* ritual to prompt the Aśoka tree to blossom in her stead. The king arrives in the garden with his second queen, Irāvatī. Together, they watch Mālavikā kick the tree until Irāvatī notices that the king is in a swoon over Mālavikā and she thereupon resolves to send her away. Dhāriṇī, the chief queen, on hearing this news, has Mālavikā thrown into prison. The king arrives but is called away on urgent business. The *vidūṣaka* arranges for Mālavikā's release but soon the queen discovers the plot and searches out the king. The Aśoka tree blossoms.

In the last act Mālavikā, in the presence of the king and the queen, is recognized by one of the court visitors. The queen, amidst the general rejoicing presents her to the king and gladly consents to their union. The match is thus approved and the play ends on a happy note.

Pārijāta-Mañjarī alias *Vijayaśrī*

In this play, dating from the thirteenth century AD and known only from inscription,[10] the proposed alliance is between King Arjunavarman and Pārijāta-Mañjarī, 'a bud from the tree of paradise' (*Pārijāta*), which falls upon Arjunavarman during battle. This bud miraculously transforms into a beautiful maiden whereupon a voice from heaven tells the king to marry her.[11]

The production opens with a monologue delivered by the stage-manager who has been instructed to script a play to be staged on the full moon day of Caitra and performed at the temple of Sarasvatī. The wonders of spring are described, the recent war is described and we become privy to the knowledge that the sovereign has handed over the maiden, Pārijāta, to the superintendent of the royal gardens. The gardener, in turn, houses her in the emerald pavilion in the royal gardens. The king retires to the uppermost room of his palace to witness the citizens celebrating the Spring Festival. Here Arjunavarman and his queen fling powder at each other until, at an auspicious moment, the queen departs for the garden to perform the ritual marriage of the Mādhavī creeper and the mango tree. In the meantime, Pārijāta-Mañjarī has fallen deeply in love with the king and pines for him in her garden prison. In the midst of the spring celebrations Arjunavarman too is overcome with love pangs for this unknown girl and these sentiments compel him towards the pleasure grove in which she is ensconced. The king catches a glimpse of Pārijāta-Mañjarī through the reflection of one of the queen's ornaments and she, in turn, notices the king's glances. The queen becomes suspicious and leaves the garden angry. King Arjunavarman promises Pārijāta-Mañjarī that he will return and rushes off to console the queen.

Unfortunately, these two acts are all that remain of the play. From the plot thus far, however, it is not difficult to guess at an ending, *viz.*, Pārijāta-Mañjarī and Arjunavarman get married.

Underlying Themes: Fertility and Marriage

The plays summarized above, though spanning several hundred years and originating in different locales in India, follow a clearly discernable pattern. That these plots are remarkably similar suggests that these particular dramatic scenarios and character relationships hold a special significance for our understanding of the *Vasantotsava*. It remains now to examine the themes of these plays with reference to the Spring Festival on which they were performed. The central motifs of both the *Vasantotsava* and the above outlined dramas cluster around the complex of fertility, eroticism and procreation. The dramatic arts attained full flower when women (originally *apsaras*) were employed in the portrayal of the sentiment of love.[12] These recurring themes must be doubly resonant when actually played out on-stage: the audience celebrates the festival of renewal and regeneration by watching a drama which reinforces this self-same theme of budding new love. These story lines are remarkably alike in both plot and detail. In every case the end result is the same: the king and a young woman fall romantically and passionately in love.

In all of these versions the end result is impending marriage, the socially sanctioned union of male and female. These matches are love matches, not simply expedient and advantageous political alliances. First, the king not only is aroused, but *must* be aroused: just as all of nature is waking up and putting forth new blossoms, so too is the king, the central figure in the kingdom, aroused when he catches a glimpse of the drudge who is really a princess. This 'awakening' of the king is provoked by the entrance of the bride-to-be, a nubile lowly servant girl. The love triangle (king/bride-to-be/servant girl) is intriguing as it involves two generations, two kingdoms and two social classes in each instance. The king's attentions are directed towards the servant girl who is 'apparently' of low birth and as such, hardly suitable for marriage to royalty. The bride-to-be, for all intents and purposes, is a stranger in the court, a stranger who is somehow particularly suited to effect his invigouration. There is something about the anonymous, vulnerable status of this young maiden that renders her so charming and so fascinating. That the king falls for a menial is a denial of, or perhaps in defiance of, hierarchical social restrictions reminiscent, though not identical to, the erasure or obfuscation of class distinctions that was noted earlier in the powder flinging rituals of the Spring Festival. This is above all a marriage provoked by desire: this union is to be born of a passion that inexorably transcends or over-comes imposed and somewhat artificial, traditional conventions.

The theme of the mum or the gagged princess and indeed, the reticence, the hush of all concerned (save the audience), echoes yet another major aspect of the Spring Festival: death and oblivion. Each year, out of the utter stillness of winter, the earth magically and beneficently yields forth new life. The lacuna, the mysterious transition between death and life akin to the transitional gap between the seasons, is essentially inexplicable. Winter and spring, like death and life, are the extremes between which the rhythms of the earth oscillate. It is this rhythmic to-and-fro which lends resonance to the festival, highlighting the sense of 'becoming' quintessential to this season. The princess suffers through her muteness and her status change, a kind of death. In the *Ratnāvalī* she is believed to be dead; in the *Priyadarśikā* she is disappeared, having been exchanged mistakenly as a tribute of war; in the *Mālavikāgnimitram* she is simply a maid, gifted to the queen who is truly a princess, and in the *Pārijāta-Mañjarī* she is forgotten, erased from memory, in the garden. In all cases her status is dramatically altered: the 'princess' is effectively in a death-like limbo. She exists in the palace environs without identity, neither who she was (an unmarried princess) nor who she is to become (a married queen). The audience to the play knows there is no conflict if the king should fall in love with this menial as there might have been should the king have fallen for a true menial. (She is the 'right' choice.) The deathlike silence of the princess is nothing but a device of plot not uncommon in Indian stories in general,[13] yet it allows the king to fall in love with the princess and she with him without the mediation of 'like' social status. Like the old year, like the winter, all is quiet and still. Akin to Kāma's fate at the third eye of Śiva, the princess' identity is dissolved and awaits resurrection which comes forth, in the case of the dramas as re-cognition, resolution and marriage (in the case of spring, as regeneration and rebirth.). Ultimately, all is resolved in the drama, the innocent princess finds her voice, is allowed to regain her identity and is now welcomed by her co-queen, through their reciprocal love of the king. The silent earth expresses its inherent nature as fertile ground ready to receive seed becoming articulated in nature simultaneous with the arrival of spring. Death (barrenness) is held in abeyance, yet again, through the blossoming of the earth. In the case of the silent princess, her inherent nature, her inherent fertility is ascribed and finds voice only in her forthcoming marriage to the king. The weapon wielded against this death, this silence, this dormancy of winter, is love.

The plot of these plays closely reflects the tangible concerns of the festivals in which they were performed. Resolution through marriage with its implied procreative course is reflected in the Spring Festival, the festival of renewal. Marriage rituals usher in and prepare for the impending union of the male and the female. The motifs of both dramas and the *Vasantotsava* exhibit a certain symmetry, a certain concord and a certain romance, especially in anticipation of new beginnings. The striking parallels between marriage ceremonies and the Spring Festival suggest that rites of this type are integrally linked.

Marriage and Renewal

Marriages in India are customarily solemnized at an auspicious time during the year, the most favoured season being spring.[14] Ancient Sanskrit ritual texts,[15] most importantly the *Gṛhya Sūtras, Dharmasūtras* and the *Smṛtis*, are nearly unanimous in maintaining that nuptials ought to be enacted during the northern course of the sun (i.e., the spring). The moment of the waxing moon, was preferred with the day of the full moon cited as the most auspicious time for such a ceremony. The *Vasantotsava* fits these parameters and is this perfect occasion on which to celebrate a marriage, both rites demanding as they do the same auspicious moment for their performance.

Like the *Vasantotsava*, general merriment and mercurial behavior is characteristic of the rites of marriage. Singing, dancing and drinking wine form part of the pre-marriage rituals according to the *Śāṅkāyana Gṛhya Sūtra*.[16] In the *Kāṭhaka Gṛhya Sūtra*[17] the bride plays musical instruments which are besmeared with water while her friends en-gage themselves playing music as well, either for one or two days and a night. The excitement and gaiety of the festivities are further described in the *Kauśītaki Gṛhya Sūtra* and in the *Mānava Gṛhya Sūtra* wherein a dance of eight *avidhavās* (unwidowed women) is followed by the feasting of

Brahmins.[18] The *Vaśiṣṭha Smṛti* tells us that after the father agrees to give his daughter in marriage the groom goes to her house accompanied by married ladies and their children, singing and playing musical instruments. Among Nepali Brahmins, the ladies keep awake all night singing and dancing. Intoxicated by the wine, they act in ways both unpredictable and impulsive, quite often in-dulging in vulgar, sexy joke-making and pranks.[19]

It is further not surprising to find that Kāmadeva, a stellar player in the *Vasantotsava* (as, for example, decribed in the *Ratnāvalī*), is also invoked during the course of the marriage ceremony.[20] The association of Kāma with marriage rites is rooted in ancient times and is confirmed in texts like the *Atharva Veda* from which we quote the following verse to be uttered during the marriage ritual.[21]

Kah idam kasmai adāt kāmaṅ kāmāya adāt /
Kāmo dātā kāmaṅ pratidrahitākāmaṅ samudram āviveśa /
kāmena tvā pratigṝhnāmi Kāma etat te

(Who hath given this and to whom? Kāma has given it to Kāma [the fulfiller, of desire, has given it to desire]; Kāma is the giver [i.e., the inspirer, or fulfiller of desire]; Kāma is the receiver. Kāma has entered into the ocean. Through Kāma I receive thee, Kāma, this is thing.) (III.29.7)

The centrality of love (*kāma*), passion (*kāma*) and desire (*kāma*) in the context of the regeneration of spring finds its equivalent symbolic paramountcy in the context of marriage rites. Kāma's association with intoxication and the awakening of passion has been established earlier.[22] During the marriage ritual, the procreative potentialities of the bride are crystallized by the sprinkling of her with wine and with the invocation of Kāma, thereby symbolically generating or stirring the passions. In the *Gobhila Gṛhya Sūtra*, the bride-to-be is sprinkled with *surā* (wine) while the following *mantra* is recited:[23]

'Kāma, I know your name, You are intoxication by name. Bring him (the bridegroom) so that he may

4. *Ragini Hindola*
Deccan (?) or Central India, *circa* A.D. 1850

> be here together with the bride. To thee there was surā. Here (may there be) the excellent birth. O Agni you are created from penance, hail!'

This sprinkling of the bride with *surā* is just one example in which substances are poured, thrown or smeared on the bride-to-be, the groom-to-be or both during the course of weddings. Wheat, rice, water, honey, ghee, curds, wine, coloured powder and confetti are commonly deployed in this context in many cultures.[24] If we understand red powder to be mimetic of blood, the substances here have much in common. They all in some way suggest regeneration as they are all regenerated substances themselves. Through the transformation which they have undergone (pollen to honey, grapes to wine, plant to seed), they have been reduced to their 'essential' nature wherein all the extraneous residue of their making and former substance has been eliminated. Nature's essences, as they have been purified and transformed, carry with them purity and transformative power. When the bride is bathed by these thrown/ applied substances, her purity and virginity are thus emphasized. She is, during the marriage ritual, in transition as she moves into her generative stage. Clearly, the notion of nurture and sustenance is one which we identify with motherhood and this is here reinforced by the sustaining power of these substances.

In the Hindu marriage ceremony, this type of ritual behavior (substance flinging) finds articulation in several ways. During *kanyādāna*, or the rite in which the father of the bride orally agrees to give the hand of his daughter to the selected bridegroom, the bride or the bride and the groom together are anointed with *ājya* (ghee),[25] *surā*,[26] which we have already encountered above and also water.[27] Although the order of the marriage rites in the *Gṛhya* and *Dharma Sūtras* is not rigidly standardized, the rites of *kanyādāna* and the bathing of the bride are usually followed by the rite of *madhuparka*[28] which consists of pouring honey into curd, mixing the two ingredients, sprinkling some of the mixture in all three directions (east, south and north) and then consuming the remaining bit.

The consumption of the sprinkled substance, *madhuparka*, is not exclusive to the marriage ceremony but, when it does take place in the context of marriage it is the bridegroom who has the honour of consuming it. In the *Vaśiṣṭha Smṛti*,[29] the friends of the couple hold a pot of water in their hands and sprinkle it on the bride and the groom with *kuśa* blades (blades of sacred grass). At the end of the ceremony both bride and groom sprinkle unhusked grains on each other's head.

Akṣata or unhusked grains are thrown at the newly married pair indicating that these seeds both help to sanctify the marital union, join the pair together and facilitate the future productivity of the couple. Grain as seed is clearly representative of fertility and the abundance of the vegetative world, a parallel for which is sought in the human world. A pot filled with water, *akṣata* grains and sometimes gold is touched by the 'woo-ers' of the bride and the bride's father (once he has given his consent to the union).[30] The couple sprinkle each other with *akṣata* to symbolize their unity and ensure their fertility. In the *Laghvāśvalāyana Smṛti*,[31] during *kanyādāna* the bride scatters *akṣata* grains on the head of the groom and then the groom scatters *akṣata* grains on hers. Following this, they exchange places and she again sprinkles *akṣata* grains on his head. Then follows a recitation of verses in which the groom is requested not to abandon the bride with respect to *dharma*, *artha* and *kāma* and then, again, *akṣata* grains are placed or poured on their heads. In more recent times *akṣata* has been replaced by husked rice grains which are coloured with turmeric and red powder. This activity is now performed by all of the guests attending the marriage ceremony. In some cases the rice has been dispensed with altogether and the throwing of red powder only remains as part of the marriage rites.

These rites are in some sense akin to the rite of throwing of coloured powder, which has been discussed above as an aspect of the family of fertility rituals. Indeed, the Sanskrit tradition is replete with references to this practice of powder throwing during the marriage ceremony. Someśvara, in his twelfth century AD text, the *Mānasollāsa*, confirms that powder throwing is a prominent part of the

Vasantotsava but he also tells us that it is integral to other festive occasions, including marriages and royal victories.[32] This same ritual is recorded in the *Nāgānanda* as part of the nuptial ceremony and in Bengal the throwing of *Halud* (turmeric powder) is an important feature of the marriage ceremony. The name of this ceremony during which the bride is anointed is *'Gaye Halud.'*[33]

Insofar as these dramas revolve around marriage and insofar as the rites of marriage correspond in many details to the celebration of the *Vasantotsava,* these dramas of marriage can be understood as metaphoric parallel enactments of the lives of audience members who are engaged in the celebration of spring. These plays operate in some manner similar to myths. Aside from their being first and foremost entertainments, both plays and myth are didactic. That they are 'unreal,' in the sense of 'fictitious' allow them to function largely as metaphor. and hence the audience views the characters of king and queen on-stage, a paradigmatic couple which ranks highest in the political order, acting in ways identifiable to the men and the women in the audience. The actions of the king and the queen, as portrayed on-stage, ensure and reinforce the continuance of both natural and social order. Parallel to these dramatic narratives of king and queen are the mythological narratives of Śiva and Pārvatī, Kāma and Rati. In the context of the *Vasantotsava,* these myths revolve around renewal thus providing models for their dramatic counterparts. As related in the *Ratnāvalī,* the *Vasantotsava* was celebrated by citizens who witnessed dramatic performances as part of the festival. The descriptions of the audience in the *Ratnāvalī,* i.e., a mass of citizens, suggest that the drama was staged before a broad cross section of the populace, reinforcing the traditional literature of the *Nāṭyaśāstra* which states that drama was created by the god Brahmā for the benefit of all *varṇas,* be they high or low, rich or poor, man or woman.[34]

NOTES

[1] See P. Kale, *The Theatric Universe* (Bombay: 1974), pp. 43-44.

[2] Though the dates of Indian texts are rarely certain, the *Nāṭya-śāstra* seems to have been composed no earlier than the third century AD. See. A. Berriedale Keith,*The Sanskrit Drama in its Origin, Development, Theory and Practice* (Reprint: London: 1964), p. 13.

[3] See below, Chapter Eleven, for a discussion of this mythological event and the festival of the *Indramahotsava* occasioned by it.

[4] Tarlekar, p. 216.

[5] There is some controversy regarding the date and authorship of the *Ratnāvalī* and the *Priyadarśikā*. C.R. Devadhar and N.G. Surû's introduction to the *Ratnāvalī* contains an overview of the evidence on this question (pp. 1-4). According to the introductory notes, the occasion is either the Spring or Autumn Festival (*Kaumudīmahotsava).* For further details on the overlapping of spring and autumn rituals, see *Bhaviṣya Purāṇa* (135) below. The same questions pertaining to the dating of texts can be raised regarding Kālidāsa's *Mālavikāgnimitram*. See R.D. Karmarkar's translation of this text (pp. i-svi). The dates of Kālidāsa range from the second century BC during the Śuṅga Empire to the fourth or fifth century AD, during the reign of Chandra Gupta II. See C. Rajan, *Kālidāsa* for a detailed discussion of the evidence for these dates (pp. 25, 307-315). For the date of the *Pārijāta-Mañjarī* , see the prefix to Dikshit's translation (pp. i-svii).

[6] Mālavikā retains her real name but she is employed as a maid-servant by the queen. Everyone seems to believe that she was sent as a present to the queen by Vīrasena, a commander of inferior caste in command of a frontier fortress. Vīrasena happens also to be the queen's brother. (Kale, *Mālavikāgnimitram, p*p. 14-15.)

[7] In the *Mālavikāgnimitram*, there are two chief queens.

[8] The summary has been taken primarily from Kālidāsa, *Mālavikāgnimitram,* translated, edited and notes by R.D. Karmarkar (Bombay: 1950) and *Mālavikāgnimitram*, trans. by M. R. Kale, revised by J.L. Dave and S.A. Upadhyaya (Delhi: 1960). Kale argues that the hero, Agnimitra is an historical person and that Mālavikā was a Malava princess (pp. xvii-xxi).

[9] Mālavikā's position in the palace is explained in Act V and is summarized by M.R. Kale, *Mālavikāgnimitram* as follows:

> In an Interlude (*praveśika)* the success of Vīrasena's expedition against the Vidarbha king is announced. In the next scene, in the presence of the King, the Queen, Mālavikā and others, two captive maid-servants brought from the Vidarbha expedition are introduced and they immediately recognize Mālavikā. She, it turns out, was none other than the missing sister of Mādhavasena. The minister of Mādhavasena, one

Sumati by name, in the confusion of Mādhavasena's capture, took flight with Mālavikā and his own sister. But Sumati was attacked by highwaymen while on his way to Agnimitra's capital and Mālavikā in the meanwhile was secured from some foresters by Vīrasena. They sent her as a present to Dhāriṇī, where she was seen and recognized by Sumati's sister, who had become a *parivrājikā* and had also happened to attach herself to Dhāriṇī's court. But she could not give out the identity of Mālavikā as she knew of a prophecy that Mālavikā would remain for a year as a servant and then be married to a suitable husband. (pp. xiii-xiv)

10 Unfortunately, the last two acts are missing.

11 The author of the introduction to the translation of this text suggests that Pārijāta-Mañjarī was the daughter of a Cālukya king whom Arjunavarman had just defeated in battle and killed.

12 See, for example, G.H. Tarlekar, *Studies in the Nāṭyaśāstrta* (Delhi: 1975), pp. 2ff; P. Kale, *The Theatric Universe: A Study of the Nāṭyaśāstra* (Bombay: 1974), pp. 8 ff; and A. Berriedale Keith, *The Sanskrit Drama* (London: 1964), pp. 9 ff.

13 See, for example, *Śākuntala*.

14 Apte, *The Sacrament of Marriage* (Delhi: 1978), p. 71.

15 Though there are a number of texts which detail the rites of marriage in the Hindu tradition, it is primarily to the *Gṛhya Sūtras* (800-400 BC, i.e., the *Gobhila Dharmasūtra, Āśvalāyana, Āpastamba* being the oldest); the *Dharmasūtras* (500-300 BC); and the *Smṛtis* (i.e., 200 BC to 100 AD [*Manusmṛti*]; 100 AD to 300 AD [*Yajñavalkyasmṛti*]; 100-400 AD; [*Nāradasmṛti*]; 300-500 AD [*Bṛhaspatismṛti*]; and 600-900 AD [the metrical *Smṛtis*]). These texts are diverse in their treatment of material pertaining to marriage rites. See B. Saraswati, *Brāhmaṇic Ritual Traditons* (Shimla: 1977), pp. xvix,xx, 165, 17 ff. and U.M. Apte, *The Sacrament of Marriage* (Delhi: 1978).

16 After the bathing of the bride-to-be, for example, four or eight women who are not widows are regaled with wine *(surā)* and food. They dance four times. *Śāṅkāyaṇa Gṛhya Sūtra* , 1.11, cited by Apte, *Marriage*, p. 85.

17 For example, *Kāṭhaka Gṛhya Sūtra*, 11.5.2, cited by Apte, *Marriage*, p. 86.

18 *Kauśītaki Gṛhya Sūtra*, 1.7; 1.11; *Mānava Gṛhya Sūtra*, 1.9.28; Apte, *Marriage*, pp. 87-88.

19 Saraswati, p. 170. This is also common among Maithili Brahmins, *Ibid*, p. 187.

20 A variety of gods and goddesses are in fact invoked at various stages during the marriage ceremony including Indra, Viṣṇu, Agni and the goddess Indrāṇī.

[21] Text and translation by J.Muir, *Original Sanskrit Texts*, Vol. 5 (Amsterdam: 1969), p. 403.

[22] See above, Kāma in the garden and also the *Sanatkumāra Saṁhitā* (302) where he is attended by *vārunī* (wine), *rāga* (love, affection, amorous or sexual feeling) and *mada* (intoxication, drunkenness).

[23] *Gobhila Gṛhya Sūtra*, 1.1.10, cited by Saraswati, p. 185.

[24] *Ājya* (ghee) is sprinkled over the bride's head in the *Vārāha Gṛhya Sūtra* (p.11), the *Gobhila Gṛhya Sūtra* (1.10.9-10), and the *Kāṭhaka Gṛhya Sūtra*. Water is found in the *Kāṭhaka Gṛhya Sūtra* and in the *Vaśiṣṭha Smṛti* (2), IV, 43-44. For *akṣata* grains, see *Laghvāśvalāyana Smṛti* (XV. 20) and the *Mānava Gṛhya Sūtra*. For *pūlya* (roasted) grains, see the *Kauśītaki Gṛhya Sūtra*. See also Saraswati and Apte for details of these rituals.

[25] *Kauśītaki Gṛhya Sūtra*, 1.8.13, cited by Apte, *Marriage*, p. 90. One *mantra* recited during the marriage ceremony suggests a comparison between sexual intercourse and melted butter (*ghee*) suggesting further, that melted butter is the symbolic equivalent of semen. *Ibid* p. 186.

[26] *Gobhila Gṛhya Sūtra*, 1.10.9-10.

[27] *Kāṭhaka Gṛhyā Sūtra* quoted in Apte, p. 83.

[28] For the order of these rites as prescribed in the *Gṛhya Sūtras*, see Saraswati, pp. 172-174.

[29] *Vaśiṣṭha Smṛti* (2), IV. 43-44, cited by Apte, *Marriage*, p. 137.

[30] *Ibid*, pp. 83, 196.

[31] *Laghvāśvalāyana Smṛti*, XV. 20, in Apte, *Marriage*, p. 134.

[32] Raghavan, *Festivals*, p. 73.

[33] Samirayet, P. Mukhopadhyay, "Sarmilar Patgṛhe Yatra" in *Desh* (July 9, 1983).

[34] P. Kale, *The Theatric Universe*, p. 9.

6

Kathāsaritsāgara

The *Kathāsaritsāgara* is a collection of stories written by the Kashmiri Brahmin, Somadeva, for the amusement of his Queen Sūryamatī.[1] It dates from the eleventh century AD and contains twenty-one thousand stanzas, divided into eighteen *laṁbhakas* with one hundred and twenty-four *taraṅgas*.[2] By the admission of its author Somadeva, the *Kathāsaritsāgara* is a condensed Sanskrit version of Gunādhya's *Bṛhatkathā*. This latter text, written in *Paiśācī prākṛt*, is the earliest known Indian compilation of stories dating perhaps to the fifth century AD.[3] Although the *Bṛhatkathā* no longer survives, we know of its contents through both the *Kathāsaritsāgara*, which begins by telling us that Gunādhya wrote the *Bṛhatkathā* while wandering in the forest in the Vindhya region,[4] as well as through the *Bṛhatkathāmañjarī* of Kṣemendra, written at the beginning of the eleventh century AD. Somadeva seems also to have incorporated other materials such as that found in the *Pañcatantra*. In addition to the main frame story, and very often obscuring that narrative altogether, is a large amount of information of almost every sort. The task of deciding which of this additional material belonged to the original of Gunādhya is difficult, if not altogether impossible.[5]

The longest collection of stories in the *Kathāsaritsāgara* and the one most relevant to the *Vasantotsava* is contained in Book Twelve, included in which is the *Vetālapañcaviṁśatikā* or the twenty-five tales of a *vetāla*. Both extant versions of the *Bṛhatkathā*, (i.e., the *Kathāsaritsāgara* and the *Bṛhatkathāmañjarī*) contain these twenty-five tales but some evidence suggests that they may originally have formed an independent cycle. (These stories are not found, for example, in Buddhasvamin's *Bṛhatkathā Ślokasaṁgraha*.[6]) The *Vetālapañcaviṁśatikā* does, however, exist independently in a variety of recensions, the most important of which is probably that of Śivadāsa and dates from the fifteenth century AD.[7] The *Vetālapañcaviṁśatikā*'s general popularity is attested to by its inclusion in the Kashmiri versions, Somadeva's *Kathāsaritsāgara*, the *Bṛhatkathamañjarī* and in its numerous independent recensions.

The frame story of this collection is simple: King Trivikramasena receives a fruit from an ascetic every year only to discover that the fruit conceals a gem. In gratitude, he summons the ascetic who asks him to go to a cemetery and fetch a corpse hanging there on a tree as the human carcass is requisite for some religious rite. The king is warned that the success of his mission depends on absolute silence. Accordingly, the king proceeds to the cemetery and recovers the corpse which is dangling from a tree there. As he is transporting the cadaver from the cemetery to the ascetic, a *vetāla* (demon or ghoul) which has entered into the lifeless body, tells the king a story. At the close of the tale the *vetāla* puts a question arising from it to the king who, naturally enough, falls into the trap and answers, thereby breaking the requirement of silence essential to the success of his mission. The corpse escapes and returns to the tree. This scenario recurs twenty-five times with the result that King Trivikramasena's task has to be repeated again and again. Finally, in the terminal story, the king is unable to solve the riddle and the *vetāla* reveals that the ascetic is planning to sacrifice the king and usurp his place. The king returns with the corpse and the ascetic bids him to prostrate himself before it. The king innocently asks the ascetic to show him how to perform the prostration. When the ascetic obligingly demonstrates the procedure, the king promptly cuts off his head.

The following story from the *Vetālapañcaviṁśatikā* contained in the *Kathāsaritsāgara* has been selected for further examination both as it is set during the celebration of the *Vasantotsava* and as it has as its focal point a narrative of the festival itself.

The *Kathāsaritsāgara*: Book XII, Story Number 17 [8]

As the number of this story suggests, this is King Trivikramasena's seventeenth journey from the cemetery, corpse on back. The *vetāla* begins with a description and adulation of the righteousness of the city Kanakpuram and its ruler, King Yaśodhana. One day, the *vetāla* continues, King Yaśodhana is approached by a merchant who wishes the king to marry his daughter, Unmādinī (literally, 'the intoxicator'). The king's interest is aroused and he dispatches his Brahmin advisors to inspect and appraise the prospective bride. Astounded by her amazing beauty, the Brahmins fear that one of such great allure would corrupt the king: she would simply be too great a diversion for him. Accordingly, they return and inform the king that Unmādinī is exceedingly ugly whereupon he orders the merchant to give his daughter in marriage to the commander of his army. The merchant's daughter, thus slighted, entertains thoughts of contempt for the king because he has rejected her.

Spring arrives. King Yaśodhana mounts a royal elephant and rides out into the city at the head of a procession in order to observe the Spring Festival. All the women residing in the city remain inside their apartments[9] except Unmādinī who shows herself. The king catches a glimpse of her and becomes disturbed by the apprehension of her great beauty. (The king is here characterized as 'Kāma' who looks 'on her form which is a weapon of victory' and he becomes infatuated.) When he discovers that he had rejected her, he banishes the Brahmin advisors who had informed him that she was ugly.

The king, however, refuses to accept Unmādinī as his wife because such an action would contravene *dharma*: she is already wed to the head of the army. The king declines even when the army chief proffers Unmādinī freely to him. In the view of the king, such a course of action would put *dharma* (his own as well as his kingdom's) in jeopardy. Unable to rid himself of desire for Unmādinī and sunk in the depths of sorrow, the king abandons his kingdom and departs from the city.

Having recounted this story to King Vikramasena, the *vetāla* asks him who is more virtuous, the king or his army chief. The king replies without hesitation that King Yaśodhana is more righteous. Vikramasena's response to the *vetāla's* query breaks the condition of silence necessary for the success of his mission and the *vetāla*, along with the corpse, vanishes and returns to the tree.

This sad tale and its variants provide us with certain new components of the *Vasantotsava* adding details to our picture of the festival not present in the *Ratnāvalī*. In the *Ratnāvalī*, the king was the convener of the festivities and the supervisor of the proceedings; in the *Kathāsaritsāgara* he is far more. In the *Kathāsaritsāgara* the king has the opposite problem to the king in the *Ratnāvalī*. In this latter text, the match between King Udayana and the Princess Ratnāvalī was a *dharmic* union, but lacked *kāma*. The arousal of the king, in anticipation of a previously established *dharmic* union, was hence a key theme in that text. Here, King Yaśodhana is overcome with *kāma* but finds himself in a set of circumstances where this *kāma* cannot be actualized without circumventing the *dharma* of the king and, by extension, the *dharma* of the kingdom. Here the king is the focal participant, much as he is in the drama plots themselves (as opposed to his role in the ritual activities which the dramas merely describe). In the *Kathāsaritsāgara* the king's sexual desire, his amour, is the motive for the tale, yet it is a desire that cannot be sated. The king's lack of success in consummating his passion, his inability to marry Unmādini threatens his realm, just as his sexual vigour ensures its prosperity. To avert the final calamity, the king chooses exile or death, echoing perhaps a ritual of expulsion or sacrifice enacted to prevent the declining powers of the king from being the cause of the downfall of the realm.

The King

We have ample evidence in Sanskrit texts of kings' functioning during festivals in a variety of capacities but especially as conveners, participants and patrons. The *Kṛtyakalpataru* of Lakṣmīdhara Bhaṭṭa, which outlines the deeds of kings, lists certain duties required of him which, if unattended, lead to drought, famine and pestilence in the kingdom.[10] Aimed at averting such calamities, one of the king's duties is to insist on the due performance of the festivals (*utsavas)* at prescribed times during the year. It is the king's duty to ensure that the celebrations be enacted correctly in order that his country and his people maintain their continued prosperity. One of the oldest of texts, the *Gautama Dharmaśāstra* records the following verse:[11]

> He (the king) shall perform in the fire-hall the rites ensuring prosperity which are connected with expiations, festivals, a prosperous march, long life, and auspiciousness; as well as those that are intended to cause enmity to subdue (enemies), to destroy (them) by incantations and to cause their misfortune. (vs. 17)

It is also clear that at festival times the absence of a king leads to anarchy. Both festivals and festival gatherings contribute to the sustenance and maintenance of the social fabric by their continuance and reinforcement of *dharma*. But if order is broken, if *dharma* is contravened, chaos ensues and the kingdom does not flourish. The *Rāmāyana* clearly states:[12]

> *nārājake janapade prahṛṣṭanaṭanartāh /*
> *utsavāśca samājaśca vardhante rāṣṭavardhanāh //*

By inaugurating festivals like the *Vasantotsava* the king represents *dharma* in spirit as well as in practice. One might suppose that the mere presence of the king is sufficient to ensure the success of the festivities.

The king is actively and specifically engaged in the *Vasantotsava* when he appears at the inaugurations as described in texts such as the *Ratnāvalī*, *Daśakumāracarita* and the *Jātakamālā*. Śulapāṇi tells us in the *Dolayatraviveka* that the Spring Festival, *Holākā*, was instituted first by King Indrayumna in Vṛndāvana.[13] In the *Bhaviṣya Purāṇa* (132), King Raghu must find out how to destroy the demoness Ḍhaunḍhā in order to protect the world. Raghu's *purohita* tells him how this can be done: 'The sin of a king,' the *purohita* tells Raghu, 'is not protecting the earth.' The sovereign must defend the earth from the demoness by convening the Spring Festival. King Raghu is told that if he observes the rites of the festival he will gain prosperity and the world will be free of sickness for the duration of the year.[14]

In the previous description in the *Ratnāvalī*, the king played only a minimal role in the festival as celebrated in the urban context but his presence is duly noted. In the garden festival in the *Ratnāvalī* the king was the object of the worship of the queen, but it was Kāma who was central: the king was worshipped insofar as he represented Kāma and then only after Kāma-worship proper had been performed. In the *Ratnāvalī*, all the king actually did was fall hopelessly in love with the princess.. That this happens however and that it is central to the development of the plot not only in the *Ratnāvalī* but in the *Priyadarśikā* and *Pārijāta-Mañjarī* as well, leads us to suspect that it is more than a mere device of plot. We have found one of the most prominent features in the spring festival pattern to be the arousal of desire and it is this feature with respect to the king in the story from the *Kathāsaritsāgara* which we shall examine in detail below. The simple act of falling in love at the Spring Festival, which in the *Ratnāvalī* leads to his marriage, is the cause in the *Kathāsaritsāgara*, of his downfall and these consequences of his emotional state are highly significant for the citizens. The *Kathāsaritsāgara*,

5. *Holī*
Bundi Raj, *circa* A.D. 1780-1800

then, enhances our understanding of the king's role, by providing a glimpse of a king's desire gone awry.

Duty or Desire

Kāma, or the satisfaction of physical and/or sexual desires and *dharma,* or performance of one's duty *vis-à-vis* society, are seen as two of the four aims of life in the Hindu tradition (*puruṣārtha*).[15] *Kāma* and *dharma* are positive and necessary conditions for the ongoing prosperity of humankind. There need not be any conflict between these two aims: the fulfillment of *kāma,* in part at least, is the *dharma* of the householder. Figuratively speaking, the satisfaction of *kāma* on the part of the king extends to the citizens in his realm. The ideal of *dharma,* too, extends from the king to all members of the social body as a *dharmic* king is necessary and requisite to ensure the ongoing stability of society. A married king may thus satisfy both *kāma* and *dharma* without difficulty.

The satisfaction of *kāma,* then, in itself is not problematic, even for kings. There are many instances in which kings are depicted as satisfying their desires with their wives or paramours during the *Vasantotsava* and it is in this sense (love sports with marital or non-marital partners) that kings may be understood as participating directly in the festival. In another story in the *Kathāsaritsāgara,* for example, King Dharmadhvaja of Ujjayini goes to the palace garden with his wives to amuse himself; in yet another tale in this same text, Prince Naravāhanadatta is entertained watching the festivities of the citizens who dance without restraint on the Spring Festival.[16] It was on the occasion of the festival of spring that King Vikramāditya married the princes of Siṁhala.[17] Both the *Daśakumāracarita* and *Priyadarśikā* describe princes joining the celebrations of the *Vasantotsava* with their beloveds.[18] In the *Tilakamañjarī* of Dhanapāla the king at this time is expected to participate with his wife in the general merrymaking characteristic of the festival.[19] According to Someśvara, kings engage in swinging with their beloveds and, in some paintings, kings are shown playing *Holī* with syringes in the palace.[20] It will be recalled that in the *Ratnāvalī* the king satisfies both *kāma* (desire for the princess) and *dharma* (social duty) by marriage. The arousal of the king, which is central in the above accounts, is a common and even a necessary ingredient in the spring celebrations. It has been suggested above that the condition of the king is intimately related to the condition of the country; and that the generative power of the king is also intimately bound up with the fertility of men, livestock and crops.[21] We might interpret the above accounts of the king's sporting activities as well as his marriage during the *Vasantotsava* as not only a matter of entertainment and amusement, but more as a public verification that he is still healthy, vigourous and above all sexually potent, qualities all essential to the security of the kingdom.

What happens when, for some reason, the king cannot fulfill his sexual needs, when he is impotent, is the real subject of this *Kathāsaritsāgara* story. The *Kathāsaritsāgara* attributes the king's inability to satisfy his desire to a conflict between *kāma* and *dharma*, rather than to any physical imperfection, perhaps because, by definition, kings had to be physically perfect. The very name of the woman evidently responsible for the king's failure in this respect suggests the source of the conflict. The woman is 'Unmādinī,' the 'Intoxicator,' she makes men crazy, she causes them to lose control. Sexual desire is essential for the maintenance of the world and the king's sexual potency is necessary for the fertility of his realm. His addiction to sexual pleasures to the exclusion of his other duties, however, would be a disaster. It is those keepers of the sacred notion of duty or *dharma*, the Brahmins, who here recall the king from the brink of the fault of excess by preventing his joining with Unmādinī. Even given the probability of Brāhmaṇical re-telling of the story, the point of the festival is that the king's potency spills over to the beautiful maidens of the realm. The reconciliation of *kāma* with the realm of social order (*dharma*) and the king's duty, abound in this moral parable of the Spring Festival, a parable in which it is acknowledged that lust is life and lust is death.

The introduction to the story emphasizes the *dharmic* qualities of the kingdom's citizens. The king himself is bound by *dharma* and dutifully follows the counsel of his Brahmin advisors who, in turn, seek to prevent the union of Unmādinī, the 'Intoxicator' and the king. The Brahmins' misplaced rationale is that by virtue of her beauty, Unmādinī would be too great a distraction even for such a great ruler as King Yaśodhana. How could he attend his *dharmic* duties, the duties to which he is obliged, with such a wife? The Brahmin counsellors fear that the king would become completely distracted by an obsession with *kāma*. Hence:

> The Brahmins went and saw that matchless beauty of the three worlds and were at once troubled and amazed, but when they had recovered their self control, they reflected: "If the king gets ahold of this maiden the kingdom is ruined, for his mind will be thrown off its balance by her and he will not regard his kingdom, so we must not tell the king that she possesses auspicious marks." (p. 319)

By virtue of her physical exquisiteness, Unmādinī is an inappropriate and undesirable match for the king. In another version of this same *Kathāsaritsāgara* story, the ministers themselves are rendered senseless by her seemliness, one is unable to speak, one unable to control his body. If these Brahmins are incapable of controlling themselves, how could the king, a mere *kṣatriya*, be expected to resist her?

Unmādinī, however, is not to be slighted and, at an opportune time, confident of success, she shows herself for the specific purpose of engendering royal passion. Although it is only by 'chance' that the king catches a glimpse of this beautiful woman (all females of good family being kept inside, out of his view), the narrative indicates that Unmādinī herself is well aware of the potency of the season.

The king falls hopelessly in love after spying her at the *Vasantotsava* only to discover that she is already married. The object of his *kāma*, his desire, is the wife of another.

Marriage is sanctioned by *dharma* and it represents a legitimate structure within society: it encourages the satisfaction of *kāma* by providing a *dharmic* channel for its expression. Yaśodhana's situation is problematic for the king and for his subjects as well. *Dharma* cannot be circumvented, Unmādinī is already married.

In a Tamil version of the same story cited by Tawney, the king sends for a soothsayer to look at the girl's horoscope. He reports simply that the king would lose his kingdom if he married her.[22] When the legitimate husband of Unmādinī freely offers her, Yaśodhana does not accept but says instead:

> How could I, being a king, do such an unrighteous deed? If I desert the path of right, who will remain loyal to his duty? (p. 320)

In a Hindi version, the *Baital Pacisī*, which describes the argument over this matter between the king and the commander of the army, the latter threatens to turn Unmādinī into a prostitute so she can no longer be considered his wife.[23] He threatens first to lead her to the palace as a gift to the king. Failing this, the husband suggests turning Unmādinī into a prostitute and by doing so giving the king *dharmic* access to her. He says:

> I will abandon her in the temple here, then, king, there will be no sin in your taking her to yourself, as there might be, if she were a matron.

Prostitutes may obviously and legitimately satisfy male desire outside of the institution of marriage. Yet even this solution is unacceptable to King Yaśodhana, perhaps because it implies that one can circumvent *dharma* by what amounts to legal maneuvering. In this same recension, the king replies to his commander:

> And how can you, though devoted to me, urge me to commit a crime, which will bring momentary pleasure but cause great misery in the next world. And if you desert your lawful wife, I shall not allow

> your crime to go unpunished, for who in my position could tolerate such an outrage on morality. (p. 320)

As the representative of *dharma* the king cannot, without endangering himself and by extension his citizens, give way to *kāma* not sanctioned by *dharmic* injunctions. Yet *kāma* also is determinative. The conflict between the two is unresolvable: the king cannot uphold *dharma* as he is afflicted by *kāma*; neither can he give way to *kāma* as this would be un-*dharmic*. The solution to the problem, death or leaving society, tips the scales on the side of *dharma*. Rather than give way to *kāma*, the king either leaves the city (as in the recension cited above) or commits suicide (as in the Hindi version, the *Baital Pacisī*). Hence the king says at the close of the story:

> So death is for me the best course.... former (ones) of noble character lose their lives sooner than abandon the path of virtue... Accordingly the king's body was gradually consumed by the fires of the grievous fever of love and only his name and fame remained. (pp. 320-1)

At the end of the story, the commander of the army and Unmādinī both throw themselves on the king's funeral pyre.

Although the source of the king's problem seems to lie with the Brahmin advisors who originally prevent the union of the king and Unmādinī, the woman Unmādinī, 'the Intoxicator,' is not above reproach. The story suggests that she consciously chooses to reveal herself to the king on the day of the *Vasantotsava* and, in so doing, anticipates the king's hopeless infatuation. Having been slighted by the king's refusal, this is her revenge.[24] Unmādinī is apparently well aware of her allure and the power that allure wields.

> Unmādinī....showed herself to the king on the roof of her palace, to revenge the insult he had offered her by refusing her and when the King saw her,

> looking like a flame shooting up from the fire of love when fanned by spring and the winds from the Malaya Mountain, he was sorely troubled.
> (p. 320)

Unmādinī's actions befit the Spring Festival: *kāma* is in the air and as even the king is not immune to its mood, her power, like the undauntable power of spring, is now manifest. As her name suggests, Unmādinī, the 'Intoxicator' may be understood as a locus of *kāma* and as such, she is evidence of both the erotic spirit of the season as well as its inevitability. The thwarted union between Unmādinī and the king as well as his subsequent dethronement and death reflect yet another modification on the theme of death and rebirth which dominates the Spring Festival. The death of the old must necessarily occur in order to make way for the new. In other parts of the world, kings are not allowed to grow old lest, with their diminishing vigour, the cattle should fall sick and the crops rot.[25] One of the fatal symptoms of decay was taken to be the incapacity to satisfy the sexual passions of women. The failure of the king to satisfy his lust with respect to Unmādinī might signal the waning of his procreative abilities and hence, elicit a corresponding failure in the continued regeneration of humanity, flora and fauna. By extension, it is important that such a king not be allowed to die a natural death as the generative powers maintained in him must surely follow a corresponding degeneration: he must therefore be put to death or exiled while he is still healthy. The *Kathāsaritsāgara* is the only evidence available for such beliefs in classical India of which I am aware and as such deserves special mention. That the king's decline and self-imposed exile are due directly to the interpretation by Brahmins of the cultural form (*dharma*) signifies the interweaving of fertility rites with a social order imposed by Brahmins. The rationale given in the story for the king's demise is his inability to uphold *dharma* which is a consequence of his failure to satisfy his lust.

The Buddhist Recension

The Pāli *Jātakas* and the Sanskrit *Jātakamālā* both contain noticeably condensed versions of this story which differ slightly from the texts of Somadeva. Brahmins, who are sent to see Unmādinī's auspicious marks, completely lose their self-control at the sight of her beauty. In the Pāli *Jātakas*, they describe her as a witch and advise the king against accepting her as a matrimonial partner. Unmādinī takes revenge by showing herself to the king. In the Pāli *Jātakas* she does so on the occasion of the *Kāttika* festival and, in the *Jātakamālā*, she does so during the *Kaumudī* festival. Here we find a thorough description of the town under the spell of festival celebrations:[26]

> Its streets and squares had been sprinkled and cleansed; their white ground was strewed with many coloured flowers: gay flags and banners were floating aloft; everywhere there was dancing and singing, representations of burlesques, ballets and music; the mingled scents of flowers, incense, odoriferous powders, perfumes, garlands, strong liquors, also of the perfumed water and the ointments used in ablutions, filled the air with fragrance; lovely articles were being exposed for sale; the principal streets were thronged by a merry crowd of townsmen and landsmen in their best dress.

The king here is overcome with passion for Unmādinī and it is only after a long conversation with his army chief that he is able to control his infatuation. Unmādinī's husband is appeased by the unwavering constancy of the king and pours praises on such a virtuous ruler.[27]

Interestingly, the Buddhist recension of this story thus resolves the problem under the over-arching structure of *dharma* and, at the same time, shifts the festival context from spring to autumn. In the *Jātakamālā*, the tension between *dharma* and *kāma* is lost: the king is able to overcome his infatuation and continue to rule successfully. Infatuation, in the Buddhist tradition, is generally considered a vice which can be overcome; hence, a final solution is possible. That the king can overcome his desire during the festival season of autumn is a feat perhaps in keeping with a season that celebrates rest rather than procreation.

NOTES

[1] Keith, *A History of Sanskrit Literature*, p. 281.

[2] K. Chaitanya, *A New History of Sanskrit Literature* (Reprint; Westport: 1975), pp. 366f. and A.Berriedale Keith, *History of Sanskrit Literature*, p. 281.

[3]Although Somadeva's text is late many of the stories are undoubtedly much older. See, Krishnamachariar, p. 419.

[4] The *Ślokasaṁgraha* on the other hand tells us that Gunādhya lived in Mathurā. See A. Berriedale Keith, *Classical Sanskrit Literature* (Calcutta: 1927), pp. 89-90.

[5] For a detailed discussion of this point see Keith, *History of Sanskrit Literature*, pp. 368f. and *Classical Sanskrit Literature*, pp. 96ff.

[6] The *Bṛhatkathāślokasaṁgraha* is another text re-telling the stories of the *Kathāsaritsāgara* discovered in Nepal in 1893. See the edition edited by F. Lacote (Paris: 1902-29).

[7] Śivadāsa, *Vetālapañcavinṁśatikā*, ed. by H. Uhle (Leipzig, 1884), cited by K. Chaitanya, p. 473.

[8] Somadeva, *Kathāsaritsāgara*, ed. by P. Durgaprasad and K.P. Parab (Bombay: 1899) and *Kathāsaritsāgara or Ocean of the Streams of Story*, trans. by C.H. Tawney (Calcutta: 1880).

[9] It is not clear why women are required to remain out of view of the king. Perhaps it is simply a question of remaining safely indoors. The sight of the king, who is exceedingly attractive, might simply be too much for women to bear. Hence, when the parade drum signifying the king's arrival in the procession is heard, women remain hidden.

[10] Lakṣmīdhara Bhaṭṭa, *Kṛtyakalpataru*, Part XI "Rājadharmakhaṇḍa" (Baroda: 1944).

[11] This particular verse is found in the *Sacred Laws of the Aryas*, *SBE* II, Part I, trans. by G. Bühler (Reprint; Delhi: 1969), II.I, p. 236. For the antiquity of the *Gautama Dharmaśāstra*, see *SBE*, II, p. lix. Haradatta further remarks on this verse that although according to the text the king must perform these rites, he is in reality only to give the necessary orders and to furnish the means for their performance. The *purohita* is to officiate as priest. *Ibid*, note 17.

[12] *Rāmāyaṇa*, 11.67.15, paraphrased above by Raghavan, *Festivals*, p. 5.

[13] Śulapani, *Dolayatraviveka*, ed. by S. Banerji in the volume of papers presented to Kane in *History of Dharmaśāstra*, p. 238.

[14] *Bhaviṣya Purāṇa*, 135.31,32.

[15] The other two *puruṣārthas* (aims of life) are *artha* (power) and *mokṣa* (release).

[16] *Kathāsaritsāgarqa*, XIV.58, p.98. Notably, King Naravāhanadatta, one of the prominent players of the Spring Festival is identified as an incarnation of Kāma. See Agrawala, *The Matsya Purāṇa: A Study* (Varanasi: 1963), p. 50.

[17] See Chattopadhyaya, "The Spring Festival and Festival of Indra," pp.1ff..

[18] *Priyadarśikā*, Act 1ff.; *Daśakumāracarita*, pp. 24-5.

[19] *Tilakamañjarī*, pp. 68-9.

[20] Someśvara, *Mānasollāsa*, 102 and Raghavan *Festivals*, p. 74. See also Thomas, *Festivals and Holidays of India*, fig. 12.11.

[21] See, for example, G. Frazer, *The Golden Bough*, p. 354.

[22] Tawney, *Kathāsaritsāgara*, p. 241.

[23] According to Keith, *Classical Sanskrit Literature*, this version rests on Śivadāsa's text. (p. 98fn.)

[24] One could interpret Unmādinī's actions as responsible for the downfall of the king. In this context the text would seem to empower her. Yet it is ultimately a negative empowerment, reflecting a somewhat conventional and standardized depiction of the danger embodied in beautiful women.

[25] See, for example, G. Frazer, *The Golden Bough*. pp. 351ff.

[26] J.S. Speyer, *Jātakamālā*, SBV, vol. I (1895), no. 13, p. 14 *et. seq.* cited by Tawney, *Kathāsaritsāgara*, p. 243.

[27] Tawney, *Kathāsaritsāgara*, pp. 243-4.

7

Vikramacarita

The *Vikramacarita*[1] or *Vikrama's Adventures* is a collection of thirty-two tales in praise of King Vikramāditya. These stories, extant in multiple renderings, are attributed to various authors. The *Vikramacarita* appears broadly in two recensions: the northern, generally known as the *Siṁhāsanadvātriṁsikā* which is comprised of a Bengali recension attributed to Vararuci, a short anonymous version and a Jain account attributed to Śiva Siddhasena Divākara Kṣemaṅkara; and the southern recension known as the *Vikramacarita*, consisting of a prose and a metrical rendering, both anonymous. The Jain version dates to the fourteenth century AD and is the most recent. Vikrama's adventures are the subject also of a variety of other works including the *Vīracarita* of Ananta and the *Vikramodaya*.[2]

The frame story of the *Vikramacarita* tells us how Bhoja, the eleventh century king of Dhārā, discovers a buried throne which had originally been given by the deity Indra to the earlier king, Vikramāditya. Grouped around this throne are thirty-two statues said to contain the spirits of thirty-two maidens who were cursed to immobility by Pārvatī. Bhoja hopes to claim the throne for himself but, as he ascends the steps to it, one of the statues comes to life and cautions that only one as magnanimous as the legendary King Vikramāditya would be able to sit upon the throne. The statue then relates a story which underscores the colossal celebrity of the dead king. Each time Bhoja tries to mount the throne one of the statues comes to life and tells a story. In the end Bhoja is successful, he ascends the throne and the maidens are released from Pārvatī's curse.[3]

The story relevant to this study of the *Vasantotsava* is number sixteen entitled "The Spring Festival and the Brahmin's Daughter."[4] It survives in three similar versions: a prose, a metrical and a Jain recension.

Story Number 16:
"The Spring Festival and the Brahmin's Daughter"

The story begins with a description of King Vikrama who has victoriously completed a military campaign against the kings of all of the four quarters. Vikrama, laden with booty, is prepared to make a grand entrance into his capital but he is prevented from so doing by a soothsayer who advises him to wait four days for an auspicious moment before re-entering the city. The king, acting upon this learned advice, retires to a nearby pleasure grove and there he constructs a tent of cloth. The time is spring and the ambiance of the season is evinced by swarms of bees, mango blossoms and budding lotuses, all typical features of the vernal landscape. Sumantra, Vikrama's minister, suggests that the king worship spring and promises Vikrama that by so doing all of the seasons would be kindly disposed towards him and prosperity in his kingdom would be ensured. The rites of spring are detailed: Sumantra builds an exceedingly beautiful assembly pavilion and summons charming women who are proficient in dance, music and song, as well as Brahmins learned in the *Śāstras* and the *Vedas*. Others join the festivities by their own volition. A throne inlaid with nine gems is placed in the pavilion and upon the throne two images, one of Lakṣmī and one of Nārāyaṇa (Viṣṇu), are installed. For the worship of Lakṣmī and Nārāyaṇa, musk, incense, aloe wood, jasmine, camphor and six types of flowers are gathered and the king has the sixteen-fold service performed.[5] Vikrama then proffers clothes and other gifts to Brahmins and those in attendance who are trained in the arts. The celebrations are accompanied by a *vasantarāga*, appropriate musical compositions for this time of year. The king, who is characteristically acclaimed for his munificence, bestows lavish gifts of gold upon the poor.

At this time of gifting, a Brahmin and his daughter approach the king. The Brahmin tells the king that he had prayed to the mother of the world for a daughter, promising to call her Ambikā and to give both her and her weight in gold to a suitor learned in the *Vedas*. Now that the time for giving had arrived, the Brahmin had come to offer his daughter to the king. In response to this offer, the king awards the Brahmin eight crores of gold in addition to the weight of the daughter in gold. Delighted, the Brahmin returns home. At an auspicious moment, the king enters the city.

Though brief in its description, the *Vikramacarita* augments the picture of the spring festivities gleaned from previous literary sources first, by adding particulars pertaining to the role of kings and second, by adding as components to the celebrations the specific worship of several figures in the Hindu mythological repertoire. The *Vikramacarita* substantiates the paramountcy of the king during the Spring Festival and, although the notion here of a regal presence differs from that in the *Kathāsaritsāgara* in some important respects, sketched in the "Spring Festival and the Brahmin's Daughter" is an image of a king who dominates the festivities. The role of the king is traditional, indeed, predictable. He possesses the qualities most esteemed and desirable in a royal figure: having just returned from a successful military campaign, Vikrama is endowed with military prowess; gifting without hesitation, he is generous beyond imagination; subjecting himself to royal duty, he is willing without question to follow the advice of his learned Brahmin advisors and remain, for the duration of the Spring Festival, outside his capital city.

The Good King

Generosity is a duty required of kings not only during festivals but on other occasions as well.[6] Corroborating texts, including the *Padma Purāṇa*, are not exceptional in prescribing gift giving as typical of all religious *vratas*.[7] Kings as well as other members of society are enjoined to provide donations for various causes on a multitude of occasions, yet it is the king especially who is required, both by virtue of his stature and by virtue of the occasion, to bestow gifts liberally. The largesse of our king in the *Vikramacarita* is not, as one would expect, an inconvenience: as he has just returned from a successful military campaign, he distributes his booty lavishly on the poor and on the rich alike, thus calling our attention in one fell swoop to his military might, the economic benefits of such campaigns and his own magnanimity as well. In a public display of both his spectacular generosity and of the awesome power he wields deriving from it, he bestows an astronomic sum of eight crores of gold on one not particularly important anonymous Brahmin who happens to offer the king his daughter in marriage.

The king *qua* king is obliged to act both as protector and benefactor of his subjects. Fulfillment of these obligations reinforces his status, his position and his power in the social hierarchy. The recipients of the gifts, especially the Brahmins who are specifically mentioned in this recension are, by reciprocation, in the king's debt: they owe him support and obedience. Hence, the allegiance of Brāhmaṇical persons substantiates and validates the king's status and power which, in turn, ensures that his position *vis-à-vis* other members of society is not only maintained, but is indeed, elevated thus cementing the bond of mutual dependence between them. Further, it is not enough for the king to be merely a great soldier as measured by the amount of booty he collects; as an obligation due his position, he must ensure that the benefits of his successful military campaign are extended to all his subjects. In this instance, the king's act of bestowing gifts as well may be one imbued with apotropaic qualities in that by so doing he disposes of impurities which might have been accrued as a result of his bloody campaigns and his absence beyond his realm. Typically, pollution accrued during the king's foray into foreign territory and by the blood on his hands from battle is erased by acts of purification which include the giving of gifts.[8]

The generosity of the king during the *Vasantotsava* can be understood then, in a quasi-magical sense, as a prelude to the prosperity the new year will bring, begat by the rituals of purification and renewal. The wealth and abundance possessed and distributed by the king are sign posts and harbingers of the coming prosperity within the reach of all members of society. Generally a requirement which upholds the religious/social hierarchy, the giving of gifts on the occasion of the *Vasantotsava* specifically renews the king's position at the zenith of the kingdom's hierarchy. A prosperous kingdom extends from a prosperous king.

The Jain Recension

A Jain recension of this identical story indicates that the festival was in vogue amongst this group as well. Here there is no mention of any *indiscriminate* generosity on the part of the king. The advent of spring is the occasion for the king to retire to his gardens and to engage in religious conversation with a Jain monk. After the discussion which revolves around philosophical questions regarding the dangers of *saṁsāra,* the king bestows upon the monk the same spectacular sum of eight crores gold. Clearly, the Jain notion of kingship and the duties of kings *vis-à-vis* his subjects differs in important respects to that given above: the Jain king's magnanimity is clearly sectarian and the story is considerably condensed, functioning simply as a framework for the propagation of Jain doctrine. Here the king's duty is to ensure the propagation of Jain doctrine espoused by its teachers.

The Seclusion of the King

Curiously, although King Vikrama has just returned to his capital from a glorious military campaign and is desirous of assuming his new position as 'Lord of the Four Quarters,' he is prevented from entering the city by Brahmin advisors and is thus unable to either celebrate his conquests or display his booty within the city walls. The time, he is told, is inauspicious for his entry into his capital: it is the occasion for the *Vasantotsava*. As we have seen in the urban context in the *Ratnāvalī*, within the walls of the city there is a temporary disruption of social order. The public celebration of the festival takes place *en masse* throughout the city streets. Although the *Vikramacarita* gives no indication of the state of the *Vasantotsava* celebrations inside the city, one can suppose that the streets are similarly choked with celebrants behaving in a manner akin to those described in the other texts we have examined wherein we found the citizens engaged in ritual revelry, dancing and powder throwing. The king, here, is refused entry and is required to undergo a period of temporary ambiguity which suspends his identity and his status much as the residents of the city from which he is barred are concurrently undergoing a similar and temporary modification in their state. As much as his citizens are subjects without a king, he is a king without subjects, a governor without a capital, a ruler without authority, a conqueror who has given away his booty. The ritual worship which the king subsequently performs outside the city walls is not described in detail in the *Vikramacarita*, but, from the little information the text does give, it seems to be a rather extensive, solemn and serious affair. The special pavilion and the sixteen types of worship (*upacāras)* required of the king indicate the ritual is strictly regulated and of some consequence. At the end of the prescribed period of ceremony, the king re-emerges, invigourated and, entering his capital, resumes his position as head of the realm. Notably, this occurs only when the festival is over and the stability of both city and king has been reestablished. The ritual pattern circumscribed by the *Vasantotsava*, in conformation here as the regeneration of the king, corresponds to a regeneration and invigouration of his entire kingdom. The *Vikramacarita* seems to suggest that his ritual seclusion and his personal celebration of the festival outside the city walls are a requisite to the maintenance of his regal status. Like the waxing and waning of spring, the king's power itself is not permanent but rather requires renewal and re-affirmation during the Spring Festival with each coming year.

Deities and Worship

A further notable aspect of this description of the *Vasantotsava* found in the *Vikramacarita* is the host of deities appearing as the focus of ritual worship in various readings of the story. In the preceding recension of this story, Lakṣmī and Nārāyaṇa are worshipped. In the Metrical recension of this same story, the king returns and honours spring by worshipping Maheśvara (Śiva). The king's pavilion is described as covered with blossoms and cloth and housing a bejewelled throne. He worships Umā and Maheśvara, Lakṣmī and Nārāyaṇa, Spring and Madana (Kāma) and Rati with camphor and Aśoka blossoms. He also glorifies Brahmins. The ease with which deities can replace each other in the *Vikramacarita* suggests that the *Vasantotsava* is not rigidly standardized with respect to the worship of deities. It is tempting to conclude that the festival has such a broad multi-sectarian base that it may be celebrated with equally as much enthusiasm by devotees of Viṣṇu, Lakṣmī, Śiva, Pārvatī or Kāma. One or more deities may be worshipped, in fact, with no contradiction and no matter which it is, they all seem to be literally plugged into the same ritual formula outlined in the *Vikramacarita*.

A variety of texts in addition to the *Vikramacarita* attest, beyond question, that the celebrants of the festival in the Hindu tradition were devotees of any of several gods, including Śiva, Viṣṇu and the minor deity, Kāma. The appearance of these deities is extremely varied: the context may be mythical or ritual. Texts such as the *Bhaviṣya Purāṇa* highlight the centrality of Śiva and Pārvatī and give us a mythological context in which we may understand the festival. Other texts, the *Virūpākṣavasantotsavacampū*, for example, are ritually oriented, describing this festival in elaborate detail as a temple festival centering around this cosmic couple. Yet Kāma, his consort Rati and his companion Spring (Vasanta) are, as we have seen elsewhere, especially central to the *Vasantotsava*. Śaivas and Vaiṣṇavas alike can worship Kāma without endangering their sectarian affiliations, although Kāma does not have a following equivalent to theirs. Notwithstanding this, he is often assigned a role significant in some texts but is rather easily and conveniently subsumed by Viṣṇu and Śiva in others. This seems particularly evident when the discussion focuses upon spring rituals.

Kāma's association with Viṣṇu in the *Matsya Purāṇa*'s description of *Madanatrayodaśī* is clearly articulated: both are worshipped on the thirteenth day of the bright fortnight. Kāma is a form of Viṣṇu. Hence in the propitiation the devotees say: 'O Lord Janārdana, in the form of Kāma' and in the final line describing this ritual the text tells us: 'Kāma is Viṣṇu.' This is corroborated in the *Nārada Purāṇa*[9] wherein at the end of the Kāma ritual one is to present a Brahmin couple with a cow uttering the following 'May God Hari in the form of Kāma be pleased' as well as in the *Matsya Purāṇa* where courtesans are to utter the following *mantra*:[10]

> As I do not make any difference between Viṣṇu and Kāma, so O Lord Viṣṇu, be pleased to always fulfil my desires.

We find this equation too in the *Padma Purāṇa*, where prostitutes worship Viṣṇu as Kāma.[11]

In the Jain recension of this text, however, all mention of worship is omitted and the festivities center around the discussion of philosophical questions of importance in the Jain tradition, i.e., in this case, the dangers of *saṁsāra*.

The multi-sectarian nature of the festival suggests thematic underpinnings which remain constant irrespective of each independent version of this story, regardless of who is worshipped. Thus ,we see that in all of these descriptions the activities revolve around the furtherance and maintenance of the fertility of the land, the people and the king. It is upon this thematic basis that elaborate structures of myth and ritual and their corresponding Śaiva, Vaiṣṇava and non-sectarian components are erected. The *Vikramacarita* illustrates the manner in which one structural setting can serve multi-sectarian purposes.

NOTES

1 *Vikrama's Adventures (Thirty-Two Tales of the Throne)*, ed. and trans. by F. Edgerton (Cambridge: 1926).

2 Keith, *History of Sanskrit Literature* (Delhi: 1973), pp. 292-3.

3 K. Chaitanya, *A New History of Sanskrit Literature*, pp. 371-2.

4 *Vikrama's Adventures*, pp. 133-141.

5 No further details are given regarding this ritual but it is probably the sixteen *upacāras* that are performed. These *upacāras* are formal ritual procedures for honouring an image, similar in many respects to ceremonies for welcoming an honoured guest. They include, for example, the offering of food, the invocation of the deities presence, washing the feet of the deity and quenching his thirst.

6 A massive body of Sanskrit literature details the duties of kings.. See, for example, Lakṣmīdhara, *Kṛtyakalpataru*, "Rājadharmakhaṇḍa," ch. 15.

7 *Padma Purāṇa*, ch. 70.

8 Heesterman in *Vrātya and Sacrifice* remarks on the giving of *dakṣiṇā* as follows:

> 'Now the *dakṣiṇā*, like the gift in general, establishes or seals a bond between giver and donee. In the case of the *dakṣiṇā* it is even possible further to define this bond as a marriage-like union. This union enables the sacrificer not only to dispose of the impurity of death, the remainder of the birth process, but also to make it productive again.' (pp. 26-7)

[9] *Nārada Purāṇa*, 121.2-16.
[10] *Matsya Purāṇa*, 70.52.
[11] *Padma Purāṇa*, ed. by V. Narayan (Poona: 1893-4), *Sṛṣṭikhaṇḍa*, ch. 23.

8

Bhaviṣya Purāṇa, 135: Kāma

The *Bhaviṣya Purāṇa,* comprised of fourteen thousand verses, is one of the eighteen *mahā* or major *purāṇas.* Like all *mahāpurāṇas,* the *Bhaviṣya* deals with a wide range of subjects recording ritual prescriptions, myths, Brāhmaṇical ceremonies, feasts, duties of caste and a number of sporadically positioned legends.[1] Due to the diversity of the material in this volume, it is extremely difficult to classify as belonging to any one distinct genre.[2] The title, *Bhaviṣya,* which translates as 'future events' bears little relation to its actual contents. Although this *purāṇa* is referred to as an early text in sources like the *Āpastambha Dharmasūtra,*[3] the extant work does not seem to correspond to the original referred to therein. Our text is almost impossible to accurately date: some sections may be as early as the eighth or eleventh centuries, others are much later.

The substance of the chapter in question, the *Madanamahotsava* (ch. 135), is the great festival of Kāma, celebrated on the thirteenth day of the bright half of Caitra, i.e., *Madanatrayodaśī.* Our *Purāṇa* specifically links the Spring Festival with the famous myth in which Kāma is reduced to ashes by fire issuing from Śiva's third eye. Kāma is subsequently revived on this Spring Festival day.

Caitrotsava (Vasantotsava) thus becomes fused with a well-known event in Hindu mythology. The same type of correlation is found in texts and oral traditions which associate holy sites with mythological events to emphasize their sanctity. The connection between this myth of the incineration and revival of Kāma and the celebration of spring is particularly *apropos*: motifs of desire, passion, eroticism and fertility which are central to the *Vasantotsava* are also axial to the broader mythology of Kāma. In the *Bhaviṣya Purāṇa* (135), Kāma provokes desire and passion in the heart of Śiva and he emerges as a symbol of eroticism and fertility *par excellence.* In this mythological sequence Kāma is the author of Śiva's desire, his erotic need for Pārvatī and Kāma's encounter with Śiva is a prelude to the production of their son, or as other texts have it, to their marriage, to their thousands of years of love making and to the eventual birth of their son. The significance of the marriage motif in this festival is clear from other texts[4] and it is thus not surprising to encounter it here, in the lives of the gods, as recorded in the *Bhaviṣya Purāṇa.* Again, there is here a clear connection between reproduction and fertility, a theme which is at the core of the *Vasantotsava.*

An interesting element which bears investigation relative to this study of the *Bhaviṣya Purāṇa* (135), is the ritual procedure, *kojāgara,* or 'staying up all night.' This is a ritual commonly connected with the worship of Lakṣmī. According to our text, however, it is performed on the *Caitrotsava* in honour of Kāma suggesting once again through the mutability of rituals, deities and the spring, that the *Vasantotsava* formula is not rigidly fixed. Our text reads:

Bhaviṣya Purāṇa, 135 : *Madanamahotsavavarnam*

1. Having married Gaurī, Śiva took the Paśupata vow. The husband of Umā, Paśupata, became intent on meditation.

2,3. Kāma was sent by Brahmā and the other gods who, delighted, had gotten together and resolved that he alone (Kāma) was fit to shake Śiva from his meditation and hence to fulfill Gaurī's desire for a son. Then the deadly one (Māra), the one who leaves behind memories (Smara), the god of love (Kāma) went to the hermitage of Śiva.

4. He was accompanied by lust, love, wild abandon and the beauty of spring (Vasanta). He was surrounded by wine, pride and amorous gestures.[5]

5,6. Kāma's crest was made of Aśoka and mango trees. His headpiece was made of jasmine. His best messengers were the female cuckoo and the music of drums, lutes and song. His treasury official was the sound of musical instruments and drums, his marvellous councillor was the spring *rāga* and he rode on women who were intoxicated with drink.[6]

7. And so, like a king of great kings, Kāma, came into the presence of Hara. Kāma was rich with the smell of the south wind, showering sidelong glances.

8. Kāma, having drawn his bow of flowers, hurled an intoxicating arrow at the slayer of the three cities, in order to interrupt his meditation.

9. Rudra knew him and knew his intention. With anger blazing from fury, Hara sent forth fire from his forehead through this third eye.

10. Kāma, when looked at by that glance, was reduced to ashes in a flash. Seeing Kāma burnt up, Rati and Prīti were frozen in grief and wailed piteously.

11. Everyone else rushed off in another direction. Then Gaurī, seeing Kāma burning, with a heart pained from grief, said to Rudra:

12. 'O lord, you have burnt Kāma because of me. Look at the two wives of Kāma, why should they weep so?

13. Be kind to Rati and Prīti, O lord of Gods, O bull-bannered one, revive Kāma! O Śambu, give him form again.'

14. Hearing that, Śiva was pleased and said to Pārvatī: "The whole world was oppressed by Kāma when he had a body.

15. How can I revive the burnt Kāma? But, dear one, I shall respect your words, I shall do as you ask.

16. In this very time of the year, in the spring, in the bright half of the moon on the thirteenth, O Devī, he who is mind-born (Kāma) will become embodied.

17. Indeed the whole world with him as the cause, will find delight." Having granted this boon to Kāma, O Yuddhiṣṭhira!

18. The beloved of Pārvatī went to the top of the Himālayas to Kailāsa. O king, I have told you the story of Kāma.

19,21 Now I will tell you about the other part (relating to) the ceremony of worship. Listen! Having bathed on this thirteenth night, one should paint the Aśoka tree with paints made from *sindūra* and then make an image of Kāma and Vasanta, either out of gold, out of wood, or painted. The image should have Rati and Prīti along with it. The god Kāma should be horse-headed and fish-bannered and accompanied by groups of *apsaras*, proud, walking in languorous, sensuous steps.[7]

22. Kāma should be intent on listening to music, songs and plays.. He should be accompanied by an auspicious sign (*svastika*), Rati, Prīti, Krīḍā, Nandyavartī and Vidhyadharas.

23. A man, along with his wife, at midday should worship this image with devotion, offering food, incense, clothes and garlands and reciting this *mantra*.

24. 'Praise to Vāma, Kāma, the lord of lords, the embodied one who causes agitation in the hearts of Indra, Śiva, Viṣṇu and Brahmā.'

25. Having done that and praised the god of gods, Kāma, then one should place sweetmeats, which are a pleasure to the mouth, in front of him.

26. And one should give various kinds of foods saying "may Kāma be pleased with me." Then one should take leave of the Brahmins having given them a pair of bullocks with the *dakṣiṇā*.

27. A woman should worship her husband with ornaments, garlands and clothes, considering him to be the god Kāma and with her mind full of happiness (i.e., thinking truly of him and not of someone else).

28. In the abode of Kāma the man of the house (sacrificer), accompanied by friends, should keep an all night vigil in such a way that the night passes in pleasure.

29. In the night the festival should occur. Offerings of areca nuts, sandal and a paste of

saffron and camphor and food of various types should be made.

30. Dancing should also occur, as should the shining of lights, public shows and repetition of dramas which are pleasing to see. This great festival, O Partha, should occur every year.

31. In the city, the king, who is delighted and pleased when the time of spring comes, celebrating this festival thus, every year, O Partha and hence ensures that for the whole year his subjects will be free from sickness.[8]

32. Clouds will rain at will and in his kingdom there will be abundance, welfare, health, prosperity, the highest pleasure and no disease.

33. The god having three eyes is greatly pleased as are Kāma, Viṣṇu, Prajāpati and Vasanta.

34. Also Candra, Sūrya and all the planets, all Brāhmaṇical sages, Yakṣas, Gandharvas and Dānavas, are pleased.

35. Asuras, Yātadhanas, Garuḍas, birds and Nāgas are pleased and bestow the highest happiness on the performer. Of this there is no doubt.

36. On the *Caitrotsava*, having praised Kāma with Rati, whose friends are the wind from the mountain Malaya and Vasanta, a man together with his wife will gain fortune, a son, beauty and fertility.

Kāma's Mythology and the *Vasantotsava*

The conflict between Kāma and Śiva and the ultimate victory of Kāma as recorded in texts like the *Bhaviṣya Purāṇa* reflect thematic motifs fundamental to the celebration of the Spring Festival. It is Kāma's fertile powers which are invoked in the *Vasantotsava* during which he reigns supreme. Kāma is desire incarnate, a symbol of creative, life-giving powers.[9] According to the *Śiva Purāṇa*:[10]

> Brahmā created all the gods and all the Prajāpatis, including Dakṣa. Then a beautiful woman named Sandhyā was born from his mind. Her beauty, which deluded the hearts of sages, aroused Brahmā but he was paralyzed by indecision, realizing that his sons were present. Then from his mind was born Kāma, with his five marvellous flower arrows. Dakṣa and the others were excited by desire and could not remain calm, but Brahmā regained control of his emotions and said to Kāma, 'Enchant men and women with your five flower arrows and your own beauty, maintaining creation eternally. No one will be able to withstand you, not even Viṣṇu nor Śiva nor I.'

In Hindu myth as in Hindu ritual, Kāma is desire and his *modus vivendi* is to sexually arouse his prey. As early as the *Atharva Veda* he is referred to as the god of sexual love.[11] Like Eros of the Greeks and Cupid of the Romans, Kāma is armed with a bow and arrow; unlike Eros and Cupid, Kāma's bow is made of sugar-cane, its string made of bees, the tips of his phallus-like arrows made of flowers. His vehicle is a parrot and the sign on his banner, a fish. His form is one of irresistible beauty. Amongst men, women, plants, animals as well as amongst the gods, he accomplishes his task by shooting his love-arrows at his many victims.

As long as his arrows are directed towards ordinary worldly mortals, Kāma's work is relatively unobstructed. He sets the world atingle. His quarry is both male and female and he pierces them indiscriminately, especially during the spring. In this capacity he is easily identified in the Indian mythology and iconography. Suffice it here to give a few examples of Kāma's expertise in succeeding in his mission. Kāma wields his power among hermits in the *Kumārasaṁbhava*. Thus:[12]

34. The hermits, dwelling in the forest of the Immovable One, seeing this untimely advance of spring, scarcely remained master of their minds, whose agitation they with difficulty repressed.
35. When the God of Love with flower-bow ready strung, together with Rati, came to that place, the loving couples revealed by their actions their state of mind, pervaded with the delight of love which had reached its peak.

From the same text Kāma's potency galvanizes the animal kingdom into action as well:

37. From joy of love the female elephant gave to the male a spray of water scented with lotus-pollen. The Cakravaka bird honoured his mate with the gift of a half-eaten lotus stalk.
38. In intervals of song, the Kinnara kissed his beloved's face, whose paint-marks were a little smeared by the drops of toil-born sweat, but bright with eyes swimming from flower-liquor.

Kāma's arrows fan the flames of passion amongst potential lovers and amongst married couples as well. In the sixteenth century AD Gujarati poem, the *Vasantavilāsa* we read:[13]

1.7 Kāma, having opened the doorway of love and pride, entered the heart of married couples.

In these passages, the passivity of Kāma's victims is notable. Kāmadeva is active, stimulating, energizing, predacious; he prowls the world of mortals, his arrows unassailable, his victims flounder, helpless and defenseless, incapable of curbing their passion. Humans, particularly, seem ill-equipped to counter the onslaught of concupiscence thus engendered. Kāma encounters little resistance when 'exciting' his mortal victims.

6. Ladies Plucking Flowers
Kangra, *circa* A.D. 1785-90

Kāma and Śiva

It is not simply Kāma's ability to instill ardor amongst mortals but it is his ability to do so amongst the gods that we find as central in the description of the *Vasantotsava* found in the *Bhaviṣya Purāṇa*. Even though Kāma plays the vital role of Cupid amongst the gods in Hindu myth, in comparative terms his exploits here are quite clearly defined: he appears in the Hindu canon primarily in connection with Śiva. Śiva is Kāma's most famous and most formidable of adversaries.[14] Unlike his mortal victims, Śiva is by no stretch of the imagination a passive target for Kāma's lusty shafts.

The position of Śiva relative to Kāma in this myth is one of opposition. Kāma is creative, productive; Śiva, destructive, extirpative. O'Flaherty in *Śiva, the Erotic Ascetic* says:

> Śiva is the natural enemy of Kāma because he is the epitome of chastity, the eternal *Brahmacarin*, the very incarnation of chastity. When Himālaya tries to bring his daughter Pārvatī to Śiva, Śiva objects with the traditional misogynist argument:
>
> > This girl with her magnificent buttocks must not come near me. I insist upon this. Wise men know that a woman is the very form of Enchantment, especially a young woman, the destruction of ascetics. I am an ascetic, a yogi, so what need have I of a woman? An ascetic must never have contact with women.
>
> Because of his chastity, Śiva is considered to be the one man in the universe who can resist Kāma. (p. 141)

Kāma's skirmish with Śiva is multi-form, recounted (with some variation) in most *purāṇas* and in a fair number of other texts as well.[15] In the majority of these stories, this encounter occurs during the spring season. In the *Kumārasaṁbhava*, with Vasanta (spring) and his consort

Rati, Kāma seeks out Śiva in the Himālaya. As they approach Śiva's hermitage the blossoms of the spring season begin to erupt in the forest. Hence:

> 25. While the sun, transgressing his ordained course, began to go towards the quarter guarded by Kubera, the south exhaled a scented breeze, likened to a sigh of sorrow.
> 26. The Aśoka tree at once gave birth to flowers and tender shoots, right from its trunk; it did not wait to be touched by the feet of beautiful women, their anklets tinkling, etc. (Canto III)

In a deviation from the *Bhaviṣya Purāṇa* where it is Brahmā who sends Kāma to Śiva, it is Indra in the *Śiva Purāṇa* who performs this function. Indra commissions Kāma also in the *Skanda Purāṇa*; Indra joins forces with Brahmā to expedite this matter in the *Liṅga Purāṇa*.[16] The appearance of Indra in this myth highlights attributes common to both Kāma and Indra: both are erotic, anti-ascetic figures. Traditionally Indra is at odds with ascetics and the Kāma/Śiva incident probably, as O'Flaherty suggests, finds precedent in the episode of Indian mythology in which Indra, fearing the powers of ascetics, sends *apsaras* (beautiful women) to dissuade holy men (ascetics) from their religious quest.[17] Other texts such as the *Matsya Purāṇa* confirm the *Bhaviṣya Purāṇa* (135) and tell us it is Brahmā who deputes Kāma.[18]

The *Matsya Purāṇa* traces the origin of this event to even earlier times. It tells how Kāma came to be burnt by Śiva: Brahmā lusted after his daughter Aṅgajā and felt ashamed at not being able to suppress his passion (Kāma). He thus cursed Kāma to be reduced to ashes by Śiva. And, in yet another rendition, the conflict between Śiva and Kāma is traced to Brahmā who gives Kāma this commission out of revenge against both Kāma and Śiva.

Whether Kāma is the emissary of Brahmā or Indra, the myths are virtually indistinguishable. All three figures (Brahmā, Kāma and Indra) are charged with the maintenance of the world, not with its destruction (particularly at the hands of a troublesome ascetic like Śiva). Even

Brahmā, though willing Kāma's destruction, promises that he will be later revived, a caveat effectively voiding his curse and putting Śiva's ascetic powers to test. O'Flaherty in her book *Śiva* drives home the point that although Śiva is primarily an ascetic, he also has an erotic side.[19] Destructive forces thus encompass potential renewal, a theme shared by myths of both Kāma and Śiva and indeed, in myths celebrating the festival of Vasanta (Caitra) with which the *Bhaviṣya Purāṇa* associates it.

Kāma not only succeeds in arousing Śiva, which should have been sufficient for the overall purposes of the myth, but additionally he must die and be reborn, an enactment analogous to seasonal renewal. Kāma's death is the requisite first step towards the conception of Śiva and Pārvatī's son. The course of these actions which lead to his demise is a result of forgetfulness, stridency and lack of fear. The *Kumārasaṁbhava* portrays Kāma as overwhelmingly confident of his prowess regarding his talent for influencing human and godly affairs:

4. Who, desirous of position, has aroused your envy by prolonged austerities: He will straightaway become obedient to the command of this my bow with its arrow held ready.
5. Who is it who against your will has set out on the path of Salvation, from fear of the pains of rebirth? Let him stand long bound by the love-glances, charming with arching of brows of beautiful women.
6. Of what enemy of yours, say, - be he taught Right Conduct by Uṣanas himself - shall I, commissioning passion as my envoy, oppress the Wealth and Righteousness, like to a swollen flood the banks of the river?
7. What lovely woman, of sorrowful mien through her vow of wifely fidelity, who has entered your wayward mind by her tender beauty, do you desire, that free from shame she should in spontaneous embrace twine her arms around your neck?

10.. Through your grace, though armed with but a flower and taking spring as my sole comrade, I shall bring low the steadfastness even of Hara who wields the bow: what are other bowmen beside me? (Canto III)

And in the *Liṅga Purāṇa* we read:

31-3. Thus advised by Brahmā, Paremeṣṭhin, Bṛhaspati of good holy rites bowed to the lord of Devas. Accompanied by Devas including Indra, he went to the peak of the mountain Meru and remembered Kāma. On being remembered by the preceptor of Devas, Kāma came along with his wife Rati. With palms joined in reverence, he spoke to Bṛhaspati sitting along with Indra, O excellent Brahmins.

34-8. 'O Bṛhaspati, since I am remembered by you I have come here in your presence. Tell me what I have to do.' Thus, he who was summoned by Bṛhaspati spoke to him. Lord Indra, too, honoured the fish-emblemed god and said: 'Unite Umā happily with Śiva today whereby the bull-emblemed lord can sport with her. Take adequate steps for the same along with your wife Rati. Mahādeva, if pleased, will grant you excellent boon. He is already separated from her. On acquiring Umā the daughter of the lord of the mountain, he will be delighted.' On being told thus, Kāma bowed to Indra the lord of Śacī and of Devas and decided to go to the penance-grove of the lord of Devas in the company of Rati. (1.101)

In the *Śiva Purāṇa* Kāma, having accepted the commission of disturbing Śiva's meditation, is confident in his ability to succeed, completely forgetting the curse (of being sizzled by Śiva) which hangs over him. Ironically it is often Kāma's wife, Rati, who is responsible for Kāma's apparent memory lapse. Hence after the curse:

> Then Brahmā vanished and Dakṣa said to Kāma, "Take this daughter of mine for your wife.." Seeing her beauty, Kāma forgot the terrible curse that Brahmā had given him and a great celebration took place.[20]

Rather than shunning Rati, Kāma is unable to resist her. He undergoes a period of temporary amnesia reminiscent of that suffered by Ratnāvalī, Priyadarśikā, Mālavikā and Pārijāta-Mañjarī in our dramas. There we included the memory loss or curious silence with those rituals that are characteristic of transition. Here too, we find Kāma is about to undergo a change in state: this time from life to death.

When Kāma becomes cognizant of the peril of his position, the gods are able to convince him that his course of actions cannot be otherwise. The *Śiva Purāṇa* shows Śiva, in a twist typical of Hindu myth, deluding Kāma into thinking he can succeed.[21] When Indra commissions Kāma to rouse Śiva from his meditation in the *Matsya Purāṇa,* Kāma reacts as follows:

> Lord of the universe! Lord Śiva is unconquerable by my resources which are terrifying to the Munis and Dānavas and do you not know this? You know the glory of the mighty Śiva very well. Perhaps the blessings and wrath of the great are also great, there is always greatness in the great. You have thought of your advantage in the enticement of Śiva. This is not right, for, such schemes against Iśvara, launch one into utter ruin. It has been witnessed many times before that. The intentions of the beings become known and those who are over anxious to gain their ends, do not attain their ambition. (*Matsya Purāṇa* 154. 212-6)

Nonetheless Kāma accepts the challenge and succeeds, if not in getting Śiva to approach Pārvatī right away, at least in disturbing his meditation. Just as inevitably though, the plan backfires: Śiva emerges from his trance in a rage and reduces Kāma to ashes. Śiva says:

> The universe must continue without Kāma, for it was he who caused all the gods, including Indra, to fall from their places and to become humble and it is Kāma who leads all creatures to hell. Without Kāma a man can do no evil and even Tāraka will be without desire from now on, although he used to be evil. I burnt Kāma in order to give peace to all creatures and I will not revive him, since he is the evil at the root of all misery. (*Skanda Purāṇa* 1.1.21.82-99 cited and trans. by O'Flaherty, *Śiva*, p. 144)

Understandably the repercussions of Kāma's death are felt throughout the universe. In the *Skanda Purāṇa* the gods respond to this crisis:

> Without Kāma the whole universe will be destroyed.[22]

Or, again, hearing the news, everyone became depressed, saying:

> Everything proceeds by intercourse and without Kāma all creatures are drying up.[23]

Kāma's death is accompanied by the mourning cries of Rati. Hence in the *Śiva Purāṇa:*

> 24. Lamenting thus and crying out various piteous words she (Rati) beat with her hands, kicked with her legs and plucked her hairs.
> 25. O Nārada, on hearing her lamentation even the beasts and residents of the forest, nay all the immobile trees and bushes became miserable. (*Rudra Saṁhitā*, 19)

The dirge sung by Rati over Kāma's death is due to her mortification over his disappearance from the earth.[24] All that remains of Kāma is ash, a powerful symbol of death as well as life. The sages in the pine forest are enjoined to cover their bodies with ash in order to burn away sin. Śiva says:

> The supreme purification of the entire universe is to be accomplished by ashes; I place my seed in ashes and sprinkle creatures with it. One who has done that which is to be done by fire will master the three worlds. By means of my ashes, my seed, one is released from all sins.... Let a man smear his body until it is pale with ashes and meditate upon Bhava in his heart and then,... by bathing in ashes, he becomes a leader of my hosts, receives all sacrifices and grasps the supreme ambrosia.[25]

In the *Matsya Purāṇa* Rati, overcome by grief, smears herself with the ash-remains of Kāma.[26] The physical contact of her body with Kāma's ashes can and indeed ought to be understood as erotic. Here, in the act of smearing her limbs with ashes, we find the union of male and female, husband and wife, life and death. Like seeds, ashes may be understood as the essence of a living thing, beyond which it can be reduced no further but, from which, it will re-emerge.

As certain as Kāma is doomed, he is fated to be reborn. Just as Kāma's suspension in ash marks the end of one cycle, so too does it mark a new beginning, a fresh start. (Śiva is somehow persuaded to reinstate Kāma.) In the *Śiva Purāṇa* it is ash, the essence of Kāma, that is preserved by Rati under instructions from the gods:

The gods said:

> 27. Take some ashes and preserve them. With effort check your fear. The lord will resuscitate your lover. You will regain your lover again.

28. There is none who gives us happiness or misery. All enjoy and experience the fruit of what they do. In vain do you curse the gods.

And later in the same text on the occasion of Śiva and Pārvatī's marriage and because he is needed Śiva, the former ascetic who is about to engage in male-female union, merely glances at the bag of ashes and Kāma, the god of love, is restored to life,[27] poised once more to inflame these lovers by shooting his flower-tipped arrows at them. Thus Kāma is revived and it is his rebirth at the beginning of the year which, in the *Bhaviṣya Purāṇa*, is cause for the celebrations which are the *Vasantotsava*, performed in anticipation of an abundant and prosperous new year through the guaranteed cycles of creation. And with each re-birth, each re-creation, Kāma is made more potent, more powerful: nothing can resist or hinder him. Kāma is reborn in the *Skanda Purāṇa* as follows:

> Śiva gave Kāma a body and Kāma performed *tapas* until Śiva, pleased, made Kāma's body more beautiful than ever before and removed all obstacles for him.'
>
> (trans. O'Flaherty, *Śiva*, p. 151)

Each *Caitrotsava* marks Kāma's death but also inherently reiterates both Kāma's revival[28] and the temporary restoration of the tension between him and Śiva. Each Spring Festival celebrates the ultimate victory of Kāma and through this victory the continued re-creation of the universe. The prelude to this creation is destruction: both are essential to the mythology of Śiva and Kāma, both are essential to the Spring Festival celebration, as it does, the end of the old and the beginning of the new. These parallels extend beyond myth directly into the palpable intricacies of the *Vasantotsava* ritual. As the *Bhaviṣya Purāṇa* tells us, the death and resurrection of Kāma is a cosmic affair, one that is re-enacted at the time of the *Vasantotsava* year upon year.

Raghavan notes that during *Kāmandī*, the South Indian festival of the new year otherwise known as 'the burning of Kāma,' a pole (*stambha*) representing Kāma is set up in an enclosure. (p. 204) It is ignited and the people divide themselves into two parties singing respectively 'Kāma is burnt' and 'Kāma is dead.' T. Bapat tells us that a caricature figure of Manmatha (Kāma) with a short turban and moustache is burned at the crossroads on this day.[29] The *Nāradīya Purāṇa* tells us that the fire consumes an effigy representing the old year. In this regard, it reads as follows:

> *saṁvatsarasya daho ayam kāmadaho matāntare.*
>
> (This is the burning of the old year; others say it is the burning of Kāma) (1.124.81)

P.V. Jagadisa Ayyar in *South Indian Festivals* describes this episode, well-known in Hindu mythology, as the backdrop for this celebration also known as *kāmadāhanam* (the burning of Kāma) in South India.[30] *Kāmadahanam* is part of the larger festival of *Paṅguṉi Uttiram* celebrated on the full moon day of Phālguna (Tamil *Paṅguṉi* and hence the *Vasantotsava*) in order to win conjugal felicity. In this particular version, following the destruction of Kāma, Rati solicits the help of Viṣṇu who advises her to journey to Sundara Tirtan (a large tank in front of a Śiva temple at Kāmarasavalli) and perform a sacrifice to Śiva. Rati does as she is directed and undergoes severe penance for approximately forty days yet, in the end, she succeeds and Kāma is restored to life with the one condition: that he be visible only to Rati.[31] In a version associated with the *Śivarātri* recorded by J. M. Christian, the myth of Śiva's encounter with Kāma is the occasion for a two-day festival (*Kāmaṇa Pandugā*) in Andhra Pradesh.[32] The festival celebrates the birth and death of Kāmaṇa (Kāma) and his wife Kāmamma.(Rati). Here, subsequent to the immolation of Kāmaṇa, Kāmaṇa's wife, Kāmamma, pleads with Śiva to restore her husband to life on the grounds that he had simply been following his *dharma*. Śiva concedes, permitting Kāmaṇa to be reborn for two days every year, but only on the condition that Kāmamma consent to join her husband on the funeral pyre. Each year for two days,

Christian tells us, the couple are allowed to live in splendour until on the third day they are ceremonially cremated.

Jāgarana

Jāgarana, ko jāgara, kaumudījāgara and *kaumudī* all require the maintenance of an all-night vigil. This is a ritual activity of some antiquity and, like the *Vasantotsava,* is referred to variously in various texts.[33] The *Bhaviṣya Purāṇa* prescribes its performance in honour of Kāma but, more often and especially in the *purāṇas,* its given focus is Lakṣmī, the goddess of wealth and good fortune. The inclusion of *jāgarana* in the *Bhaviṣya Purāṇa* (135) as an aspect of the ritual worship of Kāma, as well as an aspect of the rites of spring, draws attention to their interrelatedness.

There is, first, the overlap of ritual: *jāgarana* is typically performed in honour of Lakṣmī but is here included as a ritual of Kāma. Lakṣmī is the figure in Hindu myth most closely linked with prosperity; Kāma is worshipped through the rite of *jāgarana* in order to achieve this same prosperity. We cite here also the *Śrīpañcamī,* usually given as the worship of Lakṣmī, which is occasionally cited as the worship of Kāma and Rati (see below).

Second, *jāgarana* is usually performed in the autumn.[34] Among the various rituals associated with the *Caitrotsava* it forms part of the coherent body of transitional rituals enacted at this time of year. It, like many others in the Hindu tradition, is a ritual which reverses modalities, requiring its observers to upset their everyday routines. Rather than customarily remaining awake during the day and sleeping at night, observers of this rite remain awake all night. This disruption of order occurs at and signals the end of a ritual period (winter) creating, in Eliade's terms, a temporary return to chaos.[35] In turn, the ensuing renewal and rejuvenation flow from the following day into the coming year. The fusion of *jāgarana* and the *Vasantotsava* in our text is not completely without precedent: the *Indramahotsava* although essentially an autumn festival, is identified in several well-known texts as a festival of spring.[36] The Spring Festival thus becomes layered with many associative mythical events and multiple ritual procedures of which *jāgarana* is just one such celebration.

Although reference to *jāgarana* or *kojāgara* is made in a variety of *purāṇas* as well as other texts, the exact time when this festival is celebrated varies considerably.[37] The *Bhaviṣya Purāṇa* and the *Padma Purāṇa* tell us that the *Kaumudīmahotsava*, the Autumn Festival, is celebrated on *Kārttika Amāvasyā* (*Dīpavalī*).[38] *Kojāgara pūrṇimā*, a variant name for *Kaumudīmahotsava*, is observed in the autumn on the full moon day of Aśvina (Sept./Oct.) or the first day of the bright half of Kārttika (Oct./Nov.).[39] In this context, *jāgarana* forms part of the glorification of the autumn moon (*Kaumudīmahotsava*) and its concomitant worship of Lakṣmī.[40]

The festival is pre-eminently a Lakṣmī *vrata* and those who observe it are blessed with offspring, wealth and a long and prosperous life.[41] The *Nārada Purāṇa* tells us that Lakṣmī, the goddess of prosperity, is worshipped by keeping a jar of gold, copper, or mud in her honour, lighting lamps and staying awake all night, i.e., performing *jāgarana*.[42] Should Lakṣmī visit the house during the night and find the inhabitants asleep, she might not grant them good fortune; those who stay awake, however, will surely be granted good luck. In present day Bengal and Assam, *jāgarana* links Lakṣmī *pūjā* with the worship of Durgā. It is most often performed on the full moon night after the Durgā-*pūjā* celebrations. In this instance, too, an all-night vigil is recommended in honour of Lakṣmī, wherein she is believed to ask at midnight: '*ko jāgartti*' ('who is awake?').[43] As well as belonging to the rituals of autumn, *jāgarana* appears here in the *Bhaviṣya Purāṇa* and in the commentary on the *Kāmasūtra*, as a ritual of spring,[44] thus forging a link between the prosperity offered by Lakṣmī and that offered by Kāma.

The *Śrīpañcamī* is another instance where individual rituals associated with either Lakṣmī, Kāma, or the *Vasantotsava* become something of a *salsa*. Although the *Śrīpañcamī* is identified as celebrating Kāma and Rati in both the *Varṣakṛtydīpikā* and the *Haribhaktivilāsa*, it is a festival most usually performed in association with Lakṣmī.[45] The *Śrīpañcamī*, a ritual ensuring future prosperity, is celebrated on the fifth day of spring and is, therefore, included in the Vasanta *navarātra* (the nine days of celebrations in honour of Durgā, Lakṣmī and Sarasvatī).[46] This same celebration, in the *Purāṇasamuccaya*, is called the *Vasantapañcamī*.[47] The inclusion of Lakṣmī rituals (*jāgarana* and *Vasantapañcamī*) as one of the prescribed activities honouring Kāma at the time of the Spring Festival, indicates a degree of reciprocity with respect to the function of these two deities. It is apparent that both Kāma and Lakṣmī are worshipped for prosperity and off-spring. Both become figures of the continuance.

Navarātra

Despite their temporal distance, the commonality shared by autumn rituals and rituals of spring hinges on their parallel likeness as seasonal 'markers' identifying beginning and ending. Two important periodic events divide the year into equal parts and occur, roughly, at the time of the vernal and autumnal equinoxes. They signal, respectively, the end of winter and the beginning of spring on the one hand and the end of summer and the beginning of winter on the other. Both events are known as *navarātra* (nine nights). The first period (the vernal) occurs during the first nine days of the bright half of Caitra and the second (the autumnal), during the first nine days of the bright half of Āśvina. Gaster in *Thespis* contends that the re-emergence of the sun in spring was an obvious date from which to reckon the renewal of the world's vitality and the decline of the sun in autumn was a natural occasion from which to date the eclipse of such vitality.[48] In India, however, where two agricultural periods are not uncommon, both of these ritual periods may mark closure and commencement: one at the end of the rainy season in September/October and one at the start of spring proper in March/April.

If this were the case, we should expect these rites to be the same or similar in practice and detail.[49] Raghavan declares that in all of the *Nibandha*, as well as in practice, a Vasanta (spring) *navarātra* and a Śarada (autumn) *navarātra* is prescribed.[50] So, for example, in the *Nirṇayāmṛta*, the *Durgotsava* (festival of Durgā) must be celebrated both during the bright half of Aśvina as well as during the bright half of Caitra.[51] It will be recalled, too, that the *Indramahotsava* was prescribed in certain texts as an autumn ritual and in others as a spring ritual as, for example, in Nepal, at Bhaktapur, where there is a smaller *Indradhvaja* festival in spring and a larger one in autumn.[52] Both festivals, the spring *Vasantotsava* and the autumn *Kaumudīmahotsava*, signal particularly auspicious periods in the calendar year and perhaps it is due to this 'seasonality' that they are often related and even occasionally equated.

With respect to the fundamental characteristics of the Spring Festival as found in The *Bhaviṣya Purāṇa* (135), we can fruitfully focus our attention in two general directions. First, Kāma's destruction and resurrection provide us with a specifically delineated mythological framework: Kāma is clearly a deity associated with the Śaiva tradition. He is both subordinate to Śiva (he is destroyed by the fire of Śiva) as well as he is dependent upon him for rebirth. Śiva's power and dominion over Kāma is established and, indeed, his power over the cosmos is re-articulated. Second, Kāma is destroyed by fire, a destructive, creative and transformative force. Kāma's transformation from life to death and from death to life is the focus of spring rituals. Although Kāma is immolated, he will be reborn just as inevitably as will be the arrival of spring. Kāma's rebirth signals the success of his mission *vis-à-vis* the union of male and female in both cosmic and terrestrial realms: Śiva with Pārvatī, husband with wife. Progeny are a result of this fertile coupling thereby leading to the destruction of the demon Tāraka. Clearly expressed here is the right course of action needed in order to maintain and stabilize the cosmos.

The notions of transformation and transition, degeneration and regeneration, are given form, are shaped, in the ritual practices of the *Vasantotsava*. *Jāgarana*, the worship of Lakṣmī and the *Kaumudīmahotsava*, being mutable, being 'unfixed,' as it were, reflect the versatile accommodation of Indian ritual forms. The association of *jāgarana* with Lakṣmī and the association of the *Kaumudīmahotsava* and the *Vasantotsava* among many others help us to re-align the Spring Festival as we re-contextualize it.

NOTES

1 Winternitz, *A History of Sanskrit Literature,* I. 567.

2 There are several well-known systems of distinguishing these works. One such system maintains that each *purāṇa* aims at exalting one of the three major deities in the Hindu tradition, *viz,* Brahmā, Viṣṇu,or. Śiva. Krishnamachariar, *History of Classical Sanskrit Literature,* p. 75. The *Bhaviṣya Purāṇa* falls into the Brahmā category as it imparts instruction from Brahmā, via the Sun god Sūrya, to Manu. V. Mani, *Purāṇic Encyclopaedia* (fourth ed; Delhi: 1974), p. 128.

3 S.C. Banerji, *A Companion to Sanskrit Literature* , p. 159.

4 See for example the *Virūpākṣavasantotsavacampū* (below); the *Ratnāvalī* and the *Kathāsaritsāgara,* Book XII, No. 17 (above).

5 The meaning of *'nidhāna'* here is unclear. It could, be appropriately read as *'nidhuvāna'* in this context.

6 In these verses Kāma is described with all the attributes of a king, i.e., wearing a crown, headpiece, having messengers, treasures, councillors and mounted on an elephant.

7 I have read here *'vājivakram'* as an epithet of Kāma, 'Horse-headed.' Coomaraswamy connects the iconography of horses with the *yakṣa* motif, telling us horses (normal, fish-tailed, or water-horses) are commonly found as vehicles for *yakṣas* and *yakṣīs*. He further includes Kāma in his descriptions of *yakṣas*. (*Yakṣas,* II.31.)

8 The subject seems to switch in this verse, perhaps the text is simply bringing out that the king must also celebrate this festival.

9 According to S. Kramrisch, *The Presence of Śiva* (Princeton: 1981), 'Kāma was the urge in the creative mind toward manifestation, condensation, and substance. The arrows of Kāma, of which the *Purāṇas* speak were directed hitherward.... The arrows of Kāma flew toward this world; they would wound but not kill, they would incite passion.' p. 218.

10 Paraphrased from the *Śiva Purāṇa,* ed. by J.L. Shastri, trans. by a Board of Scholars, 4 vols. (Reprint: Delhi: 1977), 2.3.17-42.

11 *Atharva Veda,* III.25.

12 Kālidāsa, *Kumārasaṁbhava*, text and trans. by S.R. Sehgal (Delhi: 1959), Canto III. pp. 93f.

13 *Vasantavilāsa*, ed., trans. and intro. by W. Brown (New Haven: 1962), 1.7.

14 Though Śiva is the best known of Kāma's victims, he is not the only powerful figure to be on the receiving end of one of Kāma's arrows. According to the *Vāmana Purāṇa*, the penance of Nara and Nārāyaṇa was, on one occasion, disturbed by Kāma.

15 Details of it appear in the *Kathāsaritsāgara*, *Kumārasaṁbhava* and in the *Vāmana Purāṇa*. The *Śiva Purāṇa*, for example, gives us an extensive account of this episode. O'Flaherty, *Śiva*, cites thirty-four different references for this event in Sanskrit literature. (p. 321). See also *Śiva Purāṇa*, II.3.17,9,19-24; II.3.18.39; II.3.19.6-8,14,15,17; III.18.3,5,35,38 and *Kathāsaritsāgara*, III. 69-72. A similar event takes place in the *Buddhacarita* with Māra and Gautama Buddha (XII.2; I.22,53; XIII.1.6,7). The likeness of the two encounters (the Buddha and Māra; Śiva and Kāma) is striking and suggests the antiquity of the motif.

16 *Skanda Purāṇa*, 5.3.150.7-35; *Liṅga Purāṇa*, ed. by J.L. Shastri, trans. by a Board of Scholars, 2 vols. (Delhi: 1973), II. 561.

17 *op cit* p. 120. Kane in *History of Dharmaśāstra* mentions that the *apsaras'* Urvasī, Tilottamā, Menākā and Raṁbhā were utilized to disturb the concentration of ascetics trying to destabilise Indra's grip on the divine domain through their spiritual powers. (V 827)

18 *Matsya Purāṇa*, IV.12.

19 *Ibid*, p. 119.

20 O'Flaherty, *Śiva*, p.119.

21 *Śiva Purāṇa*, I.3.9.18-31.

22 O'Flaherty, *Śiva*, p. 144.

23 *Ibid*, p. 151.

24 Gaster tells us that howling and wailing are frequently associated with the rites of certain deities or spirits of fertility and are well attested at seasonal ceremonies throughout ancient civilization. Gaster, *Thespis*, pp. 30-31. See also *Bhaviṣya Purāṇa*, 132 (below).

25 *Brahmāṇḍa Purāṇa*, translated by Wendy O'Flaherty, *Hindu Myths*, pp. 147-9.

26 *Matsya Purāṇa*, 154, pp. 259-274.

27 *Śiva Purāṇa*, "Rudrasaṁhitā," 51.7.13-14.

28 Eliade calls this the "collective regeneration through repetition of the cosmographic art." Eliade, *Cosmos and History*, p. 78.

29 T. Bapat, *Rituals and Festivals of India* (Bombay: 1991), p. 65.

30 P.V. Ayyar, *South Indian Festivals* (Madras: 1921), pp. 61-4. See also, P. Younger, "Ten Days" in *Modern Asian Studies*.

[31] There are a variety of representations of this Kāma-myth in South Indian art evidencing its popularity. A bronze representation of Rati appealing to Śiva exists in the temple of Kāmarasavalli in Trichinopoly. The whole scene of Kāma's destruction is depicted in the portico near the tank in the Ekambareswarer temple at Conjeeveram. Further, in the Adipuriśvara temple at Tiruvorriyar, there is a record of King Rājakeśarivarman alias Tribbhuvanachadravartin Rājādhirājadeva (1172-1186) which mentions that this king was present at this festival during *Paṅguṉi Uttiram*. (See Ayyar, *South Indian Festivals*, p. 64.)

[32] J.M. Christian "The End is the Beginning" in G.R. Welbon and G.E. Yocum, *Religious Festivals in South India and Sri Lanka* (Delhi:1982), pp. 243-268, p. 253.

[33] Vātsyāyana, for example, in the *Kāmasūtra* refers to this ritual as *kaumudī* (1.4.27).

[34] See, for example, *The Goddess Lakṣmī*, pp. 170-1.

[35] Eliade, *Cosmos and History*, p. 68.

[36] The *Kausika Sūtra*, *Rāmāyana* and *Atharvaveda Pariśiṣṭa* refer to the *Indramahotsava* as an autumn festival. The *Sarasvatīkaṇṭhābharaṇa* and the *Śṛṅgāra Prakāśa* link it to the Spring Festival. (See Raghavan, *Festivals*, pp. 120f, 128.)

[37] Raghavan in *Festivals* cites the *Skanda Purāṇa*, *Bhaviṣya Purāṇa*, *Padma Purāṇa* and authors of *Smṛti* digests like Hemādri and Raghunanda in describing this ritual. (p. 177)

[38] *Bhaviṣya Purāṇa*, 140.6.60; *Padma Purāṇa*, 6.124.61f. cited in *The Goddess Lakṣmī*, pp. 170-4.

[39] *Padma Purāṇa*, 6.124.61f.,*The Goddess Lakṣmī* , pp. 170-1.

[40] *Śabdakalpadruma*, II, pp.200-1 cited in Upendra Nath Dhal, *The Goddess Lakṣmī* , p. 171.

[41] *Ibid*, p. 173.

[42] *Nārada Purāṇa*, 124.47.55 cited by D. Nambiar, *Nārada Purāṇa: A Critical Study* (Poona: 1968), p. 415.

[43] The term *kojāgara* is probably a contraction of *kaumudījāgarana* (staying up all night on the full moon *[kaumudī]*. K. Handiqui, *Yaśastilaka and Indian Culture*, p. 403, note 2. See also *Śabdakalpadruma* under *kojāgara*.

[44] *Kāmasūtra*, 1.31..31..

[45] See, for example, Hemādri, *Caturvargacintāmaṇi*, pp. 184-90.

[46] *Varṣakṛtydīpikā*, pp. 287-288. See also Raghavan, *Festivals*, p.187 and De, *The Early History of the Vaiṣṇava Faith in Bengal* (Calcutta: 1961), pp. 448f.

[47] Raghavan, *Festivals*, p. 252.

[48] Gaster, *Thespis*, pp. 47-8.

[49] Babb, *The Divine Hierarchy*, p. 132.

[50] Raghavan, *Festivals*, p. 150.

[51] Damodaran Nambiar, *The Nārada Purāṇa; A Critical Study*, (Poona: 1968), p. 463.

[52] Raghavan, *Festivals*, p. 150.

9

Bhaviṣya Purāṇa, 132: The Demoness

Chapter 132 of the *Bhaviṣya Purāṇa*, the *Phālgunapūrṇimotsavavarnam*, identifies the Spring Festival as the *Phalgunotsava* and specifies that it is to be staged on the full-moon day of Phālguna. On this day, all villages and cities in the world are said to commemorate and re-enact the fiery immolation of a fiendish *rākṣasī*, known variously as Ḍhaunḍhā or Holākā. The *Bhaviṣya Purāṇa* recounts the tale of this demoness who, in times past, performed such great *tapas* that she attracted the attention of Śiva and from him received the boon of invincibility. To safeguard the universe, Śiva added an apparently harmless *caveat* to the boon: her demise would be wrought by the hands of children and 'mad-ones.' So it was that Ḍhaunḍhā came to fear both children and 'mad-ones,' and, while fearing them, she torments them. The villagers, whose youth she victimizes, petition their king, Raghu, for a means to put an end to the constant harassment. Acting on the advice of the sage Vasiṣṭha, Raghu instructs children to build a fire on the full moon day of Phālguna and dance fearlessly around the flames waving pieces of wood as if they were warriors in battle wielding weapons. As they sing, laugh, clap their hands and shout '*kilākilā*' the other village members chatter incoherently (vs. 25-28). In this way, we are told, the demoness will be destroyed (by the 'unseen' blows from sticks waved by the children who circled the fire). On the following day the ashes of Ḍhaunḍhā's funeral pyre are to be worshipped and a domestic ritual is performed by married couples in which Kāma is venerated. By performing the above ceremonies, one simultaneously guarantees the destruction of sickness and assures a life of contentment in the company of one's sons.

The text reads as follows:

BHAVIŚYA PURĀṆA, 132: *Phālgunapūrṇimotsavavarnam*

Yuddhiṣṭhira said:

1. Why, O Kṛṣṇa!, is a festival celebrated in all vil–lages and all cities in the world on the day of the full moon in Phālguna?

2 Why do children in all houses jabber away without restraint and why does Holikā burn at the end of Phālguna? What is said regarding this?

3. And why do the wise say *'āḍāḍa.'* and 'hot and cold?' What god is worshipped on this day and why has this one been made to come down to earth? What is done, O Kṛṣṇa!, on that day? Tell me in detail.

Kṛṣṇa said:

4. In the *Kṛta yuga*, O Pārtha, there was a king of men named Raghu, who was brave, possessed of all good qualities, learned and the speaker of pleasant words.

5. He conquered the whole world and subjugated the kings of men; he protected his

subjects according to *dharma* as if they were his own sons.

6. There was no famine and no illness and no one died before his time while he was ruling. The citizens had no taste for *adharma*, O Pārtha!

7. While King Raghu, who was devoted to performing his royal duties, ruled the kingdom, all the citizens arrived one day and said: 'Protect us.

8. There is a *rākṣasī* named Ḍhaunḍhā in our homes. She comes night and day and torments our children without end.

9. She is not to be controlled by those great teachers knowing *mantras*, or by medicine or by protective magical devices.'

11,12. 'Who is this *rākṣasī* named Ḍhaunḍhā? What type of power does she have?' the king asked. 'How can this one who perform evil deeds be controlled by me? A king is called a king because he must protect and because he protects the world, he is a lord. The sin of the king is not protecting the earth (i.e., a king who does not protect his subjects is sinful).' The *purohita* replied: 'It is because of her *tapas*, O highest of the twice-born!'

Vasiṣṭha said:

13. Listen, O king, to a secret which has never been told before. This *rākṣasī* named Ḍhaunḍhā is the daughter of Mālin.

14,15. Formerly Lord Śiva, worshipped by her, was pleased with her great austerities and said: 'Choose a boon, O one who takes vows. I will give you what your mind desires without hesitation.'

16. Ḍhaunḍhā said to Śiva: 'If you are satisfied, O lord of the three worlds, make me incapable of being killed by *asuras*, or by men, Śaṅkara!

17. Make me not able to be killed by weapons and missiles. May I be free from danger in the time of cold, heat or the rainy season, inside or outside, during the night or day through your favour. May I be free from harm at all times through your divine favour. Let that be the boon, O Maheśvara!'

Śaṅkara said:

18. Having said 'So be it,' Śaṅkara, the bearer of the trident, again said to her, 'O fortunate one! Danger will come from children and mad-ones, you shall be afraid of these in every season, cold, hot and rainy, but do not despair.'

19. So, having granted this boon to her, the blessed one who put out the eye of Bhaga, whose words are ever true and who had appeared to her in a dream, vanished.

20. So that *rākṣasī*, taking on a form at will, obtained a boon. Everyday she, remembering the words of Śiva, torments children.

21 Thus the wife of a householder utters the *Siddhamantra 'āḍāḍa'* in her house and thus Ḍhaunḍhā in this world is called *'āḍāḍa'*.[1]

22 All these are the activities of Ḍhaunḍhā which I have told you. Now I will tell you how she can be killed.

23 Today is the fifteenth of the bright moon of Phālguna, O king of men, when winter passes; tomorrow will begin the hot season.

24 People should be protected in such a manner that, unafraid, they can enjoy themselves happily today and be content, laughing.

25. Children should go forth happily with pieces of wood and sticks in their hands like warriors to battle.

26. Children must be made to gather heaps of stones and dried wood. Then they must kindle a fire according to the rules and with *mantras* which will kill the demoness.

27. Having circled the fire three times let them make the sound *'kilākilā.'* They should sing and laugh with sounds of joy, clapping their hands with pleasure.

28. Let all people chatter at will without being afraid of anything. By these sounds and by this oblation, the evil one will be expelled. With an invisible blow from children the *rākṣasī* will be destroyed.

Kṛṣṇa said:

29. Having heard the words of the seer, that king, O son of Pāṇḍu!, did all that was told to him by that wise one.

30. The *rākṣasī* was destroyed by the fierce ritual and from that time on she (the demoness) became known in the world as *āḍāḍa*.[2]

31. A *homa* ceremony which wards off all evil and grants the cessation of all sickness, is done by

Brahmans on that day, O Pārtha!, therefore the day is known as *Holikā*.

32 O Yuddhiṣṭhira!, this was once a day more important than an other day and because it was so very important it was called *Phalgu* (beautiful), or the bringer of the highest bliss.[3]

33. Children are to be protected and they are to be kept inside, O Pārtha!, on this day at the advent of the night (i.e., at twilight). In the courtyard of the house in which there is a rectangular diagram and which is smeared with cow dung.

34. One should cause men to congregate, swords in hand, along with all the children. And these men, touching the children with sticks and singing them songs that make them laugh, will guard the children. They (the children) should be given molasses and cooked rice.

35. Thus the harm caused by Ḍhaunḍhā will be averted. Therefore protecting the young from her ought to be done at dusk.

36. At daybreak, O Lord,! what should be performed by people who strive for happiness beginning in the month of Madhava, on the first day of the rising sun (i.e., on the first day of spring)?

Yuddhiṣṭhira said:

37. One should do the obligatory duties (i.e., daily rites). Having pleased the fathers one should prostrate oneself before the ashes of Holikā to ward off evil (i.e., the ashes from the Holikā fire).

Kṛṣṇa said:

38. In a decorated, smeared courtyard, anointed with ground rice paste one should prepare a rectangle with pure, full rice grains and also paints.

39. In the middle of the rectangle one should prepare an altar covered with the best white garments and place in front of it a full pitcher brimming over with young sprouts.

40. Having put gold inside it (the pitcher) and rice grains smeared with white sandal paste in front of the pitcher, one should offer sandals and fine cloth.

41-7. The husband should sit on a seat accompanied by the sound of the Vedas. At this same time his wife, of faultless body and auspicious marks, wearing a red bodice and clothing of delicate silks, should anoint him with sandal and pour ghee with curds and grain seeds on his head, all so that he may have a long life and health. Then that wise man should drink liquor made form mango flowers with sandal. This is the way of worshipping Kāma. Those who, at the onset of spring drink (liquor) made from mango flowers mixed with sandal paste, fulfill the desires they have in their hearts. Next, the man should give gifts to Brahmins, bards, panegyrists chanting 'may Kāma be pleased with me.' Then, when it is time to eat, he should first eat rice that was prepared on the previous day; after that he can eat to his heart's content. Whoever does this, as it is said in the *Śāstras*, performs the festival of Phālguna.

48. All wishes are then easily attained; curses and sickness are destroyed immediately.

49. A man joined together with this sons and grandsons lives happily.

50. This has been told to you, O Pārtha, this is the *tithi* which is the greatest of lunar days. It is propitious, pure, victorious and destroys all obstacles.

51. It occurs when the cold season has passed on the fifteenth day of the bright moon.

53. At daybreak, in spring, a man should eat mango and sandal paste to attain happiness.

The content of the Spring Festival, here known as the *Phālgunapūrṇimotsava,* is clearly and strikingly different from those we have considered thus far. Central to the myth and to the ritual of spring herein described is a fierce and troublesome demoness named Ḍhaunḍhā or Holākā, a being whose primary function is to afflict children. At the same time, there is a discernable continuity in the thematic threads weaving the fabric of the festival. Just as Kāma was set ablaze during the *Vasantotsava* in the *Bhaviṣya Purāṇa* (135), here, in the *Bhaviṣya* (132), the celebrations revolve around the burning of the demoness. The theme of rejuvenation is reiterated: in the same way as Kāma was revived from ashes on that day, here children, the very substance of new beginnings, are granted a new lease on life as childhood disease attributable to the demoness is eradicated.

Further to and synchronous with motifs of replenishment, there is a clear indication that these rituals are designed to ward off evil, as well as to protect from curses and sins those who perform them. Just as in the *Kṛta Yuga* (132.4), Ḍhaunḍhā was destroyed, so too, Brahmins are advised to observe *Holākā* by performing a *homa* ceremony which creates a defence against all evils and grants the cessation of all sickness (132.31). They are to re-enact the occasion of the destruction of the demoness (132.32-35). It is only after her destruction at this particular ceremony that rites of renewal can commence (132.38f.). Prevalent are the mandatory ingredients of Indian renewal motifs: a full pot brimming over with young sprouts, the worship of Kāma, the imbibing of mango flowers and the like.

Ḍhauṇḍhā, Holākā and Pūtanā

This terrifying *rākṣasī* known as Ḍhauṇḍhā or Holākā is a minor being in the seemingly endless panoply of Indian deities. From most accounts she appears to be a female figure whose primary function is to torment children, particularly to inflict them with disease. The creature Ḍhauṇḍhā/Holākā elsewhere is mentioned in the company of a demoness of similar attributes named Pūtanā who is active in similar contexts. All of these *rākṣasīs*, Ḍhauṇḍhā, Holākā and Pūtanā have characteristics in common and may be considered functionally analogous. These female demonic beings who inflict sorrow and malaise on children are annihilated both by the shouting of obscenities and by fire. Evidently their destruction, as in the *Bhaviṣya Purāṇa* (132), is re-enacted coincident with the Spring Festival.

Ḍhauṇḍhā' occurs as an appellation of this *rākṣasī* least frequently in our descriptions of the *Vasantotsava*. It is found in the *Bhaviṣya Purāṇa* and in Hemādri's *Caturvargacintāmaṇi*.[4] The motive and purpose for the persecution of Ḍhauṇḍhā given in the *Caturvargacintāmaṇi*, as in the *Bhaviṣya Purāṇa*, is her propensity for abducting children: by enacting this ritual, the world is purged of her torments. In both of these texts, Ḍhauṇḍhā is unable to bear the abuse of men and women who shout obscenities in their own language while thrice circling the fire. According to Hemādri, when the *rākṣasī* is slain she falls directly into the flames. The following day her ashes are worshipped as talismans against disease.

The *Bhaviṣya Purāṇa* (132.37) clearly states that this demoness is also known as Holākā, the name found for her in the *Nāradīya Purāṇa*, *Holākāmāhātmya* and the oral Vaiṣṇava tradition of north India. The meaning of '*Holākā*,' however, is fairly obscure. It is known to the *Bhāvaprakāśa* where it means a half-baked grain of *śamī* roasted by the mild and brief fire of grass.[5] In the *Caraka Saṁhitā Sūtra*, *'Holākā'* refers to a particular method of *Śvedana* or steam bathing in which a person lies on a couch under which burning dung cakes have been placed.[6] The smoke from these is called *'Holākā.'* Raghavan suggests that this explains the use of the name *Holākā* for a festival, the central feature of which is the burning of an effigy made of cow dung and other materials.[7] The etymology, I think, is obscure. Whatever the origin of the term, Holākā emerges as a sort of chthonic deity associated with diseases of childhood. According to Mrs. Sinclair Stevenson every Brahmin baby that has been born since the previous Spring Festival is carried round the *Holākā* fire dressed in white garb. The flames have the capability of warding off illness: individuals desirous of this end take home the dung cakes and touch their livestock with them as this is said to prevent disease in the coming year. Ḍhaunḍhā is assimilated to Holākā in our text and her association with diseases, especially diseases of children, is in character with the demoness who is especially dangerous to children.[8]

The figure of Holākā achieves a further dimension when she is accorded attributes associated usually with warriors. She then becomes known variously as Devī, Holā, Kālī, Caṇḍī and Māheśvarī. In the *Holākāmāhātmya*,[9] for example, the goddess appears as victor over the *asura*, Vīrasena. This text describes the grandeur of their battle in which the goddess emerges victorious, delighting and gratifying the entire world. At the end of the battle, the Devī narrates the different sizes of her male counterpart, the *liṅga*. The goddess figure here, in the *Holākāmāhātmya*, is clearly associated with the Śaiva tradition and the battle celebrated by the festival revolves around her defeat of demons, not her personal defeat at the hand of her worshippers. This same mythic event is the narrative and ritual context of both the *navarātri*, popular in the south and *daśarah*, popular in the north.[10] Of primary importance in these like myths is the goddess Durgā's defeat of the buffalo demon (Mahiṣa). The *Holākāmāhātmya* thus translocates Holākā into the Śaiva tradition and her worship becomes relevant in both the contexts of the *Holī* festival and the *Navarātra*.

To continue this battle analogy, a tale in the *Varṣakṛtyādīpikā* quotes the *Jyotinirbandha* concerning the ritual fire in the midst of which an effigy of Ḍhauṇḍhā is to be raised consisting of a five coloured banner. This banner is reminiscent of the Indra-pole and to the festivities which revolve around the Spring Festival of Indra.[11] Indra's banner is referred to as *jarjara* in the context of Indian drama and it is traditionally explained as an instrument of destruction, used in order to chase away the enemy.[12] In the *Nāṭyaśāstra*, moreover, one should offer *pūjā* to the post to attain success at the performance of the drama and to pray as follows:[13]

> Thou art Indra's weapon killing all the demons, thou hast been fashioned by all the gods and thou art capable of destroying all the obstacles; bring victory to the king and defeat to his enemies, welfare to cows and Brahmins...

The Indra-pole, then, becomes a battle weapon used to annihilate demons, much in the same manner as the burning of Ḍhauṇḍhā banner in the *Varṣakṛtyādīpikā* destroys the evil witch.

Unlike the story of Indra's defeat of the demons or of the Devī's defeat of Mahiṣa, but like the celebration of the Indra festival, the destruction of Ḍhauṇḍhā/Holākā is the responsibility of the king. Here the king and the people enter into a sympathetic relationship: it is King Raghu who must devise the means to defeat Ḍhauṇḍhā and it is the inhabitants of Raghu's kingdom who must, in addition, perform the apropriate rituals which ensure it (*Bhaviṣya Purāṇa*, 132:11,12,29f.). The focus thus shifts in the *Bhaviṣya Purāṇa* from the arena of heaven, where the demons are restrained by the gods, to the arena of the mundane where the demons are kept at bay by the people. Ensuring the annual destruction of the demoness, the rites of spring are performed every year without fail.

In another text from south India, the *Vināyakādisarvapūjāpaddhati*, both Paraśurāma and Holākā are worshipped on this day.[14] Paraśurāma is famed for his destruction of the *kṣatriya* (warrior) caste. The connection between Paraśurāma and Holākā is unclear, although as Holākā is notorious for her destruction of children, so too is Paraśurāma occasionally, on his rampage, credited with destroying the embryos of *kṣatriya* women.[15]

A further manifestation of this same demoness, though in an explicitly sectarian context, is found occasionally in myths indigenous to Bengal and Orissa. Here Kṛṣṇa kills a demoness named either Pūtanā or Holākā during the Spring Festival. Haridas Mitra suggests that Pūtanā is connected to *'pū* (to suppurate), *puyate* and pus. In the *Mahābhārata*, the demoness Pūtanā is described as a *grahā* (grasper, i.e., a disease).[16] Pūtanā is a demoness who appears in the *Agni Purāṇa*, the *Viṣṇu Purāṇa*, the *Bhāgavata Purāṇa* and the *Skanda Purāṇa*.[17] She is described as a female *rākṣasī*, the daughter of Bali, one of the mothers (*mātṛs*) attending Skanda, a *yoginī* and a disease in children.[18] The themes of children and disease continue to remain important in Bengal and Orissa where the modern Spring Festival, *Holī*, celebrates the child Kṛṣṇa's victory over this demoness Pūtanā. Regardless of her appellation, Pūtanā/Holākā/Ḍhaunḍhā is clearly a negative and aggressive force personifying some form of disease specific to children.

The Demoness and the Gods

Pūtanā, in the mythology of the *purāṇas* and the *Mahābhārata* cited above, was sent to Vraja by Kṛṣṇa's arch-rival Kaṁsa in the guise of a beautiful woman. Her mission is to destroy the child Kṛṣṇa. She is described as a hawk (*śakunī*) perched on the wheel of a wagon which subsequently assumes the form of a beautiful woman having poisonous breasts.[19] She is intended to suckle the child Kṛṣṇa and, because her breasts are filled with poison, thereby to kill him. Kṛṣṇa, however, wise to the ways of Kaṁsa, changes his own form and himself sucks the life out of Pūtanā. In the *Bhāgavata Purāṇa* the gruesome murder of Pūtanā by Kṛṣṇa is noted as follows:[20]

> The ogress Pūtanā, a devourer of children, was sent to kill the infant Kṛṣṇa. She assumed a charming form and let him suck her breasts which she had smeared with a virulent poison. But Kṛṣṇa, pressing her breast hard with his hands, angrily drank out her life's breath with the milk and killed her, having cut off her breasts. (p. 41)

O'Flaherty commenting upon this myth, suggests an implicit connection between blood and life's breath. Just as Pūtanā reverses the fluid that she intends to give him, changing milk to poison, so he too affects a reversal, changing poison to blood, which he sucks from her.'[21] O'Flaherty cites an interesting myth in a text from Bengal wherein Kṛṣṇa in the form of Kālī kills Pūtanā:

> The gods begged Kālī to rid the realm of demonic kings and she agreed to become incarnate as Kṛṣṇa. Śiva prayed to Kālī and was given permission to become incarnate as Rādhā, in order to enjoy intercourse in reverse. 'Kṛṣṇa' resumed the form of Kālī temporarily in order to kill Pūtanā. At Śiva's wish, Rādhā's husband became impotent immediately after marriage.

Several pictorial representations of the execution of Pūtanā depict Kṛṣṇa as a small male child perched on top of Pūtanā's protruding, phallic tongue. In these drawings Pūtanā is depicted in two forms: as a beautiful women and as an hideous ogress.[22] Sudhir Kakar, in *The Inner World*, interprets Pūtanā as the epitome of the dangerous mother who refuses to allow her son to grow up; a mother who makes excessive sexual demands upon him. The manner in which Pūtanā is put to death, according to this reading, reflects the male child's fantasy of fulfilling the sexual demands of his mother and also the son's revenge upon her for making these demands.[23]

In a Śaiva scenario parallel to Kṛṣṇa's encounter with Pūtanā (i.e., sitting on Pūtanā's lap as a child), we find Śiva assuming the role of the goddess' child sitting on Pārvatī's lap. In the *Liṅga Purāṇa*, Śiva takes the form of a baby to suck the anger from the breasts of the goddess after she has slain the demon Dāruka.[24] Pūtanā appears more fully formed in the context of the Śaiva tradition as one of the seven Mothers who raises Śiva's son, Skanda. The story of the birth of Skanda is complex and numerous variants appear in both the *purāṇas* and the *Epics*. In what amounts to a postscript to the main story, the troop of Mothers which nurtures the child asks to be given control over all creatures. Such control is presently allotted to another set of Mothers who, according to Nīlakaṇṭha, are the *śāktīs* of the gods Brahmā, Śiva, etc..[25] Skanda refuses but offers to grant any other wish that they might be har–bouring. The Mothers who have nurtured him reply:[26]

> We want to devour the offspring of those Mothers give them to us, them and their Gods who are different from yourself. (15-20)

And following, Skanda replies:

> Afflict the young children of men in your various forms until they are sixteen years old. I shall give you a Rudra-like immortal soul and you shall dwell with it in complete happiness, being much worshipped. (20-25)

At this moment, out of the body of Skanda came a fiery being who was bidden by Skanda to assume horrific forms.[27] Pūtanā, the *grahā* (grasper, disease demoness), described as 'an awful Stalker of the night, evil in her ghastly shape' is one of these terrifying forms. In the *Epic*, Pūtanā is one of the disease-demonesses, a foe of children and a member of Skanda's attendants.[28] The Mothers are considered to be female ghoul-like characters who seize children and make them ill.[29]

Children

The primary function of children in this chapter of the *Bhaviṣya Purāṇa* (132) is to destroy that demoness who represents a threat to them in the form of childhood diseases. In the above text youngsters are to circle the fire with sticks and speak 'at will.' Their actions are vital to the success of this festival as by performing the ritual correctly, the destruction of the demoness is accomplished and the future prosperity of the village is ensured. While children are completely vulnerable to the whims of the evil *rākṣasī*, they are, at the same time, crucial in eliminating her. This antipodal theme of powerful/powerless is reiterated in the *Bhaviṣya Purāṇa* (135.18) where mad people also pose a challenge and a threat to the demoness.

Children and mad-ones are among the weakest members of the social order. The work of V. Turner is of assistance in interpreting the function of such figures in our myths.[30] He places much emphasis on the ritual power of the weak and on those who are hierarchically inferior. In the case of the *Bhaviṣya Purāṇa* we can interpret children and mad-ones as such beings. Turner describes children as 'mediators' between the dead and the living and claims that they, along with mad-ones, are liminal, marginal creatures whose powers in rites akin to these are due to a form of status reversal. A normative link between children and women is baby to mother. The latter gives life to and nurtures the former. Clearly this ritual reverses these traditional relationships. Rather than providing sustenance, Ḍhauṇḍhā snatches away the life-breath of children by inflicting them with disease. A common explanation in literary and popular mythology for disease and death of children is to be located in the sphere of the feminine. Sukeśin in the *Vāmana Purāṇa* (11-15), Harikeśa in the *Matsya Purāṇa* (p. 180. 5-19) and Hārīti in the Buddhist tradition[31] provide us with examples of a similar type of behavior to that exhibited by Ḍhauṇḍhā: they all afflict children. This display of female aggression, so out of character with the normative, nurturing mother, provides a startlingly effective image of what might happen should things go wrong. There exist numerous examples of women who have lost their offspring to disease or some other tragedy and who are believed to haunt villages of India as ghosts, preying particularly on helpless youngsters.[32] Children are indeed weak in the context of the social hierarchy and there is definitely a reversal of roles in the rituals of the *Bhaviṣya Purāṇa*. But Ḍhaunḍhā is, in the end, assassinated, and this must surely have some bearing on our reading of the text. Like winter which must end, each year Ḍhaunḍhā must be put to death, and with her, her deadly habits. In a parallel with spring, children, the renewers, the continuers, are perfect for the task of driving her away.

We might, as well, consider children and mad-ones as non-logical and imaginal beings who are unfettered and unencumbered by pre-determined, rational thought processes. Amongst the young, as amongst mad-ones, the world is not so rigidly ordered as it is amongst adults; a pot can become a hat, a box can become a house and so on. The power which resides in children and mad-ones is, then, their ability to 'understand,' to be capable of interacting with, to become easily amalgamated or embroiled in the magical world of gods and demons. They can, it would seem, stand in mediation between the world of gods (in this case the demoness) and the world of people. The highly symbolic nature of ritual worship in which mythical and 'real' worlds interact reveals to children and mad-ones a depth of meaning not ordinarily descriptive of rational men. It is through their access to these worlds and their concomitant intervention that Ḍhaunḍhā is destroyed. In ritual time, the weak become strong; children and mad-ones alone, in the *Bhaviṣya Purāṇa*, are capable of warding off the demoness. Their function is purificatory, protective and aggressive.

The children engage in noise-making and wild behavior in order to effect their goal. This is carried over into the adult community in texts like the *Nīlamata Purāṇa* which tells us that everyone delights in joke-playing and abusive name-calling in order to frighten the *piśācas* (demons) who were believed to enter their houses on the day of the Spring Festival. The *Caturvargacintāmaṇi* (*vrata* II, pp. 184-90) has already been mentioned in this context. The sort of ululation engaged in by the participants in this festival becomes an aggressive onomatopoeic cry of battle transforming children into front-line warriors; hence, they loudly cry *'kilākilā'* and brandish sticks about in the air. At the same time, wives of householders repeat '*āḍāḍa*' to keep the demoness away. The garbled utterances voiced by adults in the *Bhaviṣya Purāṇa* (above) are mimetic of the actions of children in a clear attempt to empower themselves *vis-à-vis* the demoness. In the 'killing of Ḍhaunḍhā,' abusive and incomprehensible language becomes a weapon hurled against a being whose base characteristic is destructive. All of these elements suggest a return to chaos where destruction reigns and a purging of the world of contamination in a relentless anticipation of renewal.

Fire and Ash

The destructive power of the fire and the regenerative power of the ash is distinctly articulated in the above myth. In the preceding description of the festival in the *Bhaviṣya Purāṇa* (135), we found that the qualities of the being who suffers immolation undergo a transformation. Thus Kāma is strengthened. In the present text, *Bhaviṣya Purāṇa* (132), the death-dealing demoness becomes a life-giving force. The residual ashes of her ritual fire are coveted for their cleansing and potent fertilizing powers. Hence, 'one should prostrate oneself before the ashes of Holākā to ward off evil.' (132:37) Despite the destruction wrought by the fire, through it evil becomes good, the impure becomes the pure.

Kane in his *History of Dharmaśāstra* reports that lighting a fire in the specific context of spring celebrations is a tradition ubiquitous throughout India, with the exception of Bengal. Rarely are the flames imbued with Brāhmaṇical significance although priests are occasionally engaged to perform *pūjā* at which coconuts are offered to the sacrificial fire.[33] The *Dolaytraviveka* declares simply that a fire should be kindled on this first day and preserved throughout the duration of the festival.[34] Other texts, including the *Varṣakṛtyādīpikā*,[35] are more specific, de-scribing what appears to be a popular rite wherein the fire is a spring bonfire kindled by children. This text adds a further dimension by telling us that the fuel for the fire is rubbish and that the fire for lighting this heap of debris is to be brought by a child from a *cāṇḍala*'s house, specifically from the lying-in chamber.[36] With this fire, ostensibly the most potent of pollutants imaginable, the *Holī* inferno is lit. In a typical ritual motif, the celebration creates an inverse consequence whereby the most impure of agents affects the purest of results.

In the ritual context of the Spring Festival, this mythic event acquires a grander significance when an effigy, a figurative element of some sort, is purposely and ceremonially placed in the blaze and thereby consumed by the flames. This destruction of an effigy is a symbolic ritual re-enactment of the end of misfortune, (personified in our myths as Kāma and Ḍhaunḍhā) performed in order to avoid calamities and grief in the coming year. Some sources explicitly equate Holākā with the year and her destruction with its termination. According to the *Nāradīya Purāṇa*, Holākā is the sister of Saṁvat (the year) and her worship (*Holākā pūjā*) is performed on the full moon day in Phālguna.[37] At this time Holākā, or *'saṁvatsara'* (the year), is burnt: on the evening before the full moon in Phālguna, an effigy of the old year is made in the form of a man, a ram, or a bamboo hut and it is subsequently and with finality reduced to ashes. The personification of a figure which exists rarely in pictures and most often in mental images formed from words, helps to focus the ritual and enables the participants to witness a tangible end to the daemonic source of crop-failures, diseases and the like.[38] In the *Bhaviṣya Purāṇa* (132, 37) the ashes of the Holākā fire are stated as the residue of past woes, a fitting substance to ward off like future evils.

Fire and the deity Holākā seem inextricable as evidenced by the tale of the demon king Hiraṇyakaśipu and Prahlāda.[39] The ancestry of the demoness, according to this account, is Vaiṣṇava: she is the elder sister of the demon Hiraṇyakaśipu who seeks her assistance in destroying his son Prahlāda. In this tale the problem with Prahlāda is that he is a devotee of Viṣṇu. Holākā here takes Prahlāda onto her lap and sits amidst the flames of the fire with the objective of torching him and hence deterring him from worshipping Viṣṇu. By the grace of Viṣṇu, however, the boy endures the conflagration unhurt while Holākā is completely incinerated.[40] In contemporary practice, the spring celebrations revolve around the activities of these two figures. The preparation of the fire is rather elaborate: the area is swept clean, a pit is dug, a pot of water and grain is buried in the pit and then fuel is stacked up to five feet high. A flag (green or red) is placed on the top, along with garlands of dung cakes. Participants circumambulate the fire three, five or seven times throwing dates and dung cakes into the blaze. Spectators sing obscene songs to show their hatred of the 'witch,' while the women of each village take an active role in burning her. To prevent other witches in the neighborhood from hearing her screams, all the men and children gather round the fire and shout loud obscenities and sing vulgar songs dedicated to the phallus.

In the *Vasantotsavanirṇaya* the burning of Holākā takes place on the full-moon evening of Phālguna and on the following day, the *Vasantotsava* is celebrated, utilizing the ashes from the fire of the previous night. The ashes are impure: they are cremation ashes of the dead Holākā. Yet, these ashes are said to assuage all misery when one pays homage to them. Lawrence Babb in the *Divine Hierarchy*, places this practice in a contemporary context when he tells us that in Chhattisgarh the demoness is burnt in the fire during the Spring Festival. Her ashes are smeared on devotees' bodies and washed off only at the noon bath on the following day.[41] The *Varṣakṛtyādīpikā* tells us that these ashes from the fire in which effigies have been thrown are to be smeared on one's body and left there until the next day if one seeks to avoid grievous trouble in the coming year.

Changing of the colour of one's skin by means of ashes is akin to the changing of the colour of one's skin by means of powder as we encountered earlier in the 'flinging of powder' episodes of spring festivities. Perhaps they are even interchangeable activities. By assuming this 'costume,' by changing one's skin, one is acting beyond the realm of reality where physical laws define and circumscribe human activities. By functioning at the 'edge' of mundane reality one enters a realm where one is able to touch upon or interact, however minimally, with the gods in their extra-physical (or metaphysical) sphere and hence, sway or influence the course of future events as they are directed and modulated by the gods themselves. Hence, a discursive relationship with the gods exists at the interstices between critical ritual moments at critical seasonal cusps. The substance (ashes), the usage (smearing) and the visual result (change in physical appearance) found in descriptions of the *Vasantotsava* are echoed fundamentally in like episodes found throughout the textual body of Hindu mythology and ritual practice.

Ashes as symbols of death are common in Indian religion. Fire is active: it destroys; ashes are passive: they signify destruction. Most importantly, in Indian society where human bodies are disposed of by means of cremation, fire signifies an end to human life. In the context of the *Vasantotsava*, the covering of participants with ashes must then be understood, on one level at least, as symbolic of termination and death. In both the *Bhaviṣya Purāṇa* and *Varṣakṛtyādīpikā* the ashes signal the demoness Holākā/Ḍhauṇḍhā and are the tangible evidence of her demise.

As such however, ashes are not in opposition to red powder as a symbol of fertility and life. As W. O'Flaherty has noted, ashes can be indicators of fertility and eroticism, as well as of destruction and asceticism. In the case of Śiva, the erotic significance of ashes is clearly discernable in that his erect phallus, smeared with ashes, is worshipped by his devotees. If we accept O'Flaherty's interpretation of ashes as both erotic [fecund] and ascetic [barren], then a thematic link between fertility and decay may be established between the ashes used by Śiva's devotees and the ashes featured in the *Vasantotsava*.

The propitiatory and fertilizing power of the ash is clearly articulated in the myth of Kāma in which he is revived through the medium of ash (*Bhaviṣya Purāṇa* 135)). Here (in the *Bhaviṣya Purāṇa* 132) children remain vigourous through its medium. S. Sinclair reports that after the fire has been put out it is customary for women to gather up the ashes and spread them in a circle. Fashioning an image of Pārvatī from the remaining cinders and placing it in the centre of the circle, they draw yet more circles around the image in various colours. Finally, they circumambulate this ritual configuration every day for fifteen days. The purpose of the rite is to gain a good husband.[42] These ashes are Holākā's ashes, the ashes of death, the ashes of the demoness; they are, under ordinary conditions, highly contaminating. Yet, instead of treating them as such, those celebrating the festival are directed to pay homage to them. The equivocality lent to the celebrations by this act is a further example of unacceptable and undesirable conditions becoming legitimized under ritual conditions. Just as the participants go about behaving like 'ghosts,' so too, do they roam about the streets covered with ash of the crematory looking like them. Although acting as if they are alive (i.e, they are ambulatory), they have taken on the mask of death.[43] They appear thus to be simultaneously both dead and alive, or, neither dead nor alive: the normal boundaries between life and death have become blurred. The arrival of spring is immanent.

Regeneration in the 'green' kingdom as well as in the human kingdom is a condition found throughout the *Vasantotsava* capable of being transferred from nature to human society, from human society to nature and within human society itself (from the king to the people). Abundance is therefore, one of the major concerns of this festival as the rituals outlined here indicate. The transition from one order to another is a predetermined annual event: the rites reflect the movement of an entire society from winter to spring.

In the *Bhaviṣya Purāṇa*, the demoness and Kāma are both destroyed by fire. Fire, though not mentioned in every description of the *Vasantotsava*, is, as we have seen in the 'killing of Ḍhaunḍhā" episode in the *Bhaviṣya Purāṇa* (132), important to its celebration even into modern times. The effect of the flames is clear: they purify and remove obstructions which may be, variously, the demoness, Kāma, or simply the old year. Ash, symbolically fertile, represents the victory of life over death as it is the essential and potent matter remaining after the process of destruction is complete. Ḍhaunḍhā/Holākā/Pūtanā inflict death and are thereby the feared and fearful symbols of death.

The primary victims of these beings are children, the virginal and innocent carriers of life who, by their conquest of her, thus mark the waning of death and the waxing triumph of new life. In a structural continuum, the annual ritual re-enactment of the destruction of the demoness during the Spring Festival ensures thus the victory of life over death, of fertility over barrenness, of germination over stagnation and of success over futility. With her murder, the seasonal cycles of the earth take their normal course, the children are protected and prosperity is guaranteed for at least another year.

NOTES

1 The use of *āḍāḍa* is fairly obscure. It is a *prākṛt* word meaning 'to exercise strength, to bully, to be high handed.'

2 I have read *āḍāḍākhyatim* as a compound 'known as *āḍāḍa*.'

3 See also the eleventh century AD text, the *Deśīnamāmālā* (VI.82), of Hemachandra which describes this festival as '*Phaggu..*'

4 Hemādri, *Caturvargacintāmaṇi, vrata* ii, pp. 184-90 quoted in Raghavan, *Festivals*, p. 177.

5 Śāradātanaya, *Bhāvaprakāśa*, 111.99.18.

6 *Caraka Saṁhitā Sūtra* 14.61.3 cited by Raghavan, p. 198.

7 *Ibid*

8 The fire is also clearly a fertility symbol: the direction in which the smoke blows is believed to mark the most fertile land in the coming year. When the fire is out and the pot of grain is dug up, the degree to which it is cooked indicates whether or not there will be sufficient food for the next year.

9 The *Holākāmāhātmya* is a text which purports to belong to the *Pātāla Khaṇḍa* of the *Padma Purāṇa* but, in all probability does not. Chatterjee in his *Critical Study of the Padma Purāṇa*, concludes that, due to the numerous references in this text to Kaliṅga (Orissa), it is most likely a work composed there. A manuscript of this text is located in the library of the Bengal Asiatic Society which confirms the above details.

10 Raghavan, *Festivals*, p. 156.

11 It is also reminiscent of the effigy of Kāma which is burnt on this same occasion. In this context the burning of an effigy of Kāma has

been interpreted as symbolic of the conquest of the passions. See L. Mohan, *Telegu Fairs and Festivals* (Hyderabad: 1988) who interprets the burning of Kāma in this way. (p. 65)

12 *Bhāratanāṭyaśāstra*, 1.53f. as cited by Gonda, "The Indra Festival According the Atharvavedins," in J. Gonda, *Selected Studies* (Leiden: 1975), p. 208.

13 *Ibid*

14 Cited by Raghavan, *Festivals*, p. 196.

15 Mani, *Purāṇic Encyclopaedia*, p. 568f.

16 *Mahābhārata*, trans. by J. van Buitenen, II. p. 834, note 25.

17 *Agni Purāṇa*, 12.14-17; *Viṣṇu Purāṇa*, V.5; *Bhāgavata Purāṇa*, p. 155 and *Skanda Purāṇa*, 10.6.

18 S. M. Gupta in *From Daityas to Devatas*, p. 69.

19 *Harivaṁśa*, 50.20 cited by O'Flaherty, *Women*, p. 182.

20 *Bhāgavata Purāṇa* 10.6.1-44; *Harivaṁśa* 50.22; *Padma Purāṇa* 6.245; *Viṣṇu Purāṇa* V.5. Cited by O'Flaherty, *Ibid*, p. 41.

21 *Ibid*, p. 342.

22 *Ibid*, p. 334.

23 S. Kakar, *Inner World* (Delhi: 1981), p. 147.

24 D. Shulman, *Tamil Temple Myths* (Princeton: 1980), p. 235.

25 See 3.230.16 of the Vulgate. Van Buitenen suggests that this rival set of mothers are the birth-mothers of the infants preyed upon by the mothers of Skanda. The *Mahābhārata*, trans., ed. by J. van Buitenen (Chicago: 1975), II. p. 834.

26 *Mahābhārata*, trans. J. van Buitenen, 3.219.14-58.

27 There are, in fact, several links between those beings who threaten children and Skanda. In the *Mahābhārata* (3.213-18) the gods fear Skanda's power and send Indra to kill him. Indra, in turn, having sent the band of Mothers unsuccessfully to kill the child, casts his thunderbolt at Skanda, splitting open his side. From the blow of the thunderbolt young men and maidens were produced who snatch away children. Shulman, *Ibid*, p. 244.

28 E. Hopkins, *Epic Mythology*, p. 229.

29 D. Shulman, *Ibid*, p. 245.

30 V. Turner, *Ritual Process*, p. 172.

31 G. Sutherland, *Yakṣas in Hinduism and Buddhism*, pp. 55-59.

32 *Ibid*, pp. 144-146.

33 P. V. Kane, *History of Dharmaśāstra*, vol. V, p. 237

34 *Ibid*, V. 238.

35 *Varṣakṛtyādīpikā*, pp. 287, 301.

36 It is interesting to note that the spring fire which is lit in association with the burning of Kāma in parts of south India is also

kindled with rubbish. T. Bapat, *Rituals and Festivals of India* (Bombay: 1991), p. 65.

[37] *Nārada Purāṇa,* 124, 76.

[38] *Nāradīya Purāṇa,* 1.124.81 also cited by V. Raghavan, *Festivals,* p. 199.

[39] The association of this myth with the Spring Festival seems to be fairly recent. Raghavan does not give us a textual reference for it. *(Festivals,* p. 196) In S. Stevenson's *Rites of the Twiceborn* (p. 288) the myth is cited in the context of village India and L. Babb in the *Divine Hierarchy* (pp. 16f.) records it in the context of the Spring Festival in Chhattisgarh.

[40] S. Stevenson *Rites of the Twiceborn,* p. 280.

[41] L. Babb, *Divine Hierarchy,* pp. 168f.

[42] S. Stevenson, *op cit.*

[43] Ascetics in the Hindu tradition also take on this mask of ash, symbolic of their break with mundane existence.

10

Virūpākṣavasantotsavacampū

The Spring Festival in Ahobala's *Virūpākṣavasantotsava-campū*[1] is an elaborate and extensive affair which unfolds on site at the Virūpākṣa temple in the ancient city of Hampi, situated in the Hemakūṭa Hills on the southern banks of the Tungabhadra river in the legendary Hindu kingdom of Vijayanagara. Our description is regional and sectarian: the festival is enacted under the auspices of the king of Vijayanagara and in honour of the god Virūpākṣa (Śiva), otherwise referred to as Pampāpati (the husband of Pampā [Pārvatī]).[2] In many respects, the festivities here correspond to those we have come to know as characteristic of spring celebrations: themes of romance, passion and marriage are brought into focus as lord Virūpākṣa is homologized as Kāma, as Virūpākṣa cavorts with the forest ladies in the environs surrounding the city and in the celebration of the eternal indivisibility of that paradigm of marital bliss, Śiva and Pārvatī. Despite these recurring references, many familiar elements which we have come to expect of the spring celebrations are absent here and new features appear. The *Vasantotsava* of the *Campū* is not primarily a festival of love, nor is it a celebration of nature. On the contrary, it is a pageant in consonance with the stalwartness and grandeur of the Vijayanagara kings. As this spectacle of royal prowess unfolds, the official star of the festivities, lord Virūpākṣa, emerges with attributes and habits constitutive of kings; he is both a victorious ruler, a champion of the city, as well as a skillful hunter.[3] The sacred heart of his kingdom is the Virūpākṣa temple and, from this sanctified encampment, his power and influence radiate in all directions. This deity and this king are, in several instances during the course of the celebrations, virtually indistinguishable and one is tempted to suspect that the Vijayanagara monarchs thrived on this sort of ambiguity, deriving much of their influence from their affinity of purpose with that of the major deities in the Hindu pantheon, i.e., expansion of their sphere of influence.

The Axis of Power : The City and The Temple

The Vijayanagara empire, which flourished from approximately the fourteenth to the sixteenth century AD, emerges in historical annals of the medieval and the modern periods as an imperium of which the overarching concern was the preservation of Hindu religion and culture. Islamic invasions of the thirteenth and the fourteenth century AD caused considerable disruption of political and religious life in south India and, throughout the history of Vijayanagara period, its kings struggled for paramountcy against both rival Muslim and Hindu rulers. The monarchs, who founded the empire in the first half of the fourteenth century AD, strove to create and sustain a political and moral order shaped by Hindu cultural values which we might sum up succinctly as the protection of Brahmins and cows.[4]

In 1570 AD the forces of the Sultanates in the Deccan united to destroy the sovereignty of the Vijayanagara kings. For six months the invaders sacked the capital city.[5] Vijayanagara was left in ruins in which condition it remained until recently when it became, under the auspices of Drs. Nagaraja Rao, Michell and Fritz and the Archaeological Survey of India, the centre of an elaborate programme of documentation and reconstruction.

The capital of the empire, Vijayanagara, 'the city of victory,' or Vidyānagara, 'the city of learning,' was one of the most magnificent capitals in medieval India yet, in its early days, Hampi was a small urban agglomeration extending east from the Virūpakṣa temple to the Mataṅga hill and south from the river to the Hemakūṭa hills. From all accounts it became a showpiece of imperial splendour.[6] Inscriptions and literary works belonging to this period compare the city with Ayodhya, the fabled capital of lord Rāma. It was also a cultural centre: Vijayanagara emperors are known to have patronized intellectual pursuits and the arts of music, literature, sculpture and architecture. Hampi and the surrounding countryside is not merely renown for the glory of Vijayanagara, it is also accorded a position of some importance in the tradition of Sanskrit literature. Its name is generally believed to be a later derivation of the Kannada 'Pampā' which, in turn, is both an alternate name of the holy Tungabhadra River as well as a local appellation for the consort of Śiva, Pārvatī.[7] The antiquity of the town and its religious sanctity can be traced to at least as early as the epic age during which, according to the *Rāmāyaṇa*, it was known as Kiṣkindhā, the city ruled by the monkey-chiefs, Sugrīva and Vāli. After Sugrīva was driven out of the city by Vāli, legend has it that he took refuge on the Mataṅga hill, south of the Tungabhadra. Rāma, in search of Sītā who had been abducted by Rāvaṇa, killed Vāli and restored Sugrīva to his kingdom. It was here also where Sītā bathed to remove the impurities accrued in Laṅkā. The city is prominent in Śaiva lore as well: according to the *Pampāmāhātmya*, Pārvatī is said to have performed penance here to win Śiva. Śiva revealed himself to her and their marriage took place on the banks of the Tungabhadra river.[8]. After the wedding, the area came to be known as *Pampākṣetra*, or simply Hampi. Because Śiva in the form of Virūpakṣa dwells here, it is also called *Virūpākṣatīrtha* (the sacred arena of lord Śiva).[9]

Ahobala, the author of our *Campū*, refers often to the hallowed place of Hampi in the Sanskritic geography of India. He calls it variously the southern Kaśī, the Kailāsa of this world, constructed by Śiva or Amarāvatī, the city of

Indra (p.12, 14, 55). Central to our description of the *Vasantotsava* as contained in this *Campū*, to the city of Hampi and to the Vijayanagara empire is the temple of Virūpakṣa. The Vijayanagara kings championed a variety of Hindu cults, including that of Virūpakṣa at Hampi.[10] Today the Virūpākṣa temple is the only major functioning sacred complex at Vijayanagara.[11] Chariot festivals are still celebrated to commemorate the betrothal and marriage of Virūpākṣa and Pampā. Indeed, historically the two celebrations to dominate the Virūpakṣa temple calendar are the betrothal of Śiva and Pārvatī and their subsequent marriage.[12] It is the separation and reunion of these two deities, together with many additional rites that our text describes under the title of the *Vasantotsava*. The spring festivities here in the *Campū* are celebrated, then, in association with a specific temple (the Virūpākṣa temple in Hampi), in honour of a specific deity (Virūpākṣa) and officiated at by priests. It is further clear that the relationship between the deity enshrined in the temple and the early kings of Vijayanagara was one of intimacy: the early rulers regarded themselves as representatives of Virūpākṣa and later rulers even signed documents in his name.[13] It is also clear that the deity enshrined in the temple is connected to the terrain outside of the city of Hampi, most likely as a tribal or folk deity. According to our text, on the occasion of the *Vasantotsava*, lord Virūpākṣa crosses the Tungabhadra river and enters the forest on the other side of its banks. There, in private, he meets celestial ladies. The domain of Virūpākṣa in this context is parallel to the domain of kings rival to those of Vijayanagara. Though Virūpākṣa's links with the forests outside of Hampi are clear, it is, in our *Campū*, the temple of Virūpākṣa that dominates the festivities, absorbing the cult of Virūpākṣa into the *purāṇic* and royal traditions of king and kingdom, but never quite eliminating what seem to be folk origins of the deity.

The main purport of our *Campū* is not to tell a story but to describe the *Vasantotsava* and, more likely, to extol the virtues of the king and the *purāṇic* Śaiva tradition.[14] Our description functions as reportage: Ahobala writes with attention to minute detail as if he himself had witnessed its performance. His *Virūpākṣavasantotsavacampū* describes a *Vasantotsava*, referred to variously as *Vasantotsava, Caitrotsava, Rathotsava, Mṛgayotsava* and *Virūpākṣadevamahotsava* which is said to last for nine days in spring.[15] It is a work in four chapters. The first two chapters and the beginning of the third chapter are lost. What remain are parts of Chapter three which describe the Chariot Festival (*Rathotsava)* on the *Paurṇimā* (full moon) and Chapter four which contains a description of the Hunt Festival (*Mṛgayotsava*). This latter chapter also details, following the *Mṛgayotsava*, the ritualized estrangement and subsequent reconciliation and re-union of Virūpakṣa and his consort, Pampā.

Chapter Three:
The Festival of the Chariot *(Rathotsava)*

The extant section of our text begins with a description of the people who have gathered to witness the car festival (*Rathotsava*) and who offer fruits for worship. The weather is hot and many take advantage of the cool river (the Tungabhadra), seating themselves in the midst of the flowing holy waters on slabs of stones. The 'chariot dragging' proper commences with the command of the *ṛtvigs* (priests) who first offer an oblation into the fire and then proceed to offer *bāli* in honour of the movable festival image of Śiva which has the form of the *liṅga* (*capalaṁ śivaliṅgamūrtim*).[16] The massive and auspicious chariot of Śiva is described: it is adorned with a high central pillar on top of which a jar of gold is placed, reminiscent of the full moon rising behind a mountain.[17] The gigantic car has four carved archways, all of which are painted and decorated with doll-like female images (*śālābhañjikā*) as well as other protective images.[18] People begin to decorate the chariot by strewing it with flags representative of the power of the god Virūpakṣa. They also bring ropes by which the car is to be pulled.[19]

It is now noon and very hot. People are warming up for the main festivities. In the bazaar, articles to propitiate

Virūpākṣa and his consort Pampā are being sold (ghee and other consumables) while Brahmins are employed to enter the temple to perform the devotions (*pūjā*) for Pampādeva. Ahobala takes time to describe the multitudes who have assembled to witness the festival. He focuses particularly on the Brahmins in attendance who seem to be of variable character: many are wealthy, yet they greedily take advantage of the legionary crowds, anticipating the gold coins they will receive as payment (*dakṣiṇā)* for performing services for the mobs.[20] So, for example, one such Brahmin, when he discovers that some of his relatives are coming from a nearby village to attend the celebrations, worriedly contemplates the expense of entertaining them. To fortify his capital reserves, he hires out his services to wealthy merchants, agreeing to perform *pūjā* in the temple of Virūpākṣa for customers and afterwards, to offer them *prasāda* of the deity. Rather than purchasing the necessary accoutrements for the *pūjā*, the Brahmin enters the temple and offers the image only water. The merchants who he has thus cheated apprehend him emerging empty-handed from the temple, without the requisite *prasāda*: however, somehow he manages to slip away. Other Brahmins are indifferent to the proceedings: some bask in the shade awaiting the main events; some occupy their time visiting numerous holy sites in the environs surrounding the city; still others are busy in their houses donning silk clothes and other costly festival garments.

A number of kings are also in attendance and Ahobala's description of these sovereigns, their tributaries and their retinues who line the city streets awaiting the *Rathotsava* to begin, is detailed. Monks, forest dwellers and *yogins* wearing garlands of *rudrākṣa* beads (beads sacred to Śiva), their bodies covered with ash, have also assembled in anticipation of this event. These religiously-minded people are described as motivated by the desire to attain *mokṣa* (p. 12), or as simply collectors of merit through performance of prescribed *Vedic* rituals, including the *Agnihotra*. They donate money to the temple and worship Virūpakṣa by dancing. Those members of the fourth caste (*turīyavarṇa*), i.e., *śūdras*, who are prohibited from entering the city streets, wait on the terraces of towering buildings outside the urban core, on the city ramparts or in trees, eager to catch a glimpse of the celebrations.

The beating of the drums and the ringing of bells commence at the command of the temple priest and this signals the beginning of the festival proper. Hordes of people surge towards the temple. White flags are unveiled and waved until the city is amass with them like the foam from the churning of the ocean of milk. The images of Śiva and Pārvatī are decorated and transported to the doorway of the temple. Brahmins wave lights before the images which are in turn circumambulated three times. Simultaneously, other officials strike sticks together and fan the images. Offerings of fruits and flowers are proffered through the media of priests (*devārcaka*) while *prasāda* of flowers is distributed to the swarming droves of people gathered there.

The car is brought out of the temple. The image of Śiva is placed on a pillow atop a pedestal inlaid with gems and then hoisted onto the car by means of pulleys. The ropes are described as aides to devotion, as if they were strings of *bhakti* which pull the god towards the devotee. Thus can Śiva, though hard to attain, be drawn nearer by the thread of love. Raising the image onto the temple chariot becomes itself a form of *sādhanā*, a meditation. All of the people fold their hands in reverence when they catch sight of the icon ascending the car. The priest secures the images of both Śiva and Pārvatī inside the vehicle.[21]

The learned preceptor Vidyāraṇya[22] and his pupils accompany Virūpākṣa atop the temple car where they worship the images. As Śaiva Brahmins take up the ropes to pull the car, people toss offerings of fruit, coconuts and water into the air until the vehicle is completely covered. Although these Brahmins strain and pull to make the chariot move, it remains stationary. The king's assistance is solicited to set the car in motion:

> O lord, if you come near the car; if you prostrate yourself before it respectfully, if you offer fruit, it will surely move. (p. 21)

With much pomp, the sovereign descends from his palace and humbles himself completely in front of the chariot. He presents an offering to the deity and then tugs at the rope. Miraculously the car begins to move and clatters, stopping and starting down the temple avenue; drums beat furiously, bugles blare, hands clap, the crowds shout 'Mahādeva! Mahādeva!' In places the mass of people is too thick for movement. Other princes and tributaries of the king join the procession mounted on elephants and horses. A few individuals in the crowds are struck by fruits hurled at the temple car and those injured slow the movement of the chariot. Clouds of heavy dust arise from the fervor of the mob and the jerking and straining of the car which quickly gains momentum, now appearing to be advancing on its own accord. Brahmins pulling the car roar 'Śiva! Śaṅkara! Lord! Great God!' and begin running to remain close to the chariot. Unable to arrest the careening car, they appeal to Śiva to bring it to a standstill in the middle of the street. Swarms of people instantly engulf the arrested vehicle bringing fresh water for the Brahmins, who drink greedily and begin fanning themselves with the ends of their garments. These Brahmins, now at a halt, recuperate from their toil by reciting passages from holy texts (*Śrutis*) and engaging in learned conversation with one another.

Meantime, while the Brahmins are thus occupied, a certain wealthy merchant known as Pampārya has constructed his own car and is preparing to mount his own *Rathotsava*. He has consecrated it by rites prescribed by the *Śaiva Āgamas* and placed upon it two images, one of Śiva and one of Pārvatī. Pampārya has recruited fellow merchants and also *śūdras* to drag his car through the streets. This latter car, the merchant/*śūdra* car, accelerates rapidly down the avenue, threatening to overtake the Brahmin car. These latter, still occupied with cooling themselves with fruit and drink, finally notice that the car towed by both merchants and *śūdras*, is swiftly approaching. The Brahmins leap to their feet and resume their positions manning the ropes of their vehicle, straining to set it in motion.

Vaiṣṇava Brahmins now join with Śaivas, bolstering the Brahmin forces and these united legions somehow manage to impel the Brahmin car towards its destination at the end of the street. The Brahmin chariot triumphs reaching the boulder on the Mataṅga hill in advance of that of the merchants/*śūdras*. In unison, the Brahmins congratulate themselves on their victory and eulogize Nandi,[23] the faithful devotee of lord Śiva, for maintaining his vigilance over lord Virūpākṣa and warning him of the approach of *daityas* (demons) who live on the other side of Mataṅga hill. Several heretics have gathered there for the express purpose of ridiculing Śiva and they are described.[24] These Bauddhas are swiftly driven away by the faithful crowds. The movers of the two cars, the merchant/*śūdra* car and the Brahmin car, engage each other in a verbal battle and *kṣatriyas*, in alliance with the Brahmins, both Śaiva and Vaiṣṇava (p. 23), assault the former denouncing them as enemies of Śiva, as merchants who attend the festival merely for financial gain and as *śūdras* who ultimately despise Śiva. During the verbal combat there is much clapping and snorting and hullabaloo amongst the swarms of people assembled there.

In preparation for the return journey to the temple, the ropes of the car are removed and attached to its other side. The images are also rotated so that they now face the temple.[25] It is evening and the car returns to the temple with great pomp and fanfare. Mobs of people jam the streets making movement impossible.

The merits of this festival including *kāma artha, dharma* and *mokṣa* are enumerated.[26] The setting of the sun is described. The king of Vidyānagara, the city of learning, circumambulates the car thrice and receives *prasāda* of lord Virūpākṣa. Following the *pūjā* and the distribution of *prasāda*, the images are brought down from the car and prepared for re-entry into the temple. A rich merchant provides lights and now the adjoining hills are illuminated. The waving of lights before the images is performed to remove any impurity incurred by the images on their sojourn outside the temple; more offerings are presented to the deities; courtesans (*vāravanitā)* entertain the crowds by dancing; and pots of gold are offered to the deities. The images are taken inside the temple and worshipped. At last the *Rathotsava* is at an end and all participants return to their homes.

The King in his City

Our description thus far is clearly dominated by the temple, the deity enshrined therein and the crowds who have gathered in the town of Hampi to witness the celebrations of spring. Here the *Vasantotsava* is composed of a *Rathotsava*. This festival of the chariot is a spectacle, a public display of the imperial magnificence linking both the deity and the king. The centre of this kingdom, the temple, is clearly the locus of power from which the eminence of the deity as well as the eminence of the king radiates. It is this centre from which the deity emerges, surveys his kingdom and to which he returns. The temple is where lord Virūpākṣa customarily receives visitors but, on the occasion of the *Rathotsava*, he ventures outside the temple compound, into the public sphere. This territory, this city is his kingdom and on this journey Virūpākṣa reinforces his claim to it as well as to the loyalty of his subjects. Ahobala places much emphasis on the crowds and the accompanying hullabaloo created when the deities emerge from the confines of the temple and journey to the end of the temple street and back again. The mobs react wildly, awed by the magnificence of Virūpākṣa's visage and by the spectacle of his conveyance. Virūpākṣa's sojourn resembles the post-battle victory march of the king as much as it resembles the annual imperial procession in which the ruler simultaneously re-establishes, symbolically, his sovereignty over a particular territory while laying claim to the loyalty of his subjects. The deity is virtually indistinguishable from the king in appearance, donning many of the attributes of accoutrement and retinue customarily assigned to kings. While both deity and king venture out of their confined quarters, they remain clearly aloof from the crowds: the deity high above the masses on his *ratha*; the ruler towering above them on his elephant. Two processes are set in motion here: the 'royalization' of gods and the 'deification' of kings.[27] By closely associating the two, this festival, this royal display, serves both to legitimize and consolidate the power of the king who is the temporal embodiment of the power of the deity and, at the same time, imbues and imparts to the deity a royal stature.

We know from previous textual descriptions that kings play vital roles in this festival. It is difficult to discern whether the emphasis placed on the king in this *Campū* is due to the eminent role he is accorded in the proceedings and resulting from the power that is inherent in his stature or whether our author, Ahobala, is being simply adulatory as regards his monarch. Our description is clear: the festival proceeds and succeeds because of the king's involvement and under his auspices. This accords with not only descriptions we have encountered elsewhere concerning the Spring Festival, but with the royal traditions associated with Vijayanagara kings as well.[28]

The power of this king extends both to the temporal and non-temporal orders. Royal symbols abound displaying regal prominence: the king's army and his flags are ubiquitous as he leads the procession on a royal elephant, his fellow kings submissively in attendance. There is no question on whom the life, prosperity and safety of this city depend. Although this king among men is alone necessary and able to move the car housing the great god Śiva and his consort Pārvatī, he completely and publicly submits to Śiva when he literally prostrates himself before the chariot. The king takes on the role of servant-devotee in recognition of and submission to Śiva's great power. In so doing he serves first as a role model for his subjects, an ideal devotee and second, he illustrates the supremacy of his power in that only his actions produce results, i.e., the car moves. These movements establish the king as not only the focal point of his kingdom, but also as one who can affect the cosmic order. Our text thus locates the king as mediator between people and gods. This conjunction of royal with religious power, the celebration of ritual sovereignty with the divine mission of the king, establishes authority and lends substance to royal claims to it.

The festival chariot housing the icons of Śiva and Pārvatī is described at length. Although the form taken by Pārvatī is not detailed, it is the iconographic form of Śiva, here a *liṅga* with five faces, which is worshipped. This icon is clearly a representation of Śiva in his creative mode as the *liṅga* is both a symbol of creation and procreation. Indeed, this is accentuated by the high central pillar upon which a jar of gold is placed (p.2). The text alludes to this imagistically as the full moon rising behind a mountain, an allusion wherein both the moon and the jar of gold contain *amṛta*, the potent nectar of immortality, the seminal elixer of life *par excellence*.[29] Further, the icons are surrounded and protected by paintings of female figures who represent the army of lustful Kāma. Surely, this conjunction of images is a clear and potent visual signifier of the themes of renewal and rejuvenation which are the very substance and heart of the festival.

Virūpākṣa's subjects, however, are hardly a unified body and there are numerous indications of rivalry amongst them of both a sectarian and a caste variety. Ahobala emphasizes the segregation and conflict between castes, a social rivalry distinctive from all other descriptions we have examined thus far. At the commencement of festivities in the *Campū*, *śūdras*, although eager to participate in the festival, are required to remain outside the city walls, excluded from the celebrations. As a united front, Śaiva and Vaiṣṇava Brahmins marshal their strength, revoking for the moment sectarian divisions and join forces with one another against the rival *vaiśya/śūdra* chariot. A broad range of Brahmins attend the festival: low ones, hard ones, charitable ones, pious ones and the like (p.21). Thus the festival, while blurring sectarian divisions, is not immune to other sorts of social antipathies. The inter-caste rivalry, in this case between Brahmins and merchants, manifests itself in a race between the two festival chariots.[30] The theme of dueling chariots becomes a ritualized re-enactment of battle and it is clear from the beginning of the race that the sanctified temple chariot will be the winner. The race reflects of course the victory of one caste over another as well as a victory of the *siatus quo* (Brahmins over *śūdras* and *vaiśyas*). More than this, however, in the context of the *Vasantotsava*, the race may be symbolic of the ultimate victory of Spring. Finally, the rigid reinforcement of caste divisions confirms what we know of extreme Vijayanagara orthodoxy. Historically, the strengthening of caste lines seems to have been a common response to threats from outside (e.g., Islam), the Sena dynasty in Bengal providing an earlier example. Vijayanagara kings themselves were constantly under pressure from rival states and their response was to struggle to unite their kingdom against these opposing forces. One obvious way to accomplish this goal was to enhance the status of Brahmins who had a vested interest in maintaining the *status quo*. At the zenith of the political hierarchy stands the king. By bolstering the image of Brahmins, by according them special status *vis-à-vis* their relationship to the deity, the king reinforces his own position and indeed our text would indicate that the king of our *Campū*, like Śiva on the *ratha*, continues pre-eminent.

Chapter Four: The Hunt Festival (*Mṛgayotsava*)

Delighted by Ahobala's account of the *Rathotsava*, the king directs him to continue. Our poet complies with a description of the people who are hurrying to the site where the remaining ritual proceedings are about to take place. In this final chapter Ahobala will describe the Hunt Festival (*Mṛgayāmahotsava*) wherein Śiva as Gaṅgādhara and the lord of the Hemakūṭa mountain, in the guise of a hunter, rides out on horseback, abandoning Gaurī. [He will also describe the ritual reunion of Śiva and Pārvatī.]

First, the *abhiṣeka* of the *liṅga* of Virūpākṣadeva[31] and the morning rites prescribed by the temple priest (*devārcaka*) are performed. Though the temple is dense with devotees, still more people, some of them in tears, try frantically for a glimpse of the deity. In the courtyard of the temple celebrants prostrate themselves in front of Pārvatī (Bhavānī), the Goddess Earth (Bhuvaneśvarī) and Sarasvatī (Vāgdevatā).[32]

The city is aflurry with people and travellers from the surrounding hills moving in and out of the city, shopping for clothes and vessels. It is now so congested that some pilgrims decide to defer their departure and call upon the hospitality of their kinsmen. Some of those who are going home make their way out of the city, glancing back at the *gopura* of the Śiva temple and chanting 'O Lord Pampā! Hara! Hara!' (58. 12-15)[33]

While the majority of people in the city are busying themselves in these ways awaiting the commencement of the *Mṛgayotsava*, Ahobala calls our attention to two friends who have decided to take advantage of the lull in the festival proceedings to take a short excursion outside the city where they explore the Śaiva sites located on the opposite banks of the Pampā (Tungabhadra) river. These two friends are identified as the son of a minister of King Śrīrāśideśa (the minister's son),[34] and a Brahmin poet.[35] They cross the river and enter a great wooded area, losing their way in the dense growth several times. The Brahmin, fearing the wildness of the forest, prays to the lord Virūpakṣa to save him from ferocious beasts residing there. He is consoled by his friend and stops for a moment to glance back at the temple of Virūpākṣadeva. The sight of the flagpole (*dhvajastaṁbha*) and the great *gopura* of the temple reassures him and, uttering the words 'Hara! Hara! Mahādeva!' (59. 24), he proceeds into the forest reciting, 'Protect me! O Great Lord!' (60. 9)

At last the two companions, realizing that much time has past, hasten to retrace their steps. As they near the edge of the forest, a huge tiger who has caught their scent lets out a roar, shakes its tail and crouches down, preparing to attack.[36] The frightened poet prays to God Virūpakṣa and miraculously a huntsman in royal dress suddenly appears mounted on a horse, sword in hand and saves them by killing the tiger. The poet extols the horseman as god himself and the latter gives him a signet ring inscribed with the name of Śrīvirūpākṣadeva.[37] The poet requests Virūpakṣa to escort them safely back to the river separating the forest from the city. On reaching Pampā their divine escort vanishes, whereupon the poet comprehends that it was Śiva himself who was responsible for their rescue, the ring with the Śiva's name on it confirming his suppositions. They cross the river and stop for twilight rites (*saṅdhyāvandana*).

While performing these rites, they overhear the voices of some divine ladies dallying in the nearby groves of the forest. Ahobala tells us that these divine women, having espied Lord Śiva riding through the forest, had journeyed to this place, overpowered by desire to cavort with him. The ladies bemoan the fact that Śiva is constantly accompanied by Pārvatī and they are delighted to find him singularly alone. They articulate their desire for his embrace and proceed to praise him: his toenails, they say, are like pearl strings on the parts of ladies' hair; the *Vedas* flow from his feet and contact with his body is akin to attaining knowledge imparted by a teacher; he is the entire universe, the destroyer and reviver of Kāma, independent of all rites and compassionate towards his devotees. The damsels entreat him not to abandon or ignore them, reminding him that Kṛṣṇa did not so treat the *gopīs*. The mere sight of Śiva, appearing in human form for the benefit of the Brahmin, his devotee, has produced in them, they say, an excess of passion. Though it is unacceptable for a woman of noble family to desire another man, these divine women consider it their good fortune that Śiva has appeared here, without Pārvatī. They extoll him as even more beautiful than Kāma, as *ardhanārīśvara* (70. 18) and they enumerate some of his incarnations including Mohinī (70. 17), a form assumed to deceive the demons; a beggar collecting alms; a lover of the wives of the sages (70. 16); and a lover of Śakti (70. 16).

In answer to their entreaties Śiva dismounts, creates the seasons according to the women's wishes and cavorts with them. Śiva becomes Kāma, taking on various attractive forms according to each woman's desire, singing songs and generally enjoying himself by making love with these heavenly damsels (to their mutual satisfaction).[38]

Gaṅgā, the daughter of the Himālaya and the greatest among the heavenly ladies, we are told, was on this occasion particularly favoured by Śiva. She pleads with him to let her accompany him and he assents, thinking 'I shall take away this very beautiful lady and keep her on my head.' (71. 19) With Gaṅgā seated comfortably in his hair and, sated at last by the love of the damsels, lord Pampāpati (Śiva) directs the heavenly women to return to their homes, mounts his horse and returns speedily to the city of Pampā, anticipating Pārvatī's anger at his extended absence.

The moon has now risen and the Brahmin, still on the banks of the river, spies a horseman in the distance crossing the river. Convinced that the horseman is Śiva, he and his companion rush back to the city, eager to partake in the Hunt Festival. Once there, these two friends approach and worship the icon of Śiva which is now situated in the streets in the garb of a hunter and mounted on a horse. The image (*mūrti*) of Dvijarājaśekhara (Śiva) is described as adorned with the attributes of royalty; as, for example, a king *(Rājaśekhara)*, a great king with vassals *(Mahāśekhara)* and a sovereign king *(Mahāsāmrājya)*.[39]

Śiva now returns to the temple to seek out Pārvatī. She refuses to see him, retreating into a sacred hall prepared especially for the festival. The image of Pārvatī is hidden and Śiva and his party pursue the goddess, trying to force their way inside. The two parties, those devotees of Śiva and those devotees of Pārvatī, throw sweets at each other and Śiva and Pārvatī engage in verbal battle. The author describes this battle at length. At first the reluctance of Pārvatī to see Śiva is explained by her shyness which is natural, we are told, to one who is inexperienced in marital life but ultimately Śiva and Śivā[40] are inseparable (both are androgynous). Śiva and Pārvatī are then worshipped separately and the stories of Śiva are retold all night long.

The next day is the last day of the festival. The argument of Śiva and Pārvatī continues. Śiva knocks at the door and Pārvatī asks this visitor to identify himself. Śiva replies variously, trying to impress her with his great accomplishments: he is *nīlakaṇṭha, girīśa, triśūlī* and *sthāṇu*.[41] Each time Pārvatī responds with a rebuke and, noticing Gaṅgā ensconced in Śiva's hair, she accuses him of infidelity. Śiva denies that he has been with other women in the forest and resorts now to praising Pārvatī by describing her beauty, her fidelity, her innocence. When

Pārvatī still refuses to open the door, Śiva plays on her sympathies. 'O Pārvatī!' laments Śiva, 'my heart belongs to you and this body of mine serves Pampā, knowing it to be another of your auspicious incarnations. It is now ornamented with paste, it is wet with the sweat of fatigue from riding a great swift horse through the forest to punish the wicked and to protect the good. My body is covered with the marks of several crescent moons, but these are the result of the claws of a tiger which pounced upon me. You accuse me of infidelity without foundation!' Pārvatī begins to mellow as Śiva now admits his dependence on this Goddess: without her he is without support, he has no form, he is unable to create progeny. He suggests even that he become androgynous (*ardhanārīśvara*).

Pārvatī is pacified and at that moment Brahmins as well become happy and they hurry to open the door separating the two images. The crowds are allowed to approach the images and the Śaiva priest transports Śiva quickly into the main temple. The icon of Pārvatī is then placed on a plank adjacent to the icon of Śiva. Everyone offers garlands of fruits and flowers uttering praises of Śiva and Pārvatī as follows:

> We are thoroughly satisfied seeing Śiva and Pārvatī together at last. We are happy! O Lord! Vibhu! Śiva! Granter of grace! Protect us, your devotees! (80. 11-12)

Śiva becomes *ardhanārīśvara* whereupon the two images are placed together on the same platform and are well-known with flowers and coloured powder. Likewise, the priest throws powder on the Brahmins in the crowd. The images are then taken to the river, bathed and thence conveyed back into the temple accompanied by Brahmins reciting the *Vedas*. It is now dark.[42] The images of Śiva and Pārvatī are decorated with garlands of red flowers, *kuṁkuma*, sandal powder, ashes, ornaments and white clothes; their foreheads are marked with musk paste. *Dakṣiṇā* is distributed to Brahmins who are busy reciting *mantras* for blessings. The priests of Śiva and Pārvatī respectively continue to decorate the *mūrtis* and present money to each deity which, in turn, is distributed to Brahmins.

Śaivas then raise the platform and convey it from house to house. Courtesans dance for lord Śiva, the husband of Rati and *prasāda* is placed into the hands of devotees. The city is alive with the sounds of Kāma: amorous songs and dances are performed; dramas with reference to erotic sentiments are enacted by those conversant with sports of kings' ladies and songs in praise of sovereign kings are sung by expert bards.[43] The streets are overflowing with people as the Śaiva priests hasten to return the platform back to the temple. Women dance in front of the images as they pass through the door of great *gopura*.[44] The pedestal is now set down near the glimmering golden flagpost in the courtyard whereupon the deities at the flagpost are invoked. This procedure marks the end of the festival.

The chief priest, invoking Nandi and declaring that Virūpākṣadeva had completed the requirements (*dīkṣā*) for the festival, lowers the bull-bannered flag. Everyone is satisfied and they clap their hands shouting, 'Hara! Hara! Mahādeva!' Hearing the din, people elsewhere surmise that the flag of Nandi had been lowered and the festival has come to a close. The ceremony of waving lights is performed and more offerings of flowers and fruits are presented to the deities. Brahmins, kings, teachers, poets and others receive the *prasāda*.

The images of Śiva and Pārvatī are then lifted up and rotated to face the *śivaliṅga*, the original image of Śrīvirūpākṣadeva, the lord of Pampā. Seeing his own reflection, Virūpākṣadeva becomes delighted, promising to be ever-present in the two ancient images. The king of Vidyānagara, the greatest of Virūpākṣa's devotees, receives *prasāda* of a jasmine garland entwined on a crown studded with gems which he then places on the head of the *śivaliṅga*. Still more offerings are proffered to Śiva and Pārvatī, the eternal couple, mother and father of the entire universe: sweet dishes prepared with milk and sugar and drown in ghee, dishes sweetened with honey and garlands of jasmine flowers are brought by Brahmin temple servants. In turn, these offerings are given as *prasāda* to the devotees who prostrate themselves in devotion. Everyone, including the Brahmins, is very happy, having completed this great sacrifice of the spring festival, the duration of which is nine nights, and they then all return home. Early the next day, the morning rituals in honour of Pampāpati are performed. Crowds of people still flock to the temple to see the image of lord Pampā and to take *prasāda* before returning to their villages outside the city.[45]

The text then closes by informing the reader that the *Vasantotsava* is a yearly festival performed on the full moon day of Madhu (Caitra).

The Śaiva Tradition and the *Vasantotsava*

A wealth of Śaiva mythology is drawn upon here and is entwined with the ritual celebration of the Spring Festival. The pervasive reference to the *purāṇic* Śaiva tradition establishes its paramountcy in the context of the worship of Virūpākṣa and more specifically in the context of the Vijayanagara empire. This chapter of the *Campū* is comprised of a Hunt Festival (*Mṛgayotsava)* in which Śiva (Virūpākṣa) appears as the locus of activity, an interlude in the forest, a quarrel between Śiva and Pārvatī, and the subsequent reunion of this cosmic couple. Śiva appears in two forms concurrently: one, as a static festival image in the attire of a hunter and mounted on a horse vehicle (*vāhana)* in the streets of the city; and two, as an active agent in the forest protecting his devotees and sporting with women.

As a hunter, particularly in the midst of the city of Vijayanagara, the deity is figuratively identified with the king whose fondness for such sports is . Virūpākṣa's foray into the forest becomes both a royal as well as a divine expedition as the actions and demeanor of Virūpākṣa (Śiva) are in consonance with those of the king. Both extend their influence beyond the banks of the Tungabhadra and into the untamed forest regions: Virūpākṣa by identifying the wooded territories as the abode of the same deity who resides in the temple (Śiva); the king who, by extension, identifies the forest as royal domain, as the hunting ground of the king.

Śiva, the royal hunter, is mounted upon a horse in the streets of Hampi and simultaneously, it seems, materializes in the forest. Here he kills a tiger in an act that is both protective and aggressive. His aggressive character is traceable to Rudra, one of the violent forms of Śiva. The association of Rudra with the heroic and warrior tradition is well-known as is his ancient identification with forests and mountain terrain.[46] Stella Kramrisch in her cosmological interpretation of Śiva as the 'Wild Hunter' in the 'pre-cosmic wilderness,' locates the meaning of this manifesation in the context of an original, primordial, paradigmatic myth of creation.[47] Implicit in this act of creation is violence, is Rudra, whose aggressive act results from disruption and leads to the disintegration of the state of wholeness, the state of undifferentiated pre-cosmic totality.[48] For example, Kramrisch says:

> Creation departs from the perfection of the unconditioned state. Creation was flawed from the moment of its origin...Rudra, the fierce god, the guardian of the Uncreate, arose himself as protector of the sacred order - the guardian of cosmic rhythms and human rites. (pp. 30-31)

Śiva as the Hunter, through his form as Rudra, is thus linked to the creation of the cosmos.

If we accept Kramrisch's equation, we must then interpret our Śiva 'the Hunter' as the bridge between the modes of creation engendered by the festival of spring and the modes of the cosmic creation/recreation of the universe. This bridge extends into mythic events as each year, with the enactment of the spring festival celebrations, Śiva appears manifest as originator thus re-establishing and reinforcing creation in the terrestrial arena.

Śiva 'the Hunter' is strong, virile, aggressive, preeminently male and as such is the deity of choice for the like-minded Vijayanagara kings. The Lord of the Cosmos, Śiva, and the terrestrial Lord of Vijayanagara, the king, fulfill their obligations and make their presence felt in like ways. As Śiva protects and keeps from harm the Brahmin poet and the minister's son, so too must the king aggressively maintain the harmonious continuance of the lives of all of his people, particularly, however, his socially powerful Brahmin subjects and the *kṣatriya* subjects who comprise his army and ministerial core. As Śiva confronts the tiger, confronts menacing and threatening forces, so too must the king wage battle against those who live outside his kingdom, in the wilderness, fending off aggressors and establishing order, safety and dominance.[49] The forest is clearly Virūpākṣa's creative and procreative domain, perhaps his original home and he must abandon both temple and city, crossing the expansive Pampā River in order to get there. This river clearly demarcates the edge of the city, the edge of the sphere of influence of both the king and the temple deity (Śiva). Too, it is a boundary demarcating the wilderness, the beginning of the natural order, Virūpākṣa's sphere of influence.[50]

In the *Campū*, this forest is ascribed with attributes and motifs which liken it to one of Śiva's favourite abodes as described in the *purāṇas*. Śiva appears at ease in this habitat and here he encounters the divine *apsaras* women. This encounter with the forest women locates Virūpākṣa, the deity of the forest and of the hunt within the Sanskrit and *purāṇic* tradition by virtue of the similarities between like narratives in which we find Śiva, the libertine, constantly under suspicion of being unfaithful to Pārvatī.[51] In a similar episode from another source, Śiva attracted the sages' wives to him in the Pine Forest whereupon they engaged in conduct both scandalous and debauched. In the *Campū* he is described by the *apsaras* women as more beautiful even than Kāma and, indeed, Śiva is referred to specifically as Kāma, the god of love, when he takes on the male form which each woman finds most desirable. We are told that he is overheard engaged in love-making with them, fulfilling their desires. In the Pine Forest myth from the *Brāhmāṇḍa Purāṇa*,[52] Śiva enters the forest:

> His body was pale and the ashes smeared on it; he was naked, and all his identifying marks were defaced; his hair was disordered and loose; he had

> enormous pointed teeth; his hands were busy with fire-brands, and his eyes were red and tawny. His penis and testicles were like red chalk, the tip ornamented with black and white chalk. Sometimes he laughed horribly; sometimes he sang, smiling; sometimes he danced erotically; sometimes he yelled again and again. As he was dancing, their wives became bewitched immediately and stood in his way as he came into the hermitage and begged for alms over and aver again. (Hindu Myths, p. 142)

This picture of Śiva in his erotic form is hardly seductive but it does present him as super-charged sexually. Śiva's dalliances in the forest with the *apsaras* women is an emphatic allusion to his 'phallic' presence in the phenomenal world and although he is not described in the *Campū* in the above manner, we can assume that a likeness is intended when he is in this mode in the pristine forest across the Pampā. Indeed, we may suppose that his relationship with Gaṅgā, the most beautiful of these *apsaras* women, is of the same ilk as was his relationship with the sages' wives. That Gaṅgā's descent onto Śiva's head, Gaṅgā's union with Śiva, occurs in the virgin wilderness is surely a sanctification and a Sanskritization of this territory.[53] The association of Virūpākṣa with the *apsaras* women and with the goddess Gaṅgā thus locates this deity in framework of Sanskrit legend. Hence, just as the Vijayanagara kings sought to expand their royal sphere of influence by absorbing rival kingdoms, so too the cult of Śiva might be viewed here, through its dominance of what are clearly wilderness territories,[54] as incorporating and subsuming local deities into the *purāṇic* tradition.

As Chapter four unfolds these sanskritic associations are reinforced: in a typical *purāṇic* scenario Śiva's sexual demeanor is seen to be inadequate *vis-à-vis* his relationship with Pārvatī. She is clearly unimpressed with the actions of her spouse for, after all, she is the Great Goddess, her domain is the temple.[55] Śiva succeeds in affecting a reconciliation with Pārvatī only when he becomes *ardhanārīśvara*: half-male, half-female. This androgynous form

7. Swinging
Jodhpur, early 19th century

assumed by Śiva is the product of either a highly sexual act or a form without sexual connotations. Thus, either the male and female (Śiva and Pārvatī) are fused in the sexual act of consummation, are 'hybridized' as it were, becoming the male/female androgynous being; or neither the male nor the female aspect is asserted in this form, resulting in an essentially neuter, non-sexual being. In the sexual/hybridized state, the iconic representation of this being is in sympathy with the aims of the festival as sexual union is a prerequisite act for procreation which ensures the on-going regeneration of the universe.[56] Thus, this androgynous form of Śiva appears here in the *Campū*, as he does most often in Hindu myth, in the creative act.[57] However, the second possibility, the androgynous a-sexual Śiva is not as powerless as we might suppose as this fused being becomes representative of the transcendent, having overcome the duality and separation of male and female. Their symbiotic relationship is cemented through marriage, a domesticating or 'civilizing' process wherein Pārvatī functions as the medium through which Virūpākṣa takes his place in the ordered cosmos, inside the temple. It is through such Sanskritic manoeuvres, absorptions and realignments such as those which seem to relocate Virūpākṣa of the temple may be validated.

NOTES

[1] Ahobala, *Virūpākṣavasantotsavacampū*, intro. by V.R.S. Panchamukhi (Dharwar: 1953). All citations refer to this edition by page and line number.

[2] 'Virūpakṣa' is one of Śiva's epithets as, for example, in the *Kumārasambhava* of Kālidāsa. It is also the name of two members of the royal family who ruled Vijayanagara in the fifteenth century AD. See R. Sewell, *A Forgotten Empire* (Reprint; Delhi: 1962), pp. 94, 95.

[3] It may be that the deity Virūpākṣa has connections with tribal deities belonging to the forest regions outside of Hampi.

[4] See, for example, S.K. Devī, *Religion in Vijayanagara Empire* (New Delhi: 1990), p. 17. Although there is no doubt that Vijayanagara kings favoured Hindu customs and practices, at the same time, given the besieged circumstances of the empire, it is to be noted that they were remarkably tolerant, patronizing simultaneously Buddhist, Jain and Islamic sects. See B. Stein, *New Cambridge History of India, I.2 Vijayanagara*, for an interpretation of this manner of contextualizing the rise of the Vijayanagara empire. pp. 13f.

[5] See, for example, George Michell and John M. Fritz, *Hampi: Splendours of Vijayanagara Empire* (Bangalore: Department of Tourism, Government of Karnataka), p. 3.

[6] See descriptions of the city as found in R. Sewell, *A Forgotten Empire (Vijayanagara)* (Delhi: 1962), pp. 236ff.

[7] *Marg*, (1982), p. 41.

[8] *Pampāmāhātmya* and Filliozat, *L'Epigraphie* (Paris: 73), p. 18.

[9] For the mythological background to the city of Hampi, see, G. Michell, "History or Myth, (Part I)"in *Marg* (1982), p. 41.

[10] Examples include the cults of Tiruvangalanātha (Venkaṭeśvara), Kṛṣṇa, Viṭṭāla and Rāma. These kings also permitted the practice of other religions at the capital. Under such enlightened leadership the city became a rich, cosmopolitan blend of different peoples with a wide variety of linguistic, ethnic and religious backgrounds. George Michell and John M. Fritz, *Hampi: Splendours of Vijayanagara Empire*, (Bangalore: Department of Tourism government of Karnataka, nd.), p. 3.

[11] Gode, *Studies in Indian Literary History*, Vol I (Bombay: 1953), p. 11.

[12] G. Michell in "Myth or History (Part I)" in *Marg*, (1982), p. 41.

[13] H. Kulke and Dietmar Rothermund, *A History of India*, Reprint of 1986 (London: 1990), p. 188.

[14] V. Raghavan maintains that the king alluded to in the *Campū* is Harihara I (or Hakka), the eldest of the five sons of Sangama, who was himself a petty chieftain credited by some sources to have founded the Vijayanagara empire. (V. Raghavan, *"The Virūpākṣa Vasantotsava Campū* of Ahobala" in *Journal of Oriental Research* XVI. pp. 17-40, p. 28. There is, however, some debate regarding both the date of the founding of the Vijayanagara empire as well as the date of our text. Some scholars convincingly argue that the *Campū* was composed much later during Vijayanagara times.

[15] The Spring Festival, for example, is referred to variously as *Vasantotsava* (75.20; 82.5; 111.2; 83.19,20), *Caitrotsava* (3.8; 10.8; 83. 8), *Rathotsava* (57.1 etc.), *Mṛgaya(mah)otsava* (57.7; 59.2; 72.8; 68.24; 66.4), *Virūpākṣadevamṛgayāmahotsava* (59.8), *Śaivamṛgayāmahotsava* (64.19) as well as a host of variant nominations. For the time period of the festival, see p. 58 of the text.

16 *Bali* is traditionally offered as a rite of protection and is a common feature of many Hindu rituals.

17 The image here, indicates the timing of the festival (i.e., the full moon).

18 The text reads *pañcājana* and *pañcāsya*. These may be explained here as protective images (p. 2). Kāmadeva is also mentioned in this context.

19 These flags also signify the power of the king.

20 The services here are *abhiṣeka*, i.e, gifts of food, flowers, etc.

21 The number of images on the chariot is unclear. At times Ahobala indicates that there are two (one of Pārvatī and one of Śiva). In other places, there seems to be only one.

22 Vidyāraṇya was a brilliant scholar, the author of numerous works such as the *Jīvanmuktiviveka*, the *Pañcadaśi*, *Vivaraṇaprameyasaṁgraha*, *Śaṅkaravijāya* and the *Devyaparahastotra*. To Vidyāraṇya are also attributed the works of Mādhava and Śāyana. Kane refers to him as the brightest star in the galaxy of *dakṣinatya* authors on *Dharmaśāstra* (p. 779). His fame stands only second to that of the great Śaṅkara. Vidyāraṇya is also remembered as far-sighted politician intimately associated with the establishment of the Vijayanagara empire as well as the guide and spiritual advisor of the early kings of the dynasty. Amongst scholars there is a fair amount of disagreement as to the exact relationship of the various kings of Vijayanagara and Vidyāraṇya. (Kane details this debate, p. 779) See also L. Anderson, "Shifting Focus of the Stories of Vidyāraṇya: A Studies in the Construction of Biographies from Late Medieval India" in *Rencontre avec l'Inde* (Delhi: ICCR, forthcoming).

23 This is probably a reference to the huge statue of Nandi at the eastern end of the Virūpakṣa temple street. This image may still be seen in modern day Hampi.

24 The heretics are identified in Ahobala's text as Bauddhas but this reference is probably an anachronism as Buddhism had all but died out in south India by this time.

25 Here we are told that the image of Śiva is five-faced.

26 The *puruṣārthas* are the aims of human existence as found in Sanskrit texts.

27 See, H. Kulke and Dietmar Rothermund, *A History of India*. (London: Routledge, 1990), p. 141 for an elaboration on the notion of 'deification of kings' and 'royalization of deities.'

28 The Vijayanagara kings have been noted for their tendency to display their royal powers in religious guise. Michell in 'History or Myth (Part I),' *Marg* (1982), pp. 43f.

29 Gold, moreover, is connected in alchemical texts with long life, while the moon is a classic symbol of renewal.

[30] The text gives us very few details regarding this merchant-made chariot.

[31] It is not clear from the text where exactly this ritual *abhiṣeka* is performed, but from the context, it would appear to take place in their homes. (57.12)

[32] 58. 1,2.

[33] There follows a lengthy description of the dense crowds in the city. (58. 16-23)

[34] This son of a minister of King Śrīrāśideśa is described as the son of a minister. It is clear throughout the story however, that he is of the warrior/*kṣatriya* caste. (59.10) See also 68.1.

[35] Perhaps Ahobala himself?

[36] 65.7-10.

[37] 68.12.

[38] Ahobala here refers to Jāyadeva and the literary works, *Śivanāṭaka* and *Śivāṣṭapadi* enumerating the stories of the amorous qualities of lord Śiva, his ability to assume various forms, young, adolescent and old alike, for the enjoyment of divine ladies. (71.15)

[39] *Rājaśekhara* (ordinary king), *Mahāśekhara* (great king with tributaries), *Mahāsāmrājya* (sovereign king). (72.6,7).

[40] Śivā is the feminine form of Śiva.

[41] The term *nīlakaṇṭha* (77.6) refers to Śiva, who drank the poison which emerged from the ocean of milk, thus saving the world. It also means peacock (i.e., one having a blue throat). Pārvatī understands it to refer to the second meaning. The term *girīśa* (77.6) refers either to Śiva or a great mountain (Meru or Mandara). Pārvatī takes it to mean the latter. *Triśūlī* refers to Śiva (the one bearing the trident) (77.7). Again Pārvatī pretends to misunderstand. She interprets *triśūlī* as 'one suffering from three types of pain *(śūla)*'. *Sthāṇu* (77.8) is an epithet of Śiva. Pārvatī takes it to mean the trunk of a tree.

[42] p. 81.

[43] This passage is difficult to construe. (pp. 82-83)

[44] The *gopura* is identified as the *Śrīviṣṭapeśagurugopura* as, for example 58.13.

[45] Our text closes with an odd story of a greedy Brahmin who is employed at the temple.

[46] See, for example, Hiltebeitel (1990), p. 302.

[47] Kramrisch, *The Presence of Śiva* (Princeton: 1981), p. 7.

[48] *Ibid*, pp. 8,20.

[49] G. Mitchell in *Marg*, tells us: "Even the briefest survey of more than two centuries of Vijayanagara's history reveals an astonishing number of wars with neighbouring Muslim kingdoms as well as a host of disputes, intrigues, rebellions, *coup d'états*, murders and general political upheavals." (p. 42)

[50] As if to confirm this, Chapter four tells of the minister's son and a Brahmin poet who, while attending the festival, wander into the forest across the Pampā. They come upon a Bilva tree, touch it and circumambulate it. Here we encounter the familiar tree motif which remains constant throughout our descriptions of the *Vasantotsava*. Bilva trees, well-known in *purāṇic* mythology, are more commonly sacred to Lakṣmī who, according to our text, worshipped Śiva with its leaves in order to win the love of Viṣṇu. After achieving a place on Viṣṇu's chest, she offered the Bilva tree to Śiva. Ahobala (pp. 61-62) says that this information is in the *Skanda Purāṇa*. The fruits of a Bilva tree are themselves worshipped as representative of the *śivaliṅga*. In the *Campū*, by circumambulating a Bilva tree, one attains the merit of worshipping Śiva; by simply touching the fruits of the tree (the *liṅga*, one will gain other fruits as well). (p. 62)

[51] O'Flaherty tells us that Pārvatī calls Śiva an adulterer and that his lascivious behaviour causes as much trouble with her as does his asceticism. He is guilty of adultery, incest and general profligacy. He refers to himself as a voluptuary, and on several occasions, Pārvatī calls him a woman-chaser. *(Śiva,* p. 226).

[52] The story of the Pine Forest sages is retold in O'Flaherty, *Hindu Myths*, pp. 141-149.

[53] See O'Flaherty, *Śiva,* p. 230. She interprets the image of Śiva and Gaṅgā as both a marriage motif and an adultery motif.

[54] Ahobala describes the wildness of the forest in detail. The Brahmin poet who enters the forest is particularly fearful of the sights and sounds there as it is not only inhabited by wild and dangerous creatures, but is, as well, inhabited by outcastes.

[55] If we look at other sources describing the *Vasantotsava* we find that sometimes only Pārvatī is mentioned in connection with the celebrations. The *Holākāmāhātmya,* for example, describes the ways of worshipping the goddess alone on this day.

[56] Ahobala gives us very few details in this regard but it might be suggested here that this fusing of Śiva and Pārvatī is a part of a wedding rite.

[57] See O'Flaherty, *Women,* pp. 310f.

11

Conclusion

At the prompting of Pārvatī, Śiva revives Kāma and in so doing the regeneration of the cosmos is achieved. Their subsequently fecund marriage establishes a mythic model by which the mundane order can achieve like ends. Hence, women worship Kāma in anticipation of the prosperity brought by bearing many children. The motif which most clearly suggests regeneration in human spheres of endeavor, be they religious, social or political, is that of union through marriage. The Śiva/Pārvatī myth in the *Bhaviṣya Purāṇa* (135) establishes the significance of this motif amongst immortals; the lengthy description of the *Vasantotsava* in the *Ratnāvalī* establishes its centrality amongst kings. These two marriages are paradigmatic: as Śiva and Pārvatī are wed in the spring, as King Udayana and the Princess Ratnāvalī are wed in the spring, so too are human marriages ideally solemnized during this season. In all of these celebrations is *kāma,* which is love and desire, and Kāma, the deity, who personifies these qualities. Kāma (desire) establishes a primary link between couples, be it erotic love, passion, conjugal love or love aimed at engendering new life.[1] Kāma embodies potentiality in anticipation of and parallel to the annual and inevitable renewal of spring.

In the mythological frameworks in the *Ratnāvalī*, the *Bhaviṣya Purāṇa* (135 and 132), and the *Campū*, we see a complex of power motifs: Kāma masters the king in the *Ratnāvalī* and in the *Bhaviṣya Purāṇa* (135); Śiva looms over Kāma but in the end is subdued by him and Kāma re-emerges from the ashes into the cosmos simultaneous with the arrival of spring. Similarly, in the *Campū*, Śiva conquers both the *aspsaras* women and Pārvatī, while in the *Bhaviṣya Purāṇa* (132), children and 'mad-ones' subdue Ḍhaunḍhā.[2] These conquests are mimetic of the inevitability of the natural order of annual, seasonal cycles, where one season 'conquers' another. That our two other major sources, detailed in Chapter Six and Seven, i.e., the *Kathāsaritsāgara* and the *Vikramacarita*, fail to make significant mention of Sanskrit mythology and that the stories in these two texts are dominated by kings would suggest that the festival here is concerned most obviously with the maintenance of political power alone. Even an interpretation of the festival in the *Campū* and the *Ratnāvalī* as being primarily of political import is not without evidence as in the *Ratnāvalī* the marriage motif is clearly linked with political regeneration. The *Kathāsaritsāgara* and the *Vikramacarita* confirm that the king most often supervises springtime renewal: it is his duty to ensure that the festivities take place. Moreover, his condition, his physical well-being, is intimately related to the maintenance and growth of his kingdom. A flourishing king, as in the *Ratnāvalī*, affects a flourishing kingdom; a debilitated king as in the *Kathāsaritsāgara*, must be deposed. It might be suggested that the Spring Festival in the Sanskrit context has, as one of its priorities, the sustenance of the power of the king and his Brahmin officials. Sanskrit mythology is here subordinated to these concerns and adapted to this purpose, with the celebration of the Spring Festival becoming a vehicle sanctioning state authority.

The susceptibility of this festival to political manipulation and reinterpretation becomes most evident in the case of the *Vasantotsava* related in the *Campū* where the supreme position of the Vijayanagara king is seen to be sanctioned by the great god Śiva. The empire celebrates the festival by extolling as paramount no mere human coupling, not even a regal coupling, but the union of the eternal celestial couple, Śiva and Pārvatī. Regeneration, affected by the unity of this binary cosmic couple, by this androgynous amalgam is generalized to the political level where the king becomes the mortal counterpart of Śiva, dominating and permeating his realm, absorbing all within his sphere. The political stability of the Vijayanagara empire, at the time of the writing of the *Campū* was, indeed, highly dependent on the personage of the king. That his rule here is tied to Śiva surely lends credence to the consolidation, maintenance and administration of his political power.

The *Vasantotsava* and Sectarianism

The mythological framework of the Spring Festival points to a reading of it both as a celebration sanctioned by and under the aegis of a variety of sectarian interests as well a festival celebrated outside the purview of any readily identifiable sectarian context. No single deity or denominational group of deities is here the consistent object of devotion. Despite private or public affiliations and regardless of any sectarian emphasis, the *Vasantotsava*, coming as it does at the end of winter, is celebratory of many things, perhaps foremost of which we may count the impending warmth and light of spring. In this regard it may be savoured by all. However, that it could in fact be celebrated by any of the Śaivas, Vaiṣṇavas or others directs a consideration of it as a pan-sectarian festival, a festival celebrated with or without evident sectarian interests. As a generic label, the *Vasantotsava* crosses sectarian boundaries and establishes thus a parameter encompassing the united group of citizens known as human society.

The textual evidence indicates that the festival could be, depending upon the orientation of the celebrants, either a Śaiva or a Vaiṣṇava festival or, as in the urban setting of the *Ratnāvalī* or the *Kathāsaritsāgara*, it could be a festival in which the worship of a deity was not required at all. Evidence in the Buddhist *Jātakas* and the Jain *Kathākośa* states further that this festival was celebrated by Buddhists and

Jains as well as by worshippers of Hindu deities. The configurations arising out of like mythological or literary episodes, while being a testament to a certain type of malleability, suggest that very often these episodes are moulded to meet sectarian ends. In the context of Hinduism, most often it is relatively minor deities in the pantheon who are denominated as central to the celebration of spring, particularly the demoness Ḍhaunḍhā/Holākā or the godling Kāma.

Although Kāma does not appear in all of our examined descriptions, he is the celestial being most frequently invoked, placing him at the thematic centre of the proceedings. When he does appear it is clearly because during springtime, he is uppermost on everyone's mind. Kāma as well as his consort Rati were regularly invoked during the celebrations: accordingly, his temple is to be visited (*Mālavikāgnimitram*), he is to be worshipped in a prescribed manner by householders and women (*Bhaviṣya Purāṇa* 135) and he is to be invoked, as well, by royalty (*Ratnāvalī*). His stories are retold at this time of year and his rebirth on this *tithi* explains the origin of the *Vasantotsava*. In the *Ratnāvalī* it is Kāma's general association with festivity, sensuality and abundance in nature that is stressed. We might recall Coomaraswamy's contention that Kāma's initial genesis was as a *yakṣa*,[3] a non-specific figure associated with nature and the fertility of nature. As the cult of Kāma in the *Ratnāvalī* does not differ substantially from our knowledge of the worship of *yakṣas*, the popularity of Kāma during this festival may indeed stem from this ancient and popular tradition of *yakṣa* worship. Kāma's appearance in the *Ratnāvalī* is as a distinctly non-sectarian deity with essentially no definitive mythology: although he is not the focus of devotion of any one sect exclusively, he is appropriated by many. If indeed the origins of Kāma' can be traced to the *yakṣa* tradition, it is precisely his pan-sectarian mythology which distinguishes him from other *yakṣas* in Sanskrit literature.

As we examine the various contexts in which Kāma appears, we find that the mythological framework underlying this festival is flexible enough to accommodate a spectrum of sectarian re-workings. Surprisingly, the amount of space in the Hindu canon devoted to the mythological adventures of Kāma is minimal, the most repeated and the most important being his endeavour to unite Śiva and Pārvatī for the purpose of procreation. Here Kāma emerges in clear association with Śaiva lore. He is both subordinate to Śiva (as he is destroyed by a burst of flames from Śiva's third eye) while being simultaneously dependent upon Śiva for his rebirth. Unlike the position of Kāma in the *Ratnāvalī*, the mythological structure of the spring festival in the *Bhaviṣya Purāṇa* (135) is specifically defined. Here, Kāma has been allotted a more vital role *vis-à-vis* the sectarian tradition: he is not in the *Bhaviṣya Purāṇa* (135) a non-specific deity worshipped only in association with nature and fertility but, by his exploits, he becomes a Śaiva deity with a broad range of associative connotations that entail.

In at least one case, *viz.*, the *Virūpākṣavasantotsavacampū*, the *Vasantotsava* is explicitly a sectarian festival focusing upon the worship of Śiva and Pārvatī alone. The Spring Festival celebrated in Vijayanagara times is a temple festival, drawing upon the textual tradition of Śiva (as Hunter, as Householder, as Great Cosmic Deity) and regional legend to give context to the celebration. In the *Campū* it is Śiva, the erotically aroused hunter who takes on the central role ascribed elsewhere to Kāma: Kāma is the sexually potent archer armed with the arrows of love and passion (*Bhaviṣya Purāṇa* 135), and Śiva, the sexually potent swordsman in the forest of the *Campū*. We can extend this parallel further to include the king of Vijayanagara so that all three, king, Kāma, and Śiva are homologized. Surely this connection facilitates the mythic transition from the *Vasantotsava* as a popular festival centering around Kāma, to the *Vasantotsava* as a Brāhmaṇical temple festival whose major concern is the worship of Śiva. At the same time, this configuration reflects the manner in which a festival can mutate as the context in which it is enacted changes.

Indeed, Kāma's mythology is so meagre in the body of Sanskrit and *purāṇic* texts that it is easily adapted to a variety of sectarian re-workings. Other versions of the story in which Śiva reduces Kāma to ashes directly connect

Kāma to the tradition of Kṛṣṇa. They tell us Kāma is to be reborn as Pradyumna. Hence in the *Śiva Purāṇa*:[4], Śiva said:

> 38. The Lord Kāma, the husband of Ratī, shall remain bodiless till Viṣṇu incarnates as Kṛṣṇa on the earth and marries Rukmiṇī.
>
> 39. Kṛṣṇa will beget Kāma in Rukmiṇī when he goes to Dvāraka and begins to procreate children.
> 40. His name will certainly be Pradyumna. The demon Śambara will abduct the boy at the time of his very birth.
>
> 42. O Rati, you shall stay in his city .... There alone you will get back your husband Pradyumna.
> 43. Kāma in the name of Pradyumna will regain his wife.... O gods, he will be happy thereafter.

The connection here between Kāma and Pradyumna links the Spring Festival of ancient and medieval times to the present day *Holī* wherein Kṛṣṇa[5] is a central figure. Although certain texts such as the *Śiva Purāṇa* cited above historically link the worship of Viṣṇu (Kṛṣṇa) to the Spring Festival, it is primarily to the modern period that we must turn for information regarding the Vaiṣṇava *Vasantotsava* still popularly celebrated as *Holī*.[6]

In tracing the origins of the modern *Holī* festival, McKim Marriott, in his well-known study of it as celebrated in Kishan Garhi in Uttar Pradesh, reports that according to the participants, it was Kṛṣṇa who first played *Holī* with the cowherd boys, Rādhā, and the *gopīs*.[7] Even given the assertions by those celebrating *Holī*, Marriott suggests that the association of Kṛṣṇa with the Spring Festival, in its modern form, can be located no earlier than the seventeenth century. It was at this time that the Gosvāmins, missionaries of the Kṛṣṇa devotional movement, immigrated to Mathurā and transformed it into a centre for Kṛṣṇa devotion (*bhakti*). In postulating the antiquity of the festival irrespective of sectarian readings

(Marriott seems to regard the association of specific mythological figures with this festival as superfluous) he says:

> Even if only some of such festivals had had the puckish, ambiguous Krishna as their presiding deity, and these only in recent centuries, many seemed since the beginning of our knowledge to have enshrined divinities who sanctioned, however briefly, some of the same riotous sorts of social behavior. (p. 210)

The mythology of the Vaiṣṇava tradition as it is associated with the *Vasantotsava* is clearly a more complicated case than that of the Śaiva tradition. Although the Kṛṣṇa-*gopī* configuration as associated with the Spring Festival is relatively recent (not appearing even in the *Bhāgavata Purāṇa),* of greater antiquity is the association of the *Holī* festival with Kṛṣṇa *via* the myth in which Kṛṣṇa slays the demoness Pūtanā or Holākā.[8] This demoness, like Kāma, is a minor deity in the Sanskrit tradition who may or may not appear in a sectarian context and who also, like Kāma, belongs to a non-specific group of beings (i.e., the demoness is a *rākṣasas* who, like *yakṣas, piśācas, kinnāras* and *gandharvas,* are relatively loosely defined). In the Vaiṣṇava context, Kṛṣṇa is responsible for Holākā's destruction. In the *Bhaviṣya Purāṇa,* it is children who perform this task.

The theme of annual renewal through destruction is echoed in the motif of ritual combat which we discussed in the context of the killing of Ḍhauṇḍhā (*Bhaviṣya Purāṇa* 132) and which persists in the celebration of *Holī* in north India in modern times. McKim Marriott remarks as follows on the Kṛṣṇa theology of love battles:[9]

> At least the Kṛṣṇāite theology of the "love battles" in Kishan Garhi, and possibly some refinements of their rustic hydrology and stick work, seemed to have been remodelled according to the famous and widely imitated public performances that had been visible in villages for the past three centuries.

It is the motif of ritual combat which, in the *Harivaṁśa*,[10] links Kṛṣṇa and Indra to the celebration of spring. Vasudeva Kṛṣṇa is here painted as an rival of Indra and described as a vociferous opponent of the celebration of the *Indramahotsava*.[11] We find a further reference in Patañjali, the author of the *Mahābhāsya* (c. 140 BC), to a ritual combat enacted in a dramatic performance in which Kṛṣṇa (the son of Vasudeva) slays Kaṁsa.[12] Confrontation such as this is central to the *Indramahotsava* as it celebrates Indra's destruction of demons. Combat persists still in the Vaiṣṇava celebration of the Spring Festival where love battles and powder wars characterize the modern *Holī*.

Indramahotsava

The *Indramahotsava*[13] is a festival of autumn celebrating Indra's defeat of Vṛtra, the demon of drought. The war between Indra and Vṛtra has been variously interpreted as a myth of invigouration aimed at securing the continuance of the universe[14]; as the re-enactment of the perennial struggle between the old year and the new, between life and death and between rain and drought.[15] In this sense, the Indra festival, like the *Vasantotsava*, is a festival of renewal and, despite the fact that the *Indramahotsava* was an autumn festival, this connection is expressed through thematic and literary affinities.

Bhoja of Dhārā in his *Sarasvatīkaṇṭhābharaṇa* and also in his *Śṛṅgāra Prakāśa*, directly connects both *Śakrārcā* (the worship of Indra) and the *Vasantotsava* (which Bhoja refers to as *suvasantaka*) by labelling them both as love festivals.[16] Other texts simply record the *Indramahotsava* as taking place in spring. Raghavan, in *Festivals*, cites the Tamil epic *Śilappatikāram* and the *Maṇimekhalai* in which the Indra festival was celebrated on Caitra Purnima (the full moon day in the spring month of Caitra). He also mentions that a small south Indian compilation from the *Dharma Nibandhas* called the *Vināyakādisarvapūjāpaddhati* cites Caitra Śukla Pratipad (the first day of the bright half of Caitra and the traditional date for the celebration of the *Vasantotsava*), as the date for the *Indramahotsava*.[17] In Nepal, there is a smaller *Indradhvaja* festival in spring and a larger one in the autumn. Further, Kane notes the prevalence in the Deccan of the practice of raising a bamboo staff (probably a vestige of the *Indradhvaja* celebration during which a pole was raised in honour of Indra) on the first of Caitra.[18]

More than just this suggested connection between the *Indramahotsava* and the *Vasantotsava,* however, is the evidence in a few texts specifically equating these two festivals. Among these we may include the Jain *Kathākośa* which contains a story set during the Spring Festival surprising in its last line which reads:

> *apanakelih śakrārcā vasantamadanotsavā*
> (the festivities of the *Vasantotsava* and the *Madanotsava* involve drinking and the worship of Indra)[19]

The account of the *Vasantotsava* in this text is typical in all other respects, conforming to descriptions previously encountered. So too does the *Bhāvaprakāśa* of Śāradātanaya include *Śakrārcā* or the worship of Indra as a component of the *Vasantotsava.*[20]

Of the *Indramahotsava* we have an abundance of information. A. K. Chatterjee in *Ancient Indian Literary and Cultural Tradition,* suggests that it was, in all probability, the earliest festival celebrated by the people in general (i.e., it was a popular festival).[21] It is mentioned in *vedic* texts such as the *Kauśītaki Brāhmaṇa* and the *Pariśiṣṭaparvan* of the *Atharva Veda.*[22] The celebration was of particular import for kings[23] as a king who performed this festival, who worshipped the Indra-pole, was promised the destruction of all of his enemies as well as the future prosperity of his realm. This emblem of Indra, the Indra-pole, is said to represent both the anticipated productivity of the realm and the vigour and power of the king. The *Kṛtyakalpataru* intimates the Indra-pole's symbolic sexual potency and power when it tells us that as long as the pole stands, the women of Indra will remain 'happy.' Thus, as the king is the centre of his kingdom and the source of its productive fertility, so too, the Indra-pole can be seen in this regard as the functional axis *vis-à-vis* the cosmos.

These striking parallels between the *Indramahotsava* and the *Vasantotsava* and the direct textual equations linking the two festivals suggest that they are not coincidentally akin. Periodically throughout this study we have encountered affinities between spring and autumn festivals, the Buddhist celebration of *Kāttika/Kaumudī* in our discussion of the *Kathāsaritsāgara*, the *Śrīpañcami* encountered in Chapter Two and the *Navarātra* in the *Nirṇayāmṛta* providing earlier examples. Both festivals ceremonialize seasonal transitions: the autumn festival celebrates the end of summer monsoon rains, the *Vasantotsava* celebrates the end of winter. They are gratefully enacted as markers of new agricultural seasons, both are celebrated as beginnings.

Vedic Precedents

There is a considerable span of time between the initial appearance of the *Vasantotsava* in Sanskrit texts[24] and the fairly elaborate descriptions of it in texts like the *Ratnāvalī* (seventh century AD). Early texts give brief acknowledgement of this festival which reveals little more than that it was known to Sanskrit authors. It is not inconceivable that very early spring festivals of various ilks were performed in concurrence with each other, that elements typical of these spring celebrations were incorporated into 'Brāhmaṇical' rituals and, indeed, that 'Brāhmaṇical' elements were incorporated into popular celebrations. The relationship between *vedic* and popular rites is not linear, nor does it move in one direction; rather it reflects a complex and organic sympathy. In later texts, the Spring Festival becomes important subject matter for Sanskrit authors and a pivotal and persuasive context for depicting various Sanskrit themes.[25] Recorded then, in the texts reviewed in Chapters Three through Ten, is the entwining of both non-orthodox, popular and Brāhmaṇical ideologies and ritual practices. Although these sources have been exclusively Sanskrit accounts of events, they undoubtedly include non-sanskritic, popular elements. It becomes evident that popular practices and pragmatic daily concerns may be amalgamated within the Sanskrit tradition, may be re-signified within the context of Sanskrit literature and religion.

The festival (*utsava)* tradition in India did not develop in cultural isolation but, rather, reflects a general shift in the Indian tradition from the sacrifice (*yajña*) of the *vedic* period to the 'festival' of the medieval and modern periods. Concurrently, it reflects the on-going exchange of various customary practices which may be formulated as popular, regional, non-sanskritic/sanskritic and little/big traditions. This shift has been investigated at length and various frameworks exist for its interpretation.[26] Whether or not the *Vasantotsava* as we find it in classical texts developed out of a tradition of *vedic* sacrifice or whether it is a festival reflective of popular celebrations that existed concurrent with *vedic* celebrations, we may never fully resolve. We cannot, however, fail to note similarities existing between the *Vasantotsava* and certain *vedic* sacrificial rituals. The seasonal sacrifices (*cāturmāsyāni*) and the *Mahāvrata* are two *vedic* celebrations which establish precedents for the *Vasantotsava* as they are characterized by shared elements we have come to associate with it.

First, both the *cāturmāsyāni* (the four-monthly sacrifices) and the *Vasantotsava* are specifically *seasonal* festivals. Just as the main *purāṇas* and *dharmaśāstra* texts deal with the seasons in order,[27] so too are the seasons connected to the *vedic* temporal sacrificial cycle (*cāturamāsyāni*)[28] described in the *Kauśītaki Brāhmaṇa* as follows:[29]

> The four-monthly sacrifices are sacrifices of healing: therefore are they performed in the joinings of the seasons, for in the joinings of the seasons pain is born. (v. 1)

Further, the *Taittirīya Brāhmaṇa* states that it is spring which is the foremost of the sacrificial seasons, the period when the spring sacrifice (*vaiśvadeva cāturmāsya*) is performed, i.e, at the beginning of the year on the full moon of Phālguna (at the end of winter and the beginning of spring).[30] Similarly, in the *Kauśītaki Brāhmaṇa*, we read:[31]

> He who prepares the four monthly sacrifices begins on the full moon night in the Phālgunis. (v. 1)

Accordingly, we must refer back to our initial discussion regarding the dates for celebrating the Spring Festival where we have established from medieval sources that indeed the *Vasantotsava* commences on the full moon night in Phālguna as a sacrifice/ritual aimed at promoting fertility.[32]

While the *vedic* spring sacrifice, like the *Vasantotsava,* celebrates renewal, the actual rituals of the early *cāturmāsya* are totally different from anything we have encountered in the Spring Festival of the medieval period. Peoples of the *vedic* period were primarily pastoral, their rituals centering around elaborate sacrifice. The *cāturmāsyāni* rituals though are comparatively minor sacrifices, their textual descriptions being neither as frequent as descriptions of other sacrifices nor as elaborate. The ritual of our medieval *Vasantotsava,* as it is described in several texts, does seem to have become much more extensive, assimilating notions of women, of procreativity, of the productiveness of the earth as well as notions emphasizing the existing political and social structures, i.e., kingship and marriage. All are essential aspects promoting the nexus of fertility. All suggest that the Spring Festival our medieval texts describe was the core of a society wishing to ensure its stable, stationary and productive continuance.

Second, the rituals of the *Mahāvrata* are often cited as precedent to the *Vasantotsava.* This celebration is described in the *Taittirīya Saṁhitā*[33] as a component of the *sattra* or sacrificial session. As all performers are consecrated Brahmins and all share in the benefits of the offering. After an initial period of ten days of preparing *soma* the *Mahāvrata* takes place and is performed variously as a one day rite or a *sattra.* It has been described elsewhere as follows:[34]

> There is beaten an earth drum, doubtless to scare away the demons who might attempt to overthrow the power of the sun; the Hotṛ sits on a swing and is swung to and fro, to represent the

8. Prince Playing *Holī* in Harem
Deccan-Golkanda, early 18th century

> path of the sun in the sky, and strengthen its power to perform it; ritual abuse is exchanged for fertility purposes, between a student or, in a later usage, a Magadha, and a *hetara*; there is actually carried out sexual intercourse; the consecrated personas are alternately praised and reviled; there is a mimic fight between an Aryan and a Sudra for the possession of a white round skin which is declared to be a symbol of the sun; the skin of an unfruitful cow is hung up or stretched out and warriors pierce through it with arrows, perhaps as a rain spell. Women celebrate to the sound of the lute in the south the patrons of the ceremony; maids dance round the fire with water pitchers, while the stotra is being performed; they pour the water on the fire, and their song shows that they desire richness in milk with water for the cows. The desire of heat and rain seems clearly united; the position of the sun nearest earth is indicated by the priest, who touches the board of the swing and the earth with one hand, and says, 'the God hath united with the Goddess.'

The likeness between these two festivals has led scholars like Sarkar to suggest that the *Mahāvrata* is the Brāhmaṇical counterpart of the popular Spring festival (*Vasantotsava*).[35] Other scholars interpret the *Mahāvrata* as a folk festival of antiquity which became attached to the *sattra* or sacrificial sessions, begging thus the question of exact *vedic* sources for the later festivals. Some scholars find the existence of such a festival sanctioned by the *Vedas* an embarrassment altogether. Thus Apte, for example, says that the *Mahāvrata* specially pertains to Prajāpati's creation of the world and the intercourse between men and women which takes place in a screened shed is probably *symbolic* of this same creation. In this light he remarks that it therefore 'cannot be justifiably maintained that the intermingling of men and women ran into extremes of promiscuity during this sacrifice.[36] Yet, as we have seen in the case of the classical Spring Festival (*Vasantotsava*), the motif of sexual creation spans both cosmic and temporal spheres. Certainly the licentious behavior in the *Mahāvrata* here has roots elsewhere but at the same time our evidence suggests that such behavior actually occurred. Hence, the mundane re-enactment of cosmic sexual intercourse (Śiva and Pārvatī, Prajāpati's creation; Śiva's revival of Kāma) is repeated *ad infinitum*.

Although no single ritual, no single figure or figure-head and no single setting circumscribes the celebration of spring, thematically the *Vasantotsava* is unified. The rites of spring reflect tone of the season: motifs of fertility, eroticism and romance freely commingle whether in the realm of immortals, in the kingdom, in the city, the forest or the garden. The ritual components of the *Vasantotsava* are not easily separable but, rather, they combine in various patterns, each configuration emerging as a distinct whole, a coherent entity. Yet these individual festivals clustering around spring often coalesce, forming larger more specific units such as festivals of Kāma, flower festivals and festivals of throwing powder. These in turn may be further absorbed into yet larger events, occasionally giving rise to an elaborately constructed *Vasantotsava* consisting of a composite of multiple elements. Our evidence suggests then that the *Vasantotsava* is appropriately understood as a generic term applied to a variety of celebrations of which each is a legitimate Spring Festival in its own right but of which none is exhaustive.

The *Vasantotsava* responds to a broad spectrum of human concerns: in the sphere of politics, it can be turned to account to celebrate and reinforce the power of the king; in the social sphere, it is a time of entertainment and merry-making indicative of the annual renewal of society through the breakdown and reorganization of social structures; and in the sphere of religion, it celebrates the exploits of the gods, establishing a link between the behavior of gods and that of mortals with human marriages echoing divine marriages, human worship renewing divine intention in the creative cycle of the universe. Themes of rejuvenation and renewal, replete throughout the *Vasantotsava*, resonate between the gods and human society, between nature and human society, and within human society between the king and his subjects.

NOTES

[1] Although the erotic and procreative are clearly not synonymous, in our descriptions of Kāma and of the *Vasantotsava*, direct links, as, for example, in the *Bhàviṣya Purāṇa* (135) between these two are established.

[2] Ḍhaunḍhā is put to death but reappears, it would seem every year at the onset of spring and must be conquered on an annual basis.

[3] A. Coomaraswamy, *Yakṣas*, pp. 43f.

[4] *Śiva Purāṇa*, "Rudrasaṁhitā" 51.7.13-14.

[5] See Sharma, p. 66; Thomas, p. 7.

[6] In addition to the male Vaiṣṇava associations cited here, there are certain texts which connect Lakṣmī with the Spring Festival. (See *Śrīpañcami*, above.) This evidence associates Lakṣmī, *via* Kāma, to the *Vasantotsava* as, for example, in the *Bhaviṣya Purāṇa* (132).

[7] See McKim Marriott, "The Feast of Love" in *Krishna: Myths, Rites and Attitudes* Chicago: 1966), pp. 201f.

[8] See *Bhaviṣya Purāṇa* (132) above.

[9] Marriott, *op. cit.*, p. 208.

[10] The *Harivaṁśa* dates to the second or third century AD.

[11] This is also a common theme in Indian iconography. See Zimmer, *The Art of Indian Asia*, 2 vols. (New York: 1960), II, pl. 291.

[12] Patañjali was a grammarian and gives this as an example to illustrate a grammatical point. This reference is cited by A. Keith, *Classical Sanskrit Literature*, pp. 31-2. Interestingly, this passage tells us that the followers of Kṛṣṇa adorn themselves in red (life), followers of Kaṁsa in black (death) and they then engage in mimetic combat.

[13] This festival is referred to variously as *Śakrārca*, *Śakramaha*, *Indramaha*, *Indramahotsava*, *Indrahvaja* and *Indrayanna*.

[14] *Ibid*, p. 26.

[15] See, for example, T. Gaster, *Thespis*, pp. 37f.

[16] V. Raghavan, *Festivals*, p. 128.

[17] *Ibid*, p. 150.

[18] Kane, *History of Dharmaśāstra*, II.ii. p. 826; and Raghavan, *Festivals*, p. 153.

[19] *Kathākośa*, (Lahore), 23.11 (page, line).

[20] Śāradātanaya, *Bhāvaprakāśa*, 111.99.

21 A. K. Chatterjee, *Ancient Indian Literary and Cultural Tradition* (Calcutta: 1974), p. 162.

22 *Kauśītaki Brāhmaṇa*, 140.16; *Pariśiṣṭaparvan of the Atharva Veda*, no. 19.

23 The *Mahābhārata* tells us that it was King Uparicara Vasu, the Cedi monarch, who ntroduced the worship of the *yaṣṭi* (stick or pole) of Indra (1.63.18-19). This is confirmed in the *Bṛhatsaṁhitā* which further tells us that a king desirous of victory must observe the Indra festival. (43.55.68) Lakṣmīdhara in his Rājadharmakhaṇḍa (the duties of kings) of the *Kṛtyakalpataru*, a twelfth century AD north Indian text, describes this festival in some detail. (ch. 17, pp. 284-290). The festivities commence with an excursion into the forest to search for a tree suitable to serve as Indra's Pole. At daybreak the next day, having found and worshipped an appropriate tree in a prescribed manner, one should cut it down, carry it back to the city, and install it with the accompaniment of dance and song. The tree is to be wrapped with cloth of various colours which serve as flags. The text tells us that as long as the pole stands, the women of Indra *(apsaras)* will remain happy. People should stay awake all night reciting the deeds of Indra.

24 *Kāmasūtra* , 3rd century BC.

25 So, for example, both Kālidāsa and Harṣa incorporate the Spring Festival in establishing a mood or sentiment.

26 Redfield, for example, in *Peasant Society and Culture* interprets Indian culture in terms of a Great Tradition and a Little Tradition; M.N. Srinivas refers to a Sanskrit and a non-Sanskrit tradition and speaks of Sanskritization as a means by which non-Sanskrit traditions filter upward into Sanskrit speaking traditions; McKim Marriot refers further to 'universalization' (movement upward into a Sanskrit tradition) and 'parochialization' (movement downward into a folk tradition). See also M. Singer, *When a Great Tradition Modernizes*, pp. 7f.

27 Someśvara, in the *Mānasollāsa*, describes festivals, treating them in order of the seasons. See Raghavan, *Festivals*, p. 61.

28 Although these sacrifices were, according to Heesterman, optional, the *cāturmāsyāni* sacrifices became an integral part of the *Rājasuya*. See Heesterman, *The Ancient Royal Consecration*, pp. 27f.

29 Cited by Keith, *Ṛgveda Brāhmaṇas*, p. 371.

30 *Ibid*, p. 370.

31 *Ibid*

32 Heesterman equates the *vedic* spring sacrifice (*vaiśvadeva)*, with the *Vasantotsava*, as a sacrifice/ritual aimed at promoting fertility. (*The Ancient Royal Consecration*, p. 28)

33 VII.5.9, Keith, *Religion and Philosophy of the Veda*, p. 351.

34 *Ibid*

35 Cited by Apte, *Marriage*, p. 55.

36 *Ibid*

Glosssary

āḍāḍa: nonsense utterance
adharma: unrighteousness, impiety, wickedness, injustice
Agni : fire, the deity of fire
Ahalyā: the wife of the sage Gautama
ājya: ghee (clarified butter)
akṣata: unhusked whole grains, entire unhusked and pounded rice washed with water used as an article of worship in religious and sacred ceremonies.
Amarāvati: the abode of Indra
āmrakusumāśana: the ritual of eating mango blossoms
Anaṅga: name of Kāma; bodilessness
amṛta: nectar of immortality, ambrosia, drink of the gods
aṅgapūjā: body worship
apsaras: a class of female deities, usually described as helpers of Indra
ārati : adoration with lamps
ardhanārīśvara: a form of Śiva, half male/ half female
artha: power, wealth
Āṣāḍha: Hindu month corresponding to June/July
Aśoka: an evergreen tree blooming in spring; Aśoka means without sorrow and it is a tree celebrated in myth and legend. The flower is one of the five flower-arrows of Kāma.
aśokadohada: kicking an Aṣoka tree to prompt it to bloom
aśokakalikābhakṣana: drinking Aśoka buds
aśokāṣṭamī: a spring ritual, drinking eight buds of the Aśoka

asura: demon, an enemy of the gods
Āśvina: name of a lunar month in which the moon is near the constellation Aśvini
avabhṛtha: an ablution at the end of a festival or a sacrifice

Bakula: *Mimusops Elengi*, a rather tall evergreen tree which puts forth blossoms when sprinkled with wine or nectar from the mouths of lovely women
bhakti:: faith, worship, homage, reverence, service
Bhuvaneśvarī: name of a goddess enshrined at the Virūpākṣa temple in Hampi
Bilva: *Aegle Marnelos*, or wood apple, associated with the cults of Sivā
Brahmā: name of the creator god
Brahmin (brāhmaṇa): one belonging to the first of the four original castes or social groups, a priest
Bṛhaspati: name of the preceptor of the gods

caccarī (or *carcari):* festival songs
Caitra: a lunar month in the Hindu calendar bridging March and April
Cakravāka: the ruddy goose
Campaka: a tree bearing yellow fragrant flowers
campū: a genre of Sanskrit narrative in mixed prose and poetry
Caṇḍi: an epithet of Durgā
caturmāsa: a period of four months reckoned from the eleventh day of the bright half of Āṣāḍha to the eleventh day in the bright half Kārtika
caturmāsyāni: the four-month sacrifices
cūtalatikā (or *navalatikā):* a spring rite in which men and women identify their lovers by tapping them with twigs

dakṣiṇā: a gift or donation given to Brahmins at the end of a religious ceremony
darbha: a kind of sacred grass used at sacrificial ceremonies (kuśa grass)
Daśara: a festival observed for nine or ten days, known in Bengal as Durgā *pūjā* and otherwise as *Navarātri*
dharma: duty, order, virtue, justice

Ḍhaunḍhā: demoness in the *Bhaviṣya Purāṇa* (132) associated with Holākā and Pūtanā

dhvajastaṁbha: flag-post

Diti: the mother of the demons

dohada: literally 'pregnancy longing,' In this context, trees are represented as feeling, like women, such longing, such desire, that they cannot blossom until their craving is satisfied. The term *dohadikā* is given in the *Sāhityamîmāṁsā* as different ways to fulfill the yearnings of trees and thus prompting them into blossom (p. 151). The Bakula tree, according to the conventions of poets, desires a mouthful of wine to be discharged at it. When this longing is fulfilled, it puts for its flowers. The Campaka craves to hear the loud laughter of a beautiful damsel.

Durgā: epithet of Pārvatī, the wife of Śiva

Durgāpūjā: a Bengal festival in honour of Durgā during the month of Āśvina

dūrva: bent grass, panic grass, a sacred grass offered to deities during worship

gandharvas: a class of demi-gods regarded as the musicians of the gods

Gaṅgā: Ganges river and the goddess who personifies this river

Gaṅgādhara: epithet of Śiva

gāyatrī: name of a sacred verse repeated during morning and evening rites and on other great occasions

gāyatrī mantra: prayers associated with the *gāyatrī*

gopī: a herdswoman, female companion of Kṛṣṇa

Halī: the plough-share, female attendant of Kāma

Harinī: loss, one of the five arrows of Kāma

Hemakūṭa: golden mountain, name of a mountain near Hampi

Holākā: a demoness in the *Bhaviṣya Purāṇa* (132) synonymous with Ḍhaunḍhā, a festival of the same name

Holī: a festival of spring celebrated in contemporary India (particularly in north and north-east India)

homa: a burnt offering, one of the five daily to be performed by a Brahmin

Indra: the king of the gods
Indrāṇi: wife of Indra

jāgara: maintaining an all-night vigil

kaivalya: final emancipation
Kāma: god of passion
kāma: variously love, passion or desire, one of the four ends of life *(puruṣārtha)*
Kāmotsava: festival of Kāma celebrated in the spring
kanyadana: the rite of giving of the daughter in the marriage ceremony
kanyavrata: a vow of an unmarried woman
Kārtika: Hindu month corresponding to October/November
Kāttika: a festival of autumn
Kaumudīmahotsava: Autumn Festival
kilākilā: nonsense utterance expressing joy or pleasure
kinnāras: a class of demi-gods
krīḍitavyam piṣācavat: the sport of behaving like a ghost
Kṛta Yuga: the first of the four ages or the Golden Age
kṣatriya: a member of the military or second caste
kuśa: an aromatic grass

lāsya: a dance of love in which the emotions of love are represented
laukikavṛtta: activities of ordinary people
liñga : the genital organ of Śiva worshipped in the form of a phallus

mada: intoxication, drunkenness, lasciviousness, rut
Madana: name of Kāma, the spring season, intoxicating
madanodyāna: the grove of Kāma, as for example, in the *Mālatîmādhava* (Act I)
Madanotsava: festival of Kāma celebrated in the spring
Mādhu: spring
Māgha: Hindu month bridging January and February
mahāvrata: a great religious observance, a *vedic* celebration
mahiṣa: name of a demon killed by Durgā, buffalo
makara: a mythical aquatic crocodile or shark-like animal which is the emblem of Kāma

makaradhvaja: the *makara*-banner, the banner of Kāma
Mālatī: *Jasimum grandiflorum,* a jasmine whose large white flowers have a powerful scent, used in garlands on all festive occasions
mandala: a kind of mystical diagram used in invoking a divinity, usually circular
mantra: mystical formula
mantrakṣara: a syllable in a spell
Mardinī: destruction, one of the five arrows of Kāma
Mataṅga: name of a sage and also a name of hills near Hampi
mātṛ: a mother
Mohinī: delusion, one of the five arrows of Kāma
moksa: freedom, release from the cycle of birth and death *(saṁsāra)*
Mṛgayotsava : Hunt Festival
mūrti: an image of a deity, icon
muṣkā: testicles, from which is derived the word musk

Navaratri: festival of nine nights, see *daśara*
Nibandhas: ritual manuals
nīlakaṇṭha: a peacock, a name of Śiva: the Blue-throated One who consumed the deadly poison which emerged from the ocean of milk. According to the myth Śiva retained the poison in his throat to save creation from destruction resulting in his throat turning blue.
nyāsa : assignment of various parts of the body to different deities which is usually accompanied with prayers and corresponding gesticulations

Pañcāṅgas: almanacs, (that which has five limbs) are manuals prepared from different astronomical texts
Pāṇḍu: the name of the father of the Pāṇḍavas
pariśiṣtha: addenda
Pārtha: a name of Arjùna, a king
Pārvatī: consort of Śiva
Phālguna: a lunar month in the Hindu calendar bridging February and March
piśācas: a malevolent being
pītha : a pedestal, the seat of a deity

Pradyumna: an epithet of Kāma, the son of Kṛṣṇa and Rukmiṇī stolen away by the demon Śambara
Prajāpati: the god presiding over creation, name of Brahmā
prākrt: vernacular or provincial dialect derived from and akin to Sanskrit
Prāmathinī: torment, one of the five arrows of Kāma
prasada: food offered to idols, remnants of the same
prastāvana: a prologue at the beginning of a drama
Pratipad: the first day of a lunar fortnight
praveśaka: a dramatic interlude explaining external events
pūjā: worship, adoration
pūrṇakalaśa: a full pitcher. The *pūrṇakalaśa* is an iconographic motif that contains and dispenses the waters of life, the *amṛta*: symbolic of the inexhaustible supply of nature.
pūrṇimā: the full moon day (also *Pūrṇimāsī* and *pūrṇamā)*
purohita: family priest who conducts all ceremonies
puruṣārtha: any one of the four principal objects of human life: *kāma, artha, dharma, mokṣa*
pūrvapakśa: the initial part of an argument or the initial objection to an argument
puṣpa: a blossom, a flower
puṣpapūjā: a ritual with flowers
Pūtanā: demoness who torments children, usually associated with Kṛṣṇa and the diseases of children, a *rākṣasī*, one of Skanda's attendants

rāga: love, affection, amorous feeling, a musical mode
rākṣasa: a demon, a goblin, a fiend
rākṣasī : female rākṣasa
ratha: a chariot, wagon
Rathotsava: chariot festival
Rati: wife of Kāma, Goddess of love
ratīkāmavrata: as detailed in the *Nārada Purāṇa*, a vow to achieve a long married life and prolific progeny
Rāvaṇa: name of the chief of the *rākśasas*, the king of Laṅkā
Rudra: terrific, frightful, name of Śiva
rudrākṣa: a tree favoured by Śiva, the berry of which is used for rosaries

Śacī: name of the wife of Indra
Śacrārcā: Festival of Indra
sādhana: a penance, self-mortification
śākta: a worshipper of śakti
śakti: power, the active power of a deity, the wife of a deity
śālabhañjikā: literally, a woman breaking the bough of a śāl tree, an Indian sculptural motif of a woman touching a tree
Śambara: name of a demon slain by Pradyumna
Śambhu: name of Śiva
saṁhitā: a systematically arranged collection of verses, a digest
samkalpa: a declaration to undertake a vow customarily made in preparation for a rite
saṁvat: a year
saṁvatsara: a year
saṇdhyā: morning or evening twilight, prayers recited at these times
Śaṅkara: name of Śiva
Śāntihoma: a sacrifice to avert or remove an evil
Śāstras: a religious or sacred treatise
sattra: a sacrificial session, especially one lasting from 13 to 100 days, a sacrifice in general
secana krīḍa: sport of splashing or squirting one another with tinted or fragrant water
siddhamantra: a magical *mantra*
sindūra: red powder
Skanda: name of a son of Śiva
Smara: name of Kāma, memory, love
soma: ambrosia of the gods, the moon
śṛṅga: syringe through which coloured water is deployed at spring festivals (water pistol)
Sthānu: epithet of Śiva
śūdra: a member of the last of the four principal castes in the service of the higher castes
śukla: the light or bright half of a lunar month
surā: wine, the most common of intoxicating drinks and usual at marriage rites
svedana: steam bath

tantra: a religious treatise teaching magical and mystical formulas for the worship of deities
tāpana: burning, inflaming, illuminating, one of the five arrows of Kāma
tapas: penance, austerities, bodily mortification
taraṅga: a section or part of a text
tirtha: a holy place, a place of pilgrimage especially on or near the bank of a sacred river
tithi : a lunar day

vāhana: a vehicle for transporting images in festival processions, a vehicle of the gods
Vaiśākha: name of a lunar month bridging April/May
vaiśvadevacaturmāsyāni: a sacrifice in which an offering is made to all deities
vaiśya: a member of the third caste, a trader and agriculturalist
Vāma: name of Kāma
vāravanitā: a woman of the multitude, a courtesan
varṇa: colour or hue, a social class, particularly applied to the four principal castes
Varuṇī: wine, female attendant of Kāma
Vasanta: spring personified as a deity, companion to Kāma
vasantābhinaya: a spring dance
Vasudeva: the father of Kṛṣṇa and a son of Sūra
vetāla: a ghost, particularly one who occupies a dead body
vidūṣaka: court jester in Sanskrit drama who is the friend and close confident of the hero
Virasena: an asura who is defeated in battle by Holākā
Virūpākṣa: name of Śiva
vrata: religious vow of which there are many different types, promising a wide diversity of of benefits
Vṛndāvana: name of a forest near Gokula
Vṛtra: name of a demon killed by Indra

yāgaśāla: sacrificial chamber
yajña: a sacrifice, a sacrificial rite, any offering or oblation
yajñaśālā: a sacrificial hall
yakṣa: name of a class of demi-gods
yakṣi: female *yakṣa*

yantra: mystical or astronomical diagram used as an amulet
yātra: a festival, festival procession
yoga: deep and abstract meditation
yoginī: female practitioner of yoga
Yuddhiṣṭhira: eldest of the Pāṇḍava princes

Dates of Texts

Throughout this work I have referred to the ancient and medieval periods. The ancient period comprises works belonging to the *Veda* (the *vedic Saṁhitās, Upaniṣads,* and the *Brāhmaṇas)* and also texts composed contemporaneous with the later *vedic* canon. Texts belonging to the medieval periods range in their composition from approximately the 5th to the 17th century AD, but the majority of these works were composed between the 7th and the 12th century AD.

There is in general much debate regarding the dating of Sanskrit texts. The following is an alphabetical list of the major texts and genres of texts consulted in this work together with approximate dates for their composition as established by scholars.

Āgamas and *Tantras:* the earliest of these texts date from 3rd to 7th century AD

Atharva Veda: c. 900 BC

Ākhyakamanikoṣa of Nemichandra: Krishnamachariar, p. 235 lists Nemichandra as a Jain author. The text dates to 1073-1083 AD

Bhāvaprakāśa of Śāradātanaya: an important work on literary criticism belonging to the 13th century AD (N. Sastri, *History of South India,* p. 349)

Bhaviṣya Purāṇa: This text is particularly difficult to date. Parts of it may be as late as the 16th or 17th century AD while others are probably earlier, dating to the 8th or 11th century AD.

Brāhmaṇas: c. 900 BC
Bṛhatkathāmañjarī of Kṣemendra: the beginning of the 11th century AD
Caraka Saṁhitā: 2nd century BC
Daśakumāracarita of Daṇḍin: 8th century AD
Deśīnamāmālā: a lexicon compiled in the 11th century AD
Dharmasūtras: c. 500-300 BC
Gaṅgāvataraṇa of Nīlakaṇṭha Dikshita: early 17th century (N. Sastri, *History of South India*, p. 351)
Gāthāsaptaśatī of Hāla: dates between the 1st and the 4th century AD
Gṛhya Sūtras: c. 800-400 BC with the *Gobhila Dharmasūtra, Āśvalāyana, Āpastamba* being the oldest
Haravijaya of Ratnākara: 9th century AD (in Kashmir)
Haribhaktivilāsa of Gopala Bhaṭṭa: a Vaiṣṇava text, written before the middle of the 16th century AD
Holikāmāhātmya: a late text belonging to the 17th or 18th century composed in north-east India
Karpūramaõjarī of Rājaṣekhara: 10th century AD composed in the Western Deccan
Kathāsaritsāgara of (the Kashmiri Brahmin) Somadeva: dates from the 10th or 11th century AD. It seems to be based on Gunādhya's *Bṛhatkathā* which is much earlier, probably composed sometime during the 5th century AD. Hence a great deal of the material contained in the *Kathāsaritsāgara* is earlier. See Krishnamachariar, pp. 419ff. See also *Bṛhatkathāmañjarī.*
Kālidāsa: *Mālavikāgnimitram, Ṛtūsamhāra* and *Śākuntala, see C Rajan (intro.) for a discussion of the dates of Kālidāsa*
Kāmasūtra of Vātsyāyana: *c.irca* the 4th century AD
Karpūramañjarī of Rājaśekhara: composed in the 10th century in the Western Deccan
Kuṭṭanīmata of Dāmodaragupta: 8th to 9th century AD
Mahābhārata: 300 BC to 300 AD
Mahābhāsya of Patañjali: 2nd BC
Mālatīmādhava of Bhavabhūti: end of the 7th, beginning of the 8th century AD (N. Sastri, *History of South India*, p. 342)
Mānasollāsa or *Abhilaśitārthacintāmaṇi:* ascribed to the Cālukya king, Someśvara and belonging to the

beginning of the 10th century AD. It consists of five books of twenty chapters each and its range is encyclopaedic (N. Śastri, *History of South India*, p. 348)

Nātyaṣāstra of Bharata: seems to have been composed no earlier than the 3rd century AD

Nyāyamālāvistara: 14th century AD

Pārijāta-Mañjarī: a play transcribed from an inscription dating from the 12th century AD. For the dating of the play, see the introduction to the *Pārijāta-Mañjarī alias Vijayaśrī*, p.vii.

Priyadarśikā: see *Ratnāvalī*

Purāṇas: These texts are almost impossible to date but range in composition from the 7th century onwards. See Hazra, *Studies in Purāṇic Records* and Ludo Rocher, *The Purāṇas.*

Puruśārthacintāmaṇi of Viśṇubhaṭṭa: a *Nibandha* which seems to post-date the *Bhaviṣya Purāṇa*

Rāmāyaṇa: between 200 BC and 200 AD

Ratnāvalī of Harṣa: c. 7th century. See the Introduction to the *Ratnāvalī* of C.R. Devadhar and N.G. Suru and as well the edition translated by M.R. Kale (pp. xx-xxi) for a discussion of the dates of Harṣa works.

Ṛg Veda: 1200 BC

Sāhityamīmāṁsā: 12th century AD (Krishnamachariar, *History of Classical Sanskrit Literature*, p. 765)

Saṇgītaratnākara of Śārṅgadeva: 12th to 13th century AD

Sarasvatīkaṇṭhābharaṇa of Bhoja: 11th century AD

Smṛtis: *Manusmṛti* (200 BC to 100 AD); *Yajñavalkyasmṛti* (100 to 300 AD); *Nāradasmṛti* ((100-400 AD); *Bṛhaspatismṛti* (300-500 AD); and the metrical *Smṛtis* (600-900 AD) (See B. Saraswati, *Brāhmaṇic Ritual Traditions* [Simla: 1977], pp. xvix, xx, 165,175 ff. and U.M.Apte, *The Sacrament of Marriage in Hindu Society* [Delhi: 1978].)

Smṛtikaustubha of Anantadeva: a *Nibandha* which post-dates the *Bhaviṣya Purāṇa,* probably belonging to the 14th century AD (See, V. Raghavan, *Festivals*, p. 203)

Śrītattvacintāmaṇi: a tantric text belonging to the 16th century AD

Śṛṅgāra Prakāśa and *Śṛṅgāramañjarīkathā* of Bhoja of Dhārā: from the 11th century AD

Tilakamañjarîsāra of Pallīpāla Dhanapāla: 10th century AD

Upamitibhāvaprapañcakathā of Siddharsi Suri: a lengthy allegory containing a great deal of folk material belonging to the 10th century (AD Krishnamachariar, p. 233)

Vasantavilāsa: a Gujarati poem belonging to the 16th century AD

Vetālapañcaviṁśatikā: exists independently in a variety of recensions, the most important of which is probably that of Śivadasa which dates from the 15th century AD

Vikramacarita or *Siṁhāsanadvātriṁsikā:* is a collection of thirty-two tales in praise of Vikramāditya which were alleged to have been discovered by Bhoja of Dhārā in the 11th century AD and probably written for or under him. Vikrama's adventures are the subject of a variety of works ranging from the 8th to the 17th century AD (Krishnamachariar, *History of Sanskrit Literature*, pp. 428-9).

Virūpākṣavasantotsavacampū: c. the 15th century AD during the Vijayanagara period

Yaśastilakacampū of Somadevasuri: middle of the 10th century AD (N. Sastri, *History of South India*, p. 347)

Bibliography

ASS	*Anandasrama Sanskrit Series*
GOS	*Gaekwad Oriental Series*
HOS	*Harvard Oriental Series*
IHQ	*Indian Historical Quarterly*
JAAR	*Journal of the American Academy of Religion*
JAOS	*Journal of the American Oriental Society*
JBORI	*Annals of the Bhandarkar Oriental Research Institute*
JRAS	*Journal of the Royal Asiatic Society*
NSP	*Nirnaya Sagara Press*
SBE	*Sacred Books of the East*
SBH	*Sacred Books of the Hindus*

Texts and Translations

Abhijñānaśākuntalam. Ed. by M.R. Kale. Delhi: Motilal Banarsidass, 1969.

Ākhyakamaṇikośa of Nemichandra. Ed. by Prākṛt Text Society. Varanasi: Vol. 5 of the Prākṛt Text Series, 1962.

Atharva Veda. Ed. by Devichand. Delhi: Munshiram Manoharlal, 1982.

(Hymns of the) Atharvaveda. Trans. by Ralph Griffith. Two vols. Chowkhamba Sanskrit Studies LXVI. Varanasi: Chowkhamba Sanskrit Series Office, 1968.

Atharvaveda Pariśiṣṭa (The Pariśiṣṭas of the Atharvaveda). Ed. by George Bölling and Julion von Negelein. Varanasi: Chowkhambha Orientalia, 1976.

Bhāṭṭacintāmaṇi. Chowkhamba Sanskrit Studies IL. Benares: Chowkhamba Sanskrit Series Office, nd.

Bhāṭṭadīpikā. Ed. by A. Mahadeva Śāstri and L. Śrīnivasa. Baroda: GOS, 1914.

Bhāvaprakāśa of Śāradātanaya. Ed. by B. Bhattacharyya. Baroda: GOS, 1930.

(Śrīmad) *Bhāgavata Purāṇa*. Trans. by J.M. Sanyal. Two vols. Second edition, reprint of 1930-34. Delhi: Munshiram Manoharlal, 1973.

Bhaviṣya Purāṇa. Bombay: NSP, 1959.

Caturvargacintāmaṇi of Hemādri. Ed. by Pandita Bharatachandra Siromani. Vol II. *Vratakhaṇḍa*, Part I. Calcutta: Asiatic Society of Bengal, 1878.

Daśakumācarita of Daṇḍin. Trans. with notes by M.R. Kale. Reprint. Delhi: Motilal Banarsidass, 1979.

Dāyabhāga of Jīmūtavāhana. Trans. by H.T. Colebrooke. Calcutta: Sreenath Banerjee and Brothers, 1868.

Deśīnamālā of Hemachandra. Ed. and notes by R. Pischel. Second ed. with intro., notes and glossary by P. V. Ramanujaswami. Bombay: The Department of Public Instruction, 1938.

Dhvanyāloka of Ānanda. With Locana of Abhinavagupta. Baroda: GOS, 1926.

Gathāsaptaśatī of Hāla. Ed., intro. and trans. by Radagovinda Basac. Calcutta: Asiatic Society of Bengal, 1971.

Gṛhya Sūtras. Trans. by Hermann Oldernberg. *SBE* XXX, Part 2. Reprint. Delhi: Motilal Banarsidass, 1973.

Haravijāya of Ratnākara. With commentary of Alaka. *Kāvyamālā* 22. Bombay: NSP, 1890 (SVII.93).

(Śrī) *Harśa's Plays*. Trans. with intro. by Bak Kau Bae. London: Asia Publishing House, 1964.

Holākāmāhātmya. Mss. Calcutta: Asiatic Society of Bengal.

Jātakamālā or Garland of Birth Stories of Āryaśūra. Trans. by J.S. Speyer. Reprint. Delhi: Motilal Banarsidass, 1971.

Jātakas or Stories of the Buddha's Former Births. Ed. and trans. by E.B. Cowell. Six vols. London: Luzac & Co. for the Pali Text Society, 1969.

Kālaviveka of Jīmūtavāhana. Ed. Pandita Pramathanātha Tarkabhūṣam. Calcutta: 1905.

(Kālidāsa) *Loom of Time*. Trans. and intro. by Chandra Rajan. Reprint. New Delhi: Penguin Books India, 1990.

Kāma Sūtra of Vātsyāyana. Varanasi: Chowkhamba Sanskrit Series Office 1961.

Kāma Sutra of Vātsyāyana. Commentary of Jayamaṇgalā. Trans. by S.C. Upadhyaya. Reprint. Bombay: Taraporevala, 1961.

Karpūramañjarī of Rājaśekhara. Ed. by Sten Konow, trans. by C.R. Lanman. Second issue. Delhi: Motilal Banarsidass, 1963.

Kāṭhaka Gṛhya Sūtra. Ed. by Dr. Willem Caland. Lahore: D.A.V. College, 1925.

Kathākośa. Lahore: Pt. Jagdish Lal Śastri, n.d.

Kathākośa or Treasury of Stories. Trans. by C.H. Tawney. Reprint of 1895. Delhi: Munshiram Manoharlal, 1975.

Kathāsaritsāgara of Somadeva. Ed. by Pandit Durgaprasad and K.P. Parab. Bombay: NSP, 1899.

Kathāsaritsāgara or Ocean of the Streams of Story. Trans. by C.H. Tawney. Calcutta: Asiatic Society of Bengal, 1880.

Kaumudīmahotsava of Queen Vijjakabhattarikā. Trans. and intro. by Śākuntala Rao Śastri: Bombay: Miss Rao Śāstri, 1952.

Kavyāmīmāṁsā. Ed. by Mr. C.D. Dalal and Pandit R.A. Śāstri. Revised and enlarged by K.S. Ramaswami Śāstri Siromani. Third edition. Baroda: Oriental Institute, 1934.

Kṛtyakalpataru of Bhaṭṭa Lakṣmīdhara. Part XI "Rājadharmakhaṇḍa." Baroda: GOS, 1944.

Kṛtyasarasamuccaya of Amṛtanātha Jha. Kasi Sanskrit Series. Bombay: Venketesvara Press, 1938.

Kumārasaṁbhava of Kālidāsa. Trans. by S.R. Sehgal. Delhi: 1959.

Liṅga Purāṇa. Trans. by a Board of Scholars. Ed. by J.L. Shastri. Delhi: Motilal Banarsidass, 1973.

Madhūravijāya of Gaṅgādevi. Delhi: Munshiram Manoharlal, 1969.

Mahābhārata. Trans. and ed. by J.A.B. van Buitenen. Three vols. Chicago: University of Chicago Press, 1973, 75, 78.

Mahābhārata of Vyāsa. Trans. by P. Chandra Roy. Five vols, third edition. Delhi: Munshiram Manoharlal, 1972.

Mālatīmādhava of Bhavabhūti. Trans., intro. and notes by R.D. Karmarkar. Poona: R.D Karmarkar, 1935.

Mālavikāgnimitram of Kālidāsa. Trans., ed. and notes by R.D. Karmarkar. Fourth revised edition. Bombay: 1950.

Mālavikāgnimitram of Kalidasa. Trans. by M. R. Kale, revised by J.L. Dave and S.A. Upadhyaya. Delhi: Motilal Banarsidass, 1960.

Mānasollāsa or *Abhilaṣitārthacintāmaṇi* of Someśvara. Ed. by B.J. Sansesara. Three vols. Baroda: GOS. No.'s 28, 84, 138, 1925, 1939, 1961.

(Laws of) Manu. SBE. Trans. by Georg Bühler. Reprint. Delhi: Motilal Banarsidass, 1964.

Manu Smṛti. Ed. by Pt. Hargovinda Shastri, comm. by Kulluka Bhaṭṭa. Third edition. Varanasi: Chowkhamba Sanskrit Series Office, 1982.

Matsya Purāṇa. Ed. by B.D. Basu, trans. by a Taluqdar of Oudh, *SBH* 17 (2 parts). New York: AMS Press Inc., 1974.

Nāṭyaśāstra. Commentary of Abhinavagupta. Ed. by G.H. Bhatt. Baroda: GOS, 1954.

Nīlamata Purāṇa. Trans. and intro. by Dr. Ved Kumari. Two vols. Srinagar-Jammu: J. and K. Academy of Art, Culture, and Language, 1968, 1973.

Nirṇayasindhu of Kamalakara. Varanasi: Ihakura Prasada, 1971.

Nityotsava of Umānandanātha. Ed. by A. Hagadeva Śāstri. Baroda: GOS, 1948.

Nyāyamālāvistara of Jaiminīyanyāyamālā. Ed. by Ānandāśrama Saṁskṛta. np., 1946.

Padmaprābhṛtaka Bhāṇa of Śūdraka. Madras: Daksinabharati Series, 1922.

Padma Purāṇa. Ed. by V. N. Mandalika. Poona: AAS, 1919.

Parameśvara Saṁhitā of Śrī Govindācarya. np., 1953.

Pārijāta-Mañjarī alias Vijayaśrī of Rāja-Guru Madana *alias* Bāla-Sarasvati. Re-ed. by S.K. Dikshit. Bhopal: S.K. Dikshit, 1963.

Priyadarśikā of Harṣa. Ed., intro., trans. and notes by N.G. Suru. Poona: 1928.

Priyadarśikā of Harṣa. Trans. by G.K. Nariman, A.V. Williams Jackson and C.J. Ogden. Reprint. New Delhi: Oriental Books Reprint Corporation, 1984.

Puruṣārthacintāmaṇi of Viṣṇubhaṭṭa. Bombay: NSP, 1927.

Puruṣārthacintāmaṇi of Viṣṇubhaṭṭa. Ed. by B.S.Pavaji. Poona: AAS, No. 55, 1907.

Pūrvamīmāṁsā Sūtra of Jaimini. Trans. by M. G. Jha. *SBH.* Volume X. Reprint. New York: AMS Press Inc., 1974.

Raghuvaṁśa. Commentary of Mallinātha. Ed. and trans. by Nandagirkar. Sixth ed. Bombay: NSP, 1917.

Rājataraṅginī of Kalhana. Trans. by M.A. Stein. Two vols., reprint. Delhi: Motilal Banarsidass, 1961.

Rāmāyaṇa of Valmīki. Trans. by M. L. Sen. Reprint, Calcutta: Firma KLM Private Limited, 1976.

Ratnāvalī of Śrī Harṣa. Preface and trans. by C.R. Devadhar and N.G. Suru. Poona: Poona Oriental Book House, 1954.

Ratnāvalī of Śrī Harṣa. Ed., intro., trans. and notes by M.R. Kale. Reprint. Delhi: Motilal Banarsidass, 1984.

(The Hymns of the) Ṛg Veda. Trans. by Ralph Griffith. Delhi: Motilal Banarsidass, 1976.

Ṛtusaṁhāra of Kālidāsa. Commentary of S.D. Gajendragadkar. Poona: A.P. Bapat and Brothers, 1916.

Śabdakalpadruma. Five vols., reprint. Varanasi: Chowkhamba Sanskrit Series Office, 1961.

Sacred Laws of the Āryas (Āpastamba, Gautama Gṛhya Sūtras). Trans. by G. Buhler. *SBE* II, Part I. Reprint. Delhi: Motilal Banarsidass, 1969.

Sanatkumāra Saṁhitā. Ed. by Pandit V. Krishnamacharya. Foreward by Dr. V. Raghavan. Madras: Adyar Library, 1969.

Saṅgītaratnākara of Śarṅgadeva. Four vols. Madras: Adyar Library, 1943, 1953, 1954, 1959.

Sarasvatīkaṇṭhābharaṇa of Dhāreśvara Bhojadeva. Commentary of Ramsimha (1-111) and Jagaddhara. Ed. by P.K. Sarma and W.L.S. Pandurang Jawaji. Bombay: NSP, 1934.

Śāstradīpikā. Commentary of Mayuravali. np. nd.

Śiva Purāṇa. Ed. by Prof. J.L. Shastri and trans. by a Board of Scholars. Four vols. Reprint. Delhi: Motilal Banarsidass, 1977.

Smṛtikaustubha of Anantadeva. Bombay: NSP, 1909.

Śrītattvacintāmaṇi of Paramahaṁsa Purnānanda. Intro. by P. Bagchi, notes by C. Bhattacharya. Calcutta: Sanskrit Series XIX. 1936.

Śṛṅgāra Prakāśa of Bhoja (*Bhoja's Śṛṅgāra Prakāśa*). Trans. by V. Raghavan. Third revised ed. Madras: Vasanta Press, 1978

Tilakamañjarīsāra of Dhanapāla. Ed. by N. M. Kansara. Lalbhai Series No. 23. Ahmedabad: Bharatiya Sanskriti Vidyamandir, 1969.

Triṣaṣṭiśalākapuruṣacaritamahākāvya of Hemachandra. Two vols. Bhavnagar: Sri Jaina-Atmananada Sabha Series, Vol. VII, 1936

Ubhayabhisarika Bhana (Caturbhani) of Vararuci. Madras: Daksinabharati Series, 1922.

Vāmana Purāṇa. Ed. by A.S. Gupta, trans. by S.M. Mukhopadhyaya, A. Bhattacharya, N.C. Nath, V.K. Verma. Varanasi: All India Kashiraj Trust, 1968.

Varṣakṛtyādīpikā (A Treatise on the Hindu Rites during the Year) of M.M.Nityānanda Pant Parvatiya. Kasi Sanskrit Series 96. Varanasi: Chowkhamba Sanskrit Series Office, 1967.

Vasanta Vilāsa. Trans. by W. Norman Brown. American Oriental Series 46. New Haven: American Oriental Society, 1962.

Vasantotsavanirṇaya of Pandit Śrīsūryanārāyaṇaśukla. np., nd.

Vikrama's Adventures (Thirty Two Tales of the Throne). Ed. and trans. by F. Edgerton. Cambridge: Harvard University Press, 1926.

Virūpākṣavasantotsavacampū of Ahobala. Intro. by V R.S. Panchamukhi. Dharwar: Kannada Research Institute, 1953.

Viṣṇu Purāṇa. Trans. by H.H. Wilson, intro. by R.C. Hazra. Reprint. Calcutta: Punthi Pustak, 1972.

Viṣṇudharmottara Purāṇa. Bombay: Venkatesvara Press Publication, 1834.

Yaśastilakacampū. Commentary of Śrutadevaśrī. Ed. by Śivadatta. Bombay: Tukaran Javi, 1916.

Yatindramatadīpikā of Srinivasadasa. Trans. and notes by Svami Adidevānanda. Madras: Śrī Rāmakrishna Math, 1949.

Secondary Sources and Journals

Adaval, Niti. *The Story of King Udayana as Gleaned From Sanskrit, Pali and Prakrit sources*. Chowkhamba Sanskrit Studies LXXIV. Varanasi: Chowkhamba Sanskrit Series Office, 1970.

Agrawala, Vasudeva S. *Ancient Indian Folk Cults*. Varanasi: Prithivi Prakashan, 1970.

______ *India As Known to Pāṇini (A Study of the Cultural Material in the Aṣṭādhyāyi)*. Lucknow: University of Lucknow, 1953.

______ *The Matsya Purāṇa: A Study*. Varanasi: All India Kashiraj Trust, 1963.

Anand, Mulk Raj. "The Rise and Fall of the Vijayanagara Empire" in *Marg* (1982), pp.1-41.

Apte, U. M. *The Sacrament of Marriage in Hindu Society*. Delhi: Ajanta Publications, 1978.

Ayyangar. S. Krishnaswami. *Sources of Vijayanagar History*. Madras: University of Madras, 1919.

Ayyar, P.V. Jagadisa. *South Indian Festivals*. Madras: Higginbothams Ltd., 1921.

Babb, Lawrence. *The Divine Hierarchy*. New York: Columbia University Press, 1975.

Bandyopadhyay, Samaresh. *Foreign Accounts of Marriage in Ancient India*. Calcutta: Firma K. L. Mukhopadhyay, 1973.

Banerjea, Jitendra Nath. *The Development of Hindu Iconography*. Calcutta: University of Calcutta, 1956.

Banerji, Sures Chandra. *Society in Ancient India*. New Delhi: D.K. Printworld (P) Ltd., 1993.

______ *A Companion to Sanskrit Literature*. Delhi: Motilal Banarsidass, 1971.

Bapat, Tara. *Rituals and Festivals of India*. Bombay: 1991

Basham, A.L. Ed. *A Cultural History of India*. Oxford: Clarendon Press, 1975.

______ *The Wonder that Was India*. New York: Grove Press, Inc., 1959.

Beck, Brenda. 'Colour and Heat in South Indian Ritual' in *Man*. 4 ; pp. 553-72.

Béteille, André. *Caste, Class and Power*. Berkeley and Los Angeles: University of California Press, 1965.

Bharati, Agehananda. *The Tantric Tradition*. New York: Anchor Books, 1970.

Bhattacharjee, Arun. *Icons and Sculpture of Early and Medieval Assam*. Delhi: Inter-India Publications, 1978.

Bhattacharji, Sukumari. *The Indian Theogony*. Reprint. Calcutta: Firma KLM Private Ltd., 1978.

Bhattacharya, Bhabutush. *Studies in the Nibandhas*. Calcutta: np., 1968.

Bhattacharyya, Narendra Nath. *Indian Puberty Rites*. Second edition. Delhi: Munshiram Manoharlal, 1975.

______ *History of Indian Erotic Literature*. New Delhi: Munshiram Manoharlal, 1975.

_______ *Ancient Indian Rituals*. Delhi: Manohar Book Service, 1975.

Bickerman, E.J. *Chronology of the Ancient World*. Ithaca, New York: Cornell University Press, 1968.

Bose, Nirmal Kumar. *Culture and Society in India*. Reprint. Bombay: Asia Publishing House, 1977.

Briffault, R. *The Mothers*. Three vols. Reprint. London: George Allen and Unwin Ltd., 1969.

Buck, C.H. *Faiths, Fairs and Festivals of India*. Reprint. Delhi: Asia Publication Services, 1979.

Burlingame, E.W. *Buddhist Legends*. HOS, 28. London: Luzac and Co., 1969.

Chaitanya, Krishna. *A New History of Sanskrit Literature*. Reprint. Connecticut: Greenwood Press, 1975.

Chatterjee, Asim Kumar. *Ancient Indian Literary and Cultural Tradition*. Calcutta: Punthi Pustak, 1974.

Chatterjee, Asoke. *Padma Purāṇa: A Study*. Calcutta College Research Series LVIII, Study # 37. Calcutta: Calcutta Sanskrit College, 1967.

Chatterjee, Chanchal Kumar. *Studies in the Rites and Rituals of Hindu Marriage in Ancient India*. Calcutta:

Shyamapada Bhattacharyya, Sanskrit Pustak Bhandar, 1978.

Chattopadhyaya, Aparna. "Spring Festival and Festivals of Indra in the Kathāsaritsāgara" in *the Journal of the Oriental Institute*. Vol. XVII, part 2 (1967), pp. 137-141.

Coomaraswamy, Ananda Kentish. *History of Indian and Indonesian Art*. Reprint of 1927. Delhi: Munshiram Manoharlal, 1972.

______ *Yaksas*. Delhi: Munshiram Manoharlal, 1971.

Crooke, William. *Religion and Folklore of Northern India*. Two vols. Third edition. New Delhi: Munshiram Manoharlal, 1926.

_______ *Tribes and Castes of North West India*. Reprint. Delhi: Cosmos Publishers, 1974.

Dallapiccola, Anna Libera in collaboration with Stephanie Zingel-Avé Lallemant. *Vijayanagara - City and Empire: New Currents of Research*. Stuttgart: Steiner Verlag Wiesbaden GMBH, 1985.

Danielou, Alain. *Hindu Polytheism*. New York: Böllingen, 1964.

Das, Kunjabehari. *A Study of Orissan Folklore*. Santiniketan: Visva Bharati, 1953.

De, S.K. *Early History of the Vaiṣṇava Faith and Movement in Bengal*. Second ed. Calcutta: Firma K. L. Mukhopadyaya, 1961.

Desai, Devangana. *Erotic Sculptures of India: A Socio-cultural Study*. Delhi: Tata McGraw-Hill Publishing Co., 1975.

Deshpande, Kamalabai. "Some Observances (*Vratas*) and Festivals (*Utsavas*) mentioned in the *Deśīnamamālā*," *AIOC*. XVII (1955), Annamalai Universitiy, Proceedings and Transactions, 1958. pp. 483ff.

Devi, Konduri Sarojini. *Religion in Vijayanagara Empire*. New Delhi: Sterling Publishers Pvt. Ltd., 1990.

Dhal, Upendra Nath. *The Goddess Lakṣmī: Origins and Development*. New Delhi: Oriental Publishers and distributors 1978.

Douglas, Mary. *Natural Symbols: Explorations in Cosmology*. Reprint of 1970. New York: Pantheon Books, 1982.

______ *Purity and Danger: An Analysis of Concepts of Pollution and Taboo.* Reprint. London: Routledge and Kegan, 1979.

Eliade, Mircea. *Cosmos and History.* New York: Harper and Row, Publishers, 1959.

______ *Patterns in Comparative Religion.* Reprint. New York: New American Library, 1974.

Eschmann, Anncharlott, H. Kulke, and G.C. Tripathi. Editors. *The Cult of Jagannath and the Regional Tradition of Orissa.* Reprint of 1978. Delhi: Manohar Publications, 1986.

Festivals of India. Government of India. Delhi: Publications Division, Ministry of Broadcasting, 1977.

Filliozat, Jean. *Le Kumāratantra de Rāvaṇa et les Textes Paralleles Indiens, Tibetains, Chinois, Cambodhien et Arabe.* Paris: Impremerie Nationale, 1937.

Filliozat, Vasundhara. *L'Épigraphie de Vijayanagar du Début à 1377.* Paris: École Française d'Extreme Orient, 1973.

______ "Relatives and Officers of Ballala III and IV who Accepted Service under the Kings of Vijayanagara" in *Itihasa* V.1(2) 1973, pp. 27-34.

______ Ed. and trans., Robert Sewell. *The Vijayanagara Empire (As seen by Domingos Paes and Fernao Nuniz, Two 16th Century Portuguese Chroniclers.* Delhi: National Book Trust, 1977.

______ "Sources of Vijayanagar Art and Architecture" in *Tamil Civilization,* Vol 2, No 3. pp. 68-73.

Frazer, George. *The Golden Bough.* Reprint. London: MacMillan Press, 1978.

Freed, Ruth S. and Stanley A. Freed. "Calendars, Ceremonies and Festivals in a North Indian Village: Necessary Calendric Information for Fieldwork" in *Southwestern Journal of Anthropology.* Albuquerque, University of New Mexico. Vol. 20 (1967), pp. 67-90.

Fritz, John M., George Michell and M.S. Nagaraja Rao. *Where Kings and Gods Meet: The Royal Centre at Vijayanagara, India.* Tuscon: University of Arizona Press, 1984.

Gaster, Theodor, H. *Myth, Legend, and Custom in the Old Testament.* New York: Harper and Row, 1969.

______ *Thespis*. Reprint, New York: Harper Torch Books, 1969.

Gnanambal, K. *Festivals of India*. Calcutta: Anthropological Survey of India, nd.

Gode, P.K. *Studies in Indian Cultural History*. Vol I, Hoshiarpur: Vishveshvaranand Vedic Research Institute, 1961; Vol. II, Poona: Prof P.K. Gode Collected Works Publication Committee, 1960.

______ *Studies in Indian Literary History*. Vol. I, Bombay: Singhi Jain Sastra Sikshapith, Bharatiya Vidya Bhavan, 1953.

Gonda Jan. "Ascetics and Courtesans" in *Adyar Library Bulletin*. 25 (1961), pp. 78-102

______ "The Indra Festival According to the Atharvavedins" in *JAOS*. 87 (1967), pp. 413-29.

______ *Medieval Religious Literature in Sanskrit*. Wiesbaden: Harrassowitz, 1972.

______ *Selected Studies*. Volume IV, History of Ancient Indian Religions. Leiden: E. J. Brill, 1975.

Goswami, S.N. "Bhatheli - A Spring Time Festival of Lower Assam" in *Folklore*. XVIII, pp. 57-61.

Grimes, Ronald, L. "Sources for the Study of Ritual" in *Religious Studies Review*. Vol. 10., no. 2. Spring (1984), pp. 134-44.

Gupta, Shakti M. *From Daityas to Devatas in Hindu Mythology*. Bombay: Somaiya Publications Pvt. Ltd., 1973.

Handiqui, Krishna Kanta. *Yaśastilaka and Indian Culture*. Sholapur: Jaina Samskriti Samrakshaka Sangha, 1968.

Hazra, R.C. *Studies in the Purāṇic Records on Hindu Rites and Customs*. Second edition. Delhi: Motilal Banarsidass, 1975.

Heesterman, J.C. *The Ancient Indian Royal Consecration*. Gravenhage: Mouton and Company, 1957.

Held, G.J. *The Mahābhārata: An Ethnological Study*. London: Kegan Paul, Trench Trubner and Co. Ltd., 1963.

Hopkins, Edward Washburn. *Epic Mythology*. Reprint of 1968. Delhi: Motilal Banarsidass, 1974.

Jha, Mahamahopadhyaya Ganganatha. *Pūrvamīmāṁsā in its Sources*. Ed. by S. Radhakrishna. Varanasi: Banaras Hindu University, 1964.

Kakar, Sudhir. *The Inner World.* Delhi: Oxford University Press, 1981.

Kale, Pramod. *The Theatric Universe (A Study of the Nāṭyaśāstra).* Bombay: Popular Prakashan Pvt. Ltd., 1974.

Kane, P. V. *History of Dharmasastra.* Five vols. Poona: Bhandarkar Oriental Research Institute, 1958.

______ *History of Sanskrit Poetics.* Fourth edition. Delhi: Motilal Banarsidass, 1977.

Keith, A. Berrierdale. *Classical Sanskrit Literature.* Second edition, Calcutta: Association Press, 1927.

______ *A History of Sanskrit Literature.* Indian edition. Delhi: Oxford University Press, 1973.

______ *Religion and Philosophy of the Veda and Upanishads.* 2 vols. London: Oxford University Press, 1925.

______ *Rig Veda Brāhmaṇas: The Aitareya and Kauśîtaki Brāhmaṇas of the Rig Veda.* Reprint of 1920. Delhi: Motilal Banarsidass, 1971.

______ *The Śānkhāyana Āraṇyaka with an Appendix on the Mahāvrata.* London: Royal Asiatic Society, 1908.

______ *The Sanskrit Drama in its Origin. Development, Theory and Practice.* Reprint. London: Oxford University Press, 1964.

Khare, R.S. *The Hindu Hearth and Home.* New Delhi: Vikas Publishing House Pvt Ltd., 1976.

Kramrisch, Stella. *The Presence of Śiva.* Princeton: Princeton University Press, 1981.

Krishnamachariar, M. *History of Classical Sanskrit Literature.* Third edition. Delhi: Motilal Banarsidass, 1974.

Kulke, Herman and Dietmar Rothermund. *A History of India.* Reprint of 1986. London: Routledge, 1990.

Kumar, Pushpendra. *Shakti Cult in Ancinet India.* Varanasi: Bharatiya Publishing House, 1974.

MacDonell, A.A. *The Vedic Mythology.* Delhi: Indological Book House, 1971.

Mani, Vetta. *Purāṇic Encyclopaedia.* First English edition. Delhi: Motilal Banarsidass, 1975.

Marriot. McKim. Ed. *Village India: Studies in the Little Community.* Chicago: University of Chicago Press, 1960.

Mauss, Marcel. *The Gift*. Glencoe, Ill. Free Press, 1954.
Meyer, Johan Jakob. *Sexual Life in Ancient India*. Two vols. New York: E. P. Dutton and Co., 1930.
Michell, George. "History or Myth (Part I)" in "Man in Nature - Town Planning" and "From Power to Pleasure" in *Marg* (1982), pp. 41-84.
Mitra, Haridas. *The Fire Works and Fire Festivals in Ancient India*. Calcutta: Abhendananda Academy of Culture, 1963.
Mitra. Kalipada. "The New Year Festivals" in *Man in India* (1938), pp. 106-21.
Muir, John. Trans. *Original Sanskrit Texts*. Vol. 5. Amsterdam: Oriental Press, 1967.
Mukerji, A.C. *Ancient Indian Fasts and Feasts*. Revised ed. Toronto: MacMillan Co. of Canada, 1932.
Mukhopadhyay, Samira. "Sarmilar Patigrhi Yatra" in *Desh* (July 9, 1983)
Müller, Max. *A History of Ancient Sanskrit Literature*. Reprint. New York: AMS Press Inc., 1978.
Murthy, H. V. Sreenivasa and R. Ramakrishnan. *A History of Karnataka*. Delhi: S. Chand and Co. Ltd., 1978.
Nambiar, Damodaran. *Nārada Purāṇa: A Critical Study*. (Thesis) Poona: Bhandarkar Oriental Research Institute, 1968.
Nilakantasastri, K.A. *Further Sources of Vijayanagar History*. Vols. I-VII. Madras: 1936.
Oberesekere, Gananath. *The Cult of the Goddess Pāttinî*. Chicago: University of Chicago Press, 1984.
______ *Medusa's Hair*. Chicago: University of Chicago Press, 1981.
O'Flaherty, Wendy Doniger. Trans. *Hindu Myths*. Reprint of 1975. Maryland: Penguin Books, 1982.
______ *Siva the Erotic Ascetic*. New York: Oxford University Press, 1981.
______ *Women, Androgynes and Other Mythical Beasts*. Chicago: University of Chicago Press, 1982.
Oman, John Campbell. *Cults, Customs, and Superstitions of India*. Philadelphia: George W. Jacobs, 1908.
Östör, Akös. *The Play of the Gods*. Chicago: University of Chicago Press, 1980.

Raghavan, V. *Festivals, Sports and Pastimes of India.* Ahmedabad: B. J. Institute of Learning and Research, 1979.

______ *Ṛtū in Sanskrit Literaure.* Delhi: Shri Lal Bahadur Shastri Kendriya Sanskrit Vidyapeetha, 1972.

______ "Variety and Integration in the Patterns of Indian Culture" in *Far Eastern Quarterly.* Vol. 15. AMS Reprint Co., New York. No. 1, pp. 497-505.

______ 'The Virūpākṣa Vasantotsava Campū of Ahobala (A Vijayanagara Kāvya)' in *Journal of Oriental Research.* XVI. pp. 17-40.

Rao, M. Rama. *Śaivite Deities of Andhradeśa.* Tirupati: Sri Venkatesvara University, 1966.

Rao, M.S. Nagaraja. *Vijayanagara. Progress of Research, 1979-1983.* Mysore: Directorate of Archaeology and Museums, 1983.

______ *Vijayanagara, Progress of Research 1983-84.* Mysore: Directorate of Archaeology and Museums, 1985.

Rao, Rajacharita V.R. B. C. H. "Kannada Literature as a Source for Vijayanagar History" in *Andhra Historical Research Society Journal.* v. 17 (1946/47), pp.149-153.

Rao. T.A. Gopinatha. *Elements of Hindu Iconography.* Two vols. Second revised ed. Varanasi: Indological Book House, 1971.

Rawlinson, H.G. *India: A Short Cultural History.* Reprint. New York: Frederick A. Praeger, Inc., 1962.

Ray, Khirod Chandra. "Aśokāṣṭami" in *Royal Asicatic Society of Great Britain* and *Ireland Journal.* Series 3 (1901), pp. 127-140.

Richards, J.F. Ed. *Kingship and Authority in South Asia.* Madison: University of Wisconsin, 1978.

Rocher, Ludo. *The Purå/as.* Wiesbaden: 1986.

Roy, Pratap Chandra. *The Mahābhārata.* Delhi: Munshiram Manoharlal, 1974.

Sahai, Bhagwant. *Iconography of Minor Hindu and Buddhist Deities.* Delhi: Abhinav Publications, 1975.

Saletore, B.A. *Social and Political Life Under Vijayanagara.* Two vols. Madras: 1934.

Saraswati, Baidyanath. *Brāhmaṇic Ritual Traditions.* Simla: Indian Institute of Advanced Study, 1977.

Sarkar, B.K. *The Folk Elements in Hindu Culture.* Reprint. Delhi: Oriental Books Reprint Corp., 1972.

Sarkar, Sukhamay. "The Hindu New Year's Day" in *Hinduism (Journal of the Bharat Sevashram Sangha).* Ed. by Swami Purnanada. London: No. 89 (summer, 1980), pp. 13-17.

______ *Some Aspects of the Earliest Social History of India.* Reprint. London: Oxford University Press, 1928.

Sastri, H. Chatterjee. *Studies in the Social Background of the Forms of Marriage in Ancient India.* Two vols. Calcutta: Sanskrit Pustak Bhandar, 1972, 1974.

Sastri, K.A. Nilakanta. *A History of South India.* Fourth edition. Delhi: Oxford University Press, 1975.

Sen Gupta, Sankar. Ed. *Tree Symbol Worship in India.* Calcutta: Indian Publications, 1965.

______ and K. Krishnaswamy. *Fire Festival of India.* Calcutta: Indian Publications, 1984.

Sewell, Robert. *A Forgotten Empire.* Reprint of 1963. Delhi: Asian Educational Services, 1984.

Sharma, Brijendra Nath. *Festivals of India.* Delhi: Abhinav Publications, 1978.

Sharma, M.H. Rama. *The History of the Vijayanagara Empire.* Ed. by M.H. Gopal. Bombay: 1980.

Shastri, A.M. *India as Seen in the Kuṭṭanīmata of Dāmodaragupta.* Delhi: Motilal Banarsidass, 1975.

Shastri, D.R. "The Lokāyatikas and Kāpalikas" in *IHQ.* VII, 1931.

Shulman, David Dean. *The King and the Clown in South Indian Myth and Poetry.* Princeton: Princeton University Press, 1986.

_______. *Tamil Temple Myths: Sacrifice and Divine Marriage in the South Indian Śaiva Tradition.* Princeton: Princeton University Press, 1980.

Singer, Milton B. Ed. *Krishna: Myths, Rites and Attitudes.* Chicago: University of Chicago Press, 1966.

______ *When a Great Tradition Modernizes.* New York: Praeger Publishers Inc.,1973.

Singh, Amal Dhari. *Kālidāsa: A Critical Study.* Delhi: Bharatiya Vidya Prakashan, 1977.

Sinha, Binod Chandra. *Tree Worship in Ancient India.* Delhi: Books Today (Oriental Publishers), 1979.

Sörensen, S. *An Index to the Names in the Mahābhārata*. Reprint Delhi: Motilal Banarsidass, 1978.

Srinivas, M.N. *Religion and Society Among the Coorgs of South India*. London and New York: Oxford University Press, 1952.

Srivastava, M.C.P. *Mother Goddess*. Delhi: Agam Kala Prakashan, 1979.

Srivastava, S.L. *Folk Culture and Oral Tradition*. Delhi: Abhinav Publications, 1974.

Stein, Burton. *The New Cambridge History of India I.2 Vijayanagara*. Published in association with Orient Longman. Cambridge: Cambridge University Press, nd.

Stevenson, Margaret. *Jaina Festivals and Fasts*. np., nd.

Stevenson, Mrs. Sinclair. *Rites of the Twice-Born*. Second ed. Delhi: Oriental Books Reprint Corp., 1971.

Stutley, Margaret. *The Illustrated Dictionary of Hindu Iconography*. London, Boston, Melbourne, Henley: Routledge & Kegan Paul, 1985.

Sutherland, Gail Hinich. *Yakṣa in Hinduism and Buddhism*. Delhi: Manohar Publications, 1992.

Tarlekar, G.H. *Studies in the Nāṭyaśāstra*. Delhi: Motilal Banarsidass, 1975.

Thomas, P. *Festivals and Holidays of India*. Bombay: D.B. Taraporevala Sons and Co. Private, Ltd., 1971.

Turner, Victor. *The Ritual Process: Structure and Anti-structure*. Reprint. Ithaca: Cornell University Press, 1977.

Underhill, M.M. *The Hindu Religious Year*. Calcutta: Association Press, 1921.

Viennot, Odette. *Le Culte de l'Arbre dans L'Inde Ancienne*. Paris: Presses Universitaires de France, 1954.

Vijayanagara Sextenary Commemoration Volume. Dharwar: Vijayanagara Empire Sextenary Association, 1936.

Vogel, Jean Philippe. "The Makara dans la sculpture de l'Inde" in *Revue des Artes Asiatiques* (1930), pp. 128-133.

_______. "The Woman and Tree or Śālabhañjikā in Indian Literature and Art" in *AO*. 7 (1929), pp. 201-31.

Welbon, Guy R. and Glen E. Yocum. Eds. *Religious Festivals in South India and Sri Lanka*. Delhi: Manohar Publications, 1982.

Wells, Henry, W. Ed. *Six Sanskrit Plays.* London: Asia Publishing House, 1964.

Winternitz, M. A *History of Indian Literature.* Two vols. New York: 1972.

Younger, Paul. "A Temple Festival of Mariyamman" in *JAAR.* (1980), pp. 493-518.

_______. "Ten Days of Wandering and Romance with Lord Raṇkanātan: The Paṇkuṇi Festival in Śrīrankam Temple, South India" in *Modern Asian Studies* (1982), 16, pp. 623-57.

Zimmer, Heinrich. *The Art of Indian Asia; Its Mythology and Transformation.* Ed. and completed by Joseph Campbell. Böllingen Series no. XXXIX. Two vols. New York: Pantheon Books, 1955.

Index